UKKUSIKSALIK

DAVID F. PELLY

UKKUSIKSALIK

ᐅᒃᑯᓯᒃᓴᓕᒃ

The People’s Story

DUNDURN
TORONTO

Project editor: Kathryn Lane
Copy editor: Natalie Meditsky
Cover designer: Laura Boyle
Interior design: Courtney Horner
Printer: Friesens
All photography by the author unless otherwise noted.

Library and Archives Canada Cataloguing in Publication

Pelly, David F. (David Fraser), 1948-, author
    Ukkusiksalik : the people's story / David F. Pelly.

Includes bibliographical references and index.
Issued in print and electronic formats.
ISBN 978-1-4597-2989-6 (bound).--ISBN 978-1-4597-2990-2 (pdf).--
ISBN 978-1-4597-2991-9 (epub)

    1. Ukkusiksalik National Park (Nunavut)--History. 2. Inuit--
Nunavut--History. 3. Oral history--Nunavut. 4. Nunavut--History.
I. Title.

| FC4314.U45P44 2016 | 971.9'58 | C2015-906121-0 |
| | | C2015-906122-9 |

1   2   3   4   5   20   19   18   17   16

We acknowledge the support of the **Canada Council for the Arts** and the **Ontario Arts Council** for our publishing program. We also acknowledge the financial support of the **Government of Canada** through the **Canada Book Fund** and **Livres Canada Books**, and the **Government of Ontario** through the **Ontario Book Publishing Tax Credit** and the **Ontario Media Development Corporation**.

Care has been taken to trace the ownership of copyright material used in this book. The author and the publisher welcome any information enabling them to rectify any references or credits in subsequent editions.

— *J. Kirk Howard, President*

The publisher is not responsible for websites or their content unless they are owned by the publisher.

Printed and bound in Canada.

VISIT US AT
Dundurn.com | @dundurnpress | Facebook.com/dundurnpress | Pinterest.com/dundurnpress

Dundurn
3 Church Street, Suite 500
Toronto, Ontario, Canada
M5E 1M2

Parks   Parcs
Canada   Canada

This book is dedicated to the Ukkusiksalingmiut elders, whose generosity with their knowledge informed this work, even as they enriched my life.

Our shared commitment to pass their stories on to their grandchildren, and beyond, is now fulfilled.

CONTENTS

FOREWORD

When I was a little girl, we lived in Ukkusiksalik as a nomadic Inuit family. My father, Marc Tungilik, and my brother, Kadluk, hunted for all our daily essentials. We were dependent on the animals for both clothing and food, and in the winter seal fat provided the oil for our *qulliq* (seal-oil lamp), which gave us light and heat. My mother, Angugatsiaq, prepared the sealskins to make waterproof boots and mitts, and double-sided pack bags for our dogs. We were free to roam the boundless land. Everyone had the freedom to live where they wanted. This is why Ukkusiksalik feels to me like a place of freedom and beauty.

I first met David Pelly in Naujaat (Repulse Bay) when he came to our house in the summer of 1986. I was visiting from Rankin Inlet to see my dad, to help him out and spend time with him. My mother had passed away the year before, and my father would follow her just a few weeks after this visit. It was a pleasure to interpret for David as he asked about Ukkusiksalik, and to hear the stories of my father, who was normally a quiet fellow.

Over the years, David befriended and interviewed many of the people who once lived in Ukkusiksalik. The storytellers were people like Leonie Sammurtok, who became a mother to many children in Chesterfield Inlet; Tuinnaq Kanayuk Bruce, who had memories of life at the Hudson's Bay Company post in Ukkusiksalik; and Mariano Aupilarjuq, the late Inuit historian who was so instrumental in the creation of Nunavut. Several other elders who have left us now told their stories in order to leave behind a record and a sense of how so many of these families were connected.

All the people who were interviewed by David reminisced about their past, remembering how hard it was, but how joyous and free it felt at the time. I, too, was interviewed, which allowed me to look back at my childhood in Ukkusiksalik. I have such fond memories. It was an innocent and joyful time, living in such a beautiful and bountiful place.

I remember one autumn my father was building a rock and sod *qarmaq* (sod house) for us to live in. I watched him carry very big rocks. I was about three years old. I had just learned to walk again after recovering from polio. But at times I was running after him as fast as I could, sometimes holding my mother's hand. I remember saying to her, "My dad is the strongest man on Earth" — in Inuktitut,* of course. I gleamed with pride. I remember when we first occupied the *qarmaq*, how warm and bright and cozy it felt when my mother lit the *qulliq*. I was only back there once, forty years later, when I saw that they really were big rocks!

I hope you will enjoy this book. It is a timeless and valuable work of true Inuit history. The land tells its story, as witnessed through the eyes of those we knew who lived in Ukkusiksalik, and those who came before them.

Theresie Tungilik
Ukkusiksalingmiut, Rankin Inlet, Nunavut
Former chair of the Ukkusiksalik Park Management Committee

---

* The language of the Inuit is known as Inuktitut, which literally means "sounds like an Inuk."

PREFACE

Henry Naulaq is a veteran Inuit Broadcasting Corporation cameraman who travelled the North for thirty years. Some years ago, when he saw Ukkusiksalik for the first time, he said, "How am I going to do any justice to this *kajaanaqtuq* in my camera and show it to people who will never see it in person?" *Kajaanaqtuq* means "the most beautiful, scenic place in memory," but even as he explains that, he says, he knows the area's significance is rooted more deeply in "the people who were there … at that wonderful time."

Ukkusiksalik means "a place where there is soapstone," or, more literally, "the material for a cooking pot." It refers to the whole area surrounding the body of water named Wager Inlet by Captain Christopher Middleton during his 1742 search for the Northwest Passage. Over time, the ancient name came to conjur up much more than just a place where one might find the soapstone needed to make his next pot. It resonates still today as a land of plenty with older people in the Kivalliq region, the mainland part of Nunavut on the west side of Hudson Bay. It calls out to Inuit and *qablunaat* (white men) alike who have seen it as a beautiful place to visit. Most recently, it has become the name of one of Canada's newest national parks. When the name is used in this book, it refers simply to the area — this is the story of that land; it is not the story of a park.

A wise Inuit elder once explained to me that Inuit did not live on the land with any sense of ownership, although their connection to the land could not have been stronger. "We have all belonged to this land," he said, turning the Western notion of land ownership on its head. This philosophical perspective underlies the stories captured here. These are stories from the land, as shared with us by some of the elders whose families lived and travelled and hunted in Ukkusiksalik.

———

This volume is divided into three sections. Part one, "A Prehistoric Glimpse," briefly sets the scene, providing some background to the real heart of the book, by reaching back further in time than the oral tradition permits. Part two, "*Inuit Unipkausingit* — the People's Story," delivers the oral accounts from former residents of Ukkusiksalik; in this section, you will read personal histories as far back as living memory could provide in the 1990s. Part three, "A Landscape of Stories," follows up by gathering the first-person reflections, augmented by archival research, to paint the landscape of stories.

Where it made most sense, I used Inuit terminology. You will find a glossary of Inuit words near the end of the book.

There is some repetition. This reflects the Inuit way of storytelling — repetition provides emphasis — as do other attributes, like the unspoken thoughts that hang in the air above some stories, offering the reader an opportunity to read between the lines, or the long pauses for silence one would have heard in the original oral accounts, or the matter-of-fact style of storytelling, which leaves it to the listener's imagination to provide the drama inherent in tales of starvation, or spiritual intervention, or even murder. Beyond that, the book's structure requires the repetition. Each informant's story in part two has an inviolable integrity; you will almost hear the individual voices. Certain excerpts from these accounts necessarily and unapologetically reappear in the stories from the land in part three. I trust you will appreciate the emphasis.

I believe that the sum of all this is more than simply the history of Ukkusiksalik. For me, it is also a manifestation of the power of the oral tradition. It has the potential, I hope, to change your perspective of the northern landscape as a whole, in a broader way than just that area surrounding Ukkusiksalik. That said, it also celebrates one of the most beautiful places on Earth.

I first went to Wager Bay in 1986. Together with some companions, I hiked in the hills and travelled by *qajaq* (kayak) along the shores of this magnificent fjord. I ate Arctic char caught at the mouth of the river at Piqsimaniq. I sat blithely in my *qajaq* as a polar bear stalked along the rocky shoreline. I stood on the hillside overlooking Tinittuqtuq with a friend who told me, "I grew up here. My grandfather is buried just up behind us." I also met and spent time with some of the people who later became essential in a variety of ways to the research underlying this work. On that first trip, I heard the first few snippets of the stories from this land. I was hooked. I returned the next summer and on a number of subsequent occasions over the next twenty-five years. I began immediately to collect the stories, even as they forged my sense of connection to this land and its people.

What a privilege it has been, to know the people and to know the land, inseparable as they are.

D.F.P.
February 2014

ACKNOWLEDGEMENTS

There are many people to acknowledge for their contributions to this work. Going back to the beginning, the informants whose stories were documented in the 1990s offered their time and knowledge unselfishly and enthusiastically. Without them, there would be no volume of Ukkusiksalik history today, and this knowledge would have been lost. Gaining access to their stories was possible only with the assistance of interpreters, translators, and transcribers, often family members, who worked alongside me throughout the process: Paul Sammurtok, Pasha Bruce, Thomas Tiktak, Simeoni Natseck, Stephen Kopak, Steve Mapsalak, Manitok Thompson, Leonie Duffy, Veronica Dewar, Bernice Malliki, Shauna Tatty, Carol Nanordluk, Dolly Mablik, and Nicole Camphaug.

Many people at Parks Canada recognized the importance of this work and found ways to support it. Most particularly, Elizabethe Seale in the 1990s and Lynn Cousins in recent years both played key roles in advancing aspects of this project. Without Lynn's vision and determination to champion the concept, you would not now be holding this book in your hands.

Several people reviewed an early draft of the manuscript and offered me constructive suggestions that all served to improve the final product. I am indebted for this assistance to Theresie Tungilik, Joan Scottie, Jackie Nakoolak, Gary Mouland, Margaret Bertulli, Karen Routledge, Kenn Harper, John MacDonald, and Peter Irniq. These people worked diligently with me in a joint effort to correct mistakes, especially to get the names of people and places correct. Nonetheless, there will no doubt remain some errors or misjudgments, for which I apologize and accept complete responsibility. I value most highly the forthright and thoughtful nature of the reviewers' input. Thank you all.

As always, the folks at the Hudson's Bay Company Archives in Winnipeg were most helpful in finding and arranging for the use of photographs.

Parks Canada staff in Iqaluit worked with Dundurn in support of publication, which efforts helped to ensure that the production values of the book are a suitable reflection of the respect we all hold for the informants' collective wisdom.

I'm grateful also to friends Barry Penhale and Jane Gibson, who immediately saw the value of this work as a publishing project, and took it to Dundurn, where Kirk Howard's superb team of editors and designers has succeeded in turning the raw material into a fine volume which will preserve the historical legacy of Ukkusiksalik.

Thank you all.

LIST OF MAPS

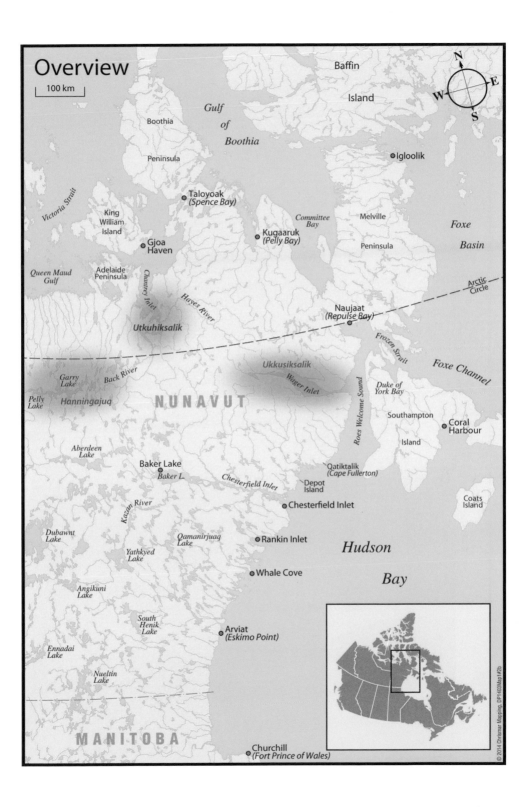

Overview

100 km

N
E
W
S

Baffin

Island

Gulf

of

Boothia

Boothia

Peninsula

Igloolik

Victoria Strait

Taloyoak
(Spence Bay)

Committee
Bay

Melville

Foxe

King
William
Island

Kugaaruk
(Pelly Bay)

Peninsula

Basin

Gjoa
Haven

*Queen Maud
Gulf*

Adelaide
Peninsula

Chantrey Inlet

Hayes River

Arctic
Circle

Naujaat
(Repulse Bay)

Utkuhiksalik

Frozen Strait

Foxe Channel

Garry
Lake

Back River

Ukkusiksalik

Wager Inlet

Duke of
York Bay

Pelly
Lake

Hanningajuq

N U N A V U T

Southampton

Coral
Harbour

Roes Welcome Sound

Island

Aberdeen
Lake

Baker Lake
Baker L.

Chesterfield Inlet

Qatiktalik
(Cape Fullerton)

Coats
Island

Kazan River

Depot
Island

Chesterfield Inlet

Dubawnt
Lake

Qamanirjuaq
Lake

Rankin Inlet

Hudson

Yathkyed
Lake

Whale Cove

Bay

Angikuni
Lake

South
Henik
Lake

Ennadai
Lake

Arviat
(Eskimo Point)

Nueltin
Lake

M A N I T O B A

Churchill
(Fort Prince of Wales)

© 2014 Chrismar Mapping, DP1403Map1#2b

Ukkusiksalik

25 km

Kugajuk

Qamanikuluk

Qamanaaluk

HBC
Trading
Post

Tasiujaq *(Ford Lake)*

Sarvaq

Qaurnak

Iglurjuarnaaq

Tinittuqtuq

Bennett.
Bay

Tikirajuaq

Kingarjuaq

South shore of Wager Inlet

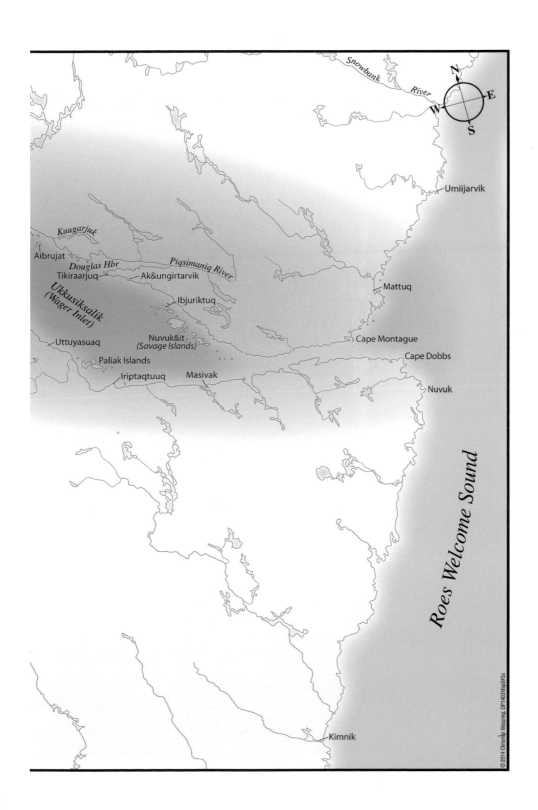

Snowbank River

N
W   E
S

Umiijarvik

Kuugarjuk

Aibrujat
Douglas Hbr
Tikiraarjuq
Piqsimaniq River
Ak&ungirtarvik

Mattuq

Ibjuriktuq

Ukkusiksalik
(Wager Inlet)

Uttuyasuaq
Nuvuk&it
(Savage Islands)

Cape Montague

Cape Dobbs

Paliak Islands

Iriptaqtuuq
Masivak

Nuvuk

Roes Welcome Sound

Kimnik

A PREHISTORIC GLIMPSE

ONE

THE LAND EMERGES

Seven thousand years ago, the area surrounding Ukkusiksalik was covered with mile-thick ice, the last remnant of the Laurentide Ice Sheet, which had once covered all of northern Canada. The ice age, which had lasted about eighty thousand years, was coming to a close. The ice was retreating. By seven thousand years ago, most of what we now call the central tundra of Canada's mainland Arctic was ice-free, the ice sheet having melted during the previous three to five thousand years, leaving behind a vast, flooded plain — in effect, an extension of present-day Hudson Bay. It covered more than one hundred thousand square kilometres, with today's hilltops showing only as islands in what geologists call the Tyrrell Sea. As the great sea retreated, it left behind the valleys and basins for the mighty barrenlands lakes and rivers of the Back, Kazan, Dubawnt, and Thelon watersheds.

Inevitably, the last of the mainland ice melted, and the land once depressed under the weight of ice began to rebound. The surface now exposed around Ukkusiksalik is largely granite, sometimes metamorphosed to gneiss, rocks more than 2.5 billion years old, among the oldest on Earth. The rock itself dates back to a time when the continents as we know them today did not exist, when the world was essentially lifeless, when there was much less oxygen in the Earth's atmosphere.

The bedrock surface was altered by the ice. Advancing ice scraped off loose material in places, picked up huge chunks of granite, ground solid bedrock to sand and clay, and deposited it all in new locations. Moving very slowly — perhaps one metre in a year — across the rock surface, armed with massive rock tools and weighted down by the thickness of pure ice, the glacial action caused erosion and scouring of the granite surface. During the ice age, some of the granite bedrock, never before uncovered, was exhumed from beneath younger overlay and remains exposed today. The evidence of the glacial action is etched on the polished, striated surfaces of rock.

Initially, as the warming climate melted the Laurentide Ice Sheet, the newly exposed landscape had little to offer. The ice-scoured, ancient rock lay bare in most places, with occasional pockets of loose till on top. Slowly, over millenia, it came to life. In the crevices on the hillsides surrounding Ukkusiksalik and in the valleys left behind by the glacial melt, there were places where tiny airborne particles of life-giving minerals came to rest. Lichens, the vanguard of natural colonization, were able to derive sustenance from this material and from the rock itself. A natural succession began. Wind-blown material accumulated. Dead lichen provided nutrients. The process picked up speed. Certain pioneer plants were established by seeds blowing in on the winds. Only plants that could survive in the shallow active layer of soil atop the permafrost had a chance of survival. Mosses, grasses, herbs took root. This northern landscape is one of the youngest on Earth, although the underlying rock itself is among the world's oldest. Over time, these new pastures became the feeding grounds for an invasion of new species: the first avian and mammalian colonizers, followed by larger species, and in turn by *their* predators, eventually including humans.

TWO

THE FIRST PEOPLE

W hile we cannot know when it happened, exactly, we can
be certain that the first people to venture into the Ukkusiksalik area did so in
pursuit of the animals they depended upon for food and clothing, and the raw
materials needed for the other necessities of life. On land, that meant caribou
and muskoxen; in the ocean, primarily seals; and at the river mouths, Arctic char.

This could have occurred as long as four thousand years ago, when some
early peoples ventured into parts of Canada's Arctic, but at Ukkusiksalik it is
likely to have been no earlier — and quite possibly later — than the so-called
Dorset* cultural period, 500 B.C.E. to 1200 C.E. High in the hills between
Masivak and Iriptaqtuuq, on the south shore of Ukkusiksalik, there is an
ancient cobble beach that was once at the edge of the sea, at some point after
deglaciation when the sea level was much much higher than it is today. The site
is covered in dead black lichen, which suggests that whatever human activity
took place here happened a long time ago, as does the inaccessibility afforded
by the inconvenient height, some ninety metres above today's sea level. On the
gentle bedrock slope, there are stone structures used as meat caches and rings of
rocks used to hold down the bottom of a skin tent. One of the tent rings was

---

* The Paeleo-Eskimo people who lived in the Arctic during this period are now
referred to as the "Dorset" culture because the first physical evidence of their
presence was discovered near Cape Dorset (Kinngait) on Baffin Island.

described by archaeologist Karlis Karklins as a "strong" construction, meaning that the walls were formed by a circle of heavy, contiguous boulders standing as much as a metre high. Such construction, he suggested, is probably from an earlier period, though exactly how early remains a question that cannot be answered without excavation to find buried clues in the form of old tools or animal residue that could be dated. One large oval tent ring at this site is divided internally, he says, in a manner which specifically relates to the cultural methods of the Dorset people who preceded today's Inuit across northern Canada.

Karklins wrote: "At least twenty tent rings and six cache cairns are present. One of the former is of the strong variety, but most consist of low circular or oval configurations composed of cobbles and small boulders.... Arctic archaeologist Robert McGhee (personal communication, 1992) believes that this site may date to Dorset or Pre-Dorset times."[1]

Inuit call these people "Tuniit"; they have mythical status among Inuit still today. We know that the Tuniit lived somewhat differently from the direct ancestors of Inuit, who arrived in our Arctic from the west about eight hundred to a thousand years ago. Inuit believe the Tuniit were very strong people, able to move heavy rocks into the ancient formations still evident in the landscape today.

Francis Kaput, who was born in 1930 in the Qamanaaluk area at the inland head of Ukkusiksalik, claimed that "Inuit always lived in Ukkusiksalik — long, long before our time." It is unseemly to argue with him. In considering his statement, it is important to respect the traditional Inuit perspective, that even the people who preceded them in the Arctic were in some measure "their own people" or their cultural ancestors, if not blood relatives. Inuit generally do not differentiate in the manner of anthropologists between themselves and their Dorset or Pre-Dorset predecessors. While they recognize that the Tuniit were different — smaller but stronger than Inuit, it is often said — there is also a sense of brotherhood or connection to these previous Arctic dwellers that permits modern-day Inuit to say, "Our people have been living here for millenia."

From historical records dating to the mid-nineteenth century, we know that the Aivilingmiut (the Inuit group occupying the northwest corner of Hudson Bay, including the coastal area both north and south of Ukkusiksalik) followed a semi-nomadic lifestyle, with their movements largely dictated by the availability of different animals for food. As Mary Nuvak in Chesterfield Inlet said: "People used to travel to survive. They had to travel." Caribou and muskox hunting during the summer, inland from the coast, provided not only a time of plenty but also the opportunity — particularly in late summer as the temperatures cooled — to establish meat caches of winter provisions. Similarly, seal and walrus hunted in summer provided blubber that could be stored in sealskin bags and saved for winter use in the soapstone *qulliq* that every family owned, the principal source of heat and light during the dark, cold months. Seal hunting for these people was largely conducted at the floe edge, in open water, or in the spring months when the seals climbed up onto the sea ice to bask in the sun.* There were specifically timed events that mobilized people greatly: the char runs in the rivers, the fall migration of caribou. Both of these offered not only an abundance of food but equally a relative ease for the catch. So it was essential to take maximum advantage of the opportunity. The winter months ahead were survived largely by having put up sufficient food in advance, as hunting in that season was both more difficult and less productive.

Peter Katokra, whose family lived and hunted around Ukkusiksalik when he was a teenager in the 1940s, described the cycle this way: "Inuit, before the white men or the trading post, lived where there was game. They didn't necessarily stay in one area. They just moved according to where they could survive." Katokra, like the others, reflects the wisdom of his elders and those who came before.

One can imagine, then, that the Ukkusiksalik region has long been an important hunting ground, long thought of as a land of plenty. The extensive body of water, today called Wager Bay, stretches well inland, affording relatively easy access to the inland herds of caribou and muskoxen. The saltwaters of Ukkusiksalik's principal fjord itself are full of ringed seals, and the river mouths thick with Arctic char at certain times. Just as there was a natural ebb and flow to the presence of particular prey animals, Inuit experienced a similar and related cycle in their food supply. Felix Kopak, who was born about 1918 and in later years lived in Repulse Bay, recalled how this phenomenon was described to him many years ago by his grandparents. "There would be times

---

* In 1998, while doing research for my book *Sacred Hunt*, a pan-Arctic examination of the relationship between Inuit and seals, I turned to an Aivilingmiut man, Mikitok Bruce, who at the time was considered the last of the great *aurnaq* hunters. He described in detail the technique for *aurnaq*, or *auriaq* — lying on your side and slowly inching across the sea ice toward a basking seal, tricking the prey into believing that you, the hunter, are just another seal, scratching the ice with your heel and grunting to make seal-like noises, or as Mikitok put it "communicating with the seal."

when game would be plentiful, and other times there would be nothing. It fluctuated. At that time, before the *qablunaat* came, animals were our only source of livelihood, so what we did was hunt all the time. Our elders used to tell us when the game got scarce, it was not that they were going extinct, it was just that they had gathered in another land, seal or caribou or what have you. They were not here because they were there, in another place. The ones before us used to say that even if the animals are not in the immediate area, that does not mean that this land is not good for anything. They used to say that the animals will come back to this place again, sometime in the future."

Archaeological findings, which include more than 440 sites around Ukkusiksalik, suggest that the region was well used by early Inuit arrivals in this corner of Hudson Bay, going back several hundred years. Archaeologist Margaret Bertulli wrote: "Wager Bay was used by both Thule* and historic Inuit over the last several hundred years."[2] Several of the known archaeological sites are well encrusted with lichen and overgrown with moss, suggesting occupation a very long time ago. There are Thule-style summer tent rings, with stone platforms across the rear and sunken stone-lined passageways at the entrance. There are also semi-subterranean houses, with rock walls built into the ground, which would have been topped with whale ribs to support a roof made of sod and skins — the sort of dwelling often used by Thule from autumn through to spring. Excavation of one or more of these winter houses may someday provide confirmed dates for the early Thule occupation of Ukkusiksalik. Without that, the first arrivals remain a mystery, but one which the oral history suggests lies a very long time in the past.

FURTHER READING

Franz Boas, *The Central Eskimo* (Washington: Smithsonian Institute, 1888).

Renée Fossett, *In Order to Live Untroubled: Inuit of the Central Arctic, 1550 to 1940* (Winnipeg: University of Manitoba Press, 2001).

Karlis Karklins, *The Wager Bay Archaeological Survey, 1991–92* (Ottawa: Parks Canada, 1998).

David F. Pelly, *Sacred Hunt: A Portrait of the Relationship between Seals and Inuit* (Vancouver: Grey Stone Books, 2001).

---

* Thule people, the direct ancestors of today's Inuit, migrated across Canada's Arctic in the thirteenth century.

THREE

THE EARLY *QABLUNAAT*

W hen Captain Christopher Middleton sailed his ship, the *Furnace*, accompanied by the *Discovery*, under the command of William Moor, through the mouth of what he named Wager Inlet, in July 1742, he was in search of the Northwest Passage. This was the first party of *qablunaat* to enter Ukkusiksalik. So confident of success were his masters at the British Admiralty that his orders included advice on how to conduct himself should he encounter Japanese shipping.

Both Middleton and Moor were actually Hudson's Bay Company (HBC) men. Middleton, the senior of the two, went to sea as a boy seaman, served with privateers before joining the HBC in about 1720 as a second mate, and rose to command within five or six years. He quickly became one of the most trusted captains in the HBC fleet. At least sixteen times his ships made the round trip from Britain to Hudson Bay, delivering supplies and men, returning each time with a load of fur pelts. He was an accomplished mariner and a capable astronomer, among the first navigators to calculate how to determine a ship's longitude at sea using a sextant and chronometer. In 1726, Middleton published a paper on the magnetic variations in Hudson Bay, which ultimately led to his appointment as a Fellow of the Royal Society — just the man to lead an expedition in search of the Northwest Passage, it would seem.

The HBC was not at all keen about this endeavour, as there seemed to be no advantage to the Company's business; in fact, there was a real possibility that it might undermine the Company's monopoly. As the Governor of the HBC at the time, Sir Bibye Lake wrote to shareholders, the expedition "might affect their Property and be Prejudicial to the Company in their Trade."[1] A noted parliamentarian at the time, Arthur Dobbs, argued strenuously in favour of pursuing the search for the Northwest Passage along the west side of Hudson Bay; he was convinced by fragments of data about tidal currents, ice movements, and whale sightings that this must be where the passage lay. He strongly resented the HBC's monopoly and campaigned vigorously against it, as he lobbied in favour of a new expedition with people "who I believe will undertake it chearfully [sic], as they are convinced it will be a national Benefit."[2] In the end, he convinced the admiralty to take up his proposal, and he further convinced Captain Middleton to abandon his long-time employer and accept a commission with the Royal Navy in order to lead the expedition — in fact, the first of many naval expeditions that Britain mounted in search of the Northwest Passage. Middleton's younger cousin, William Moor, followed his mentor.

On June 8, 1741, the two ships left England, many among the crew press-ganged into service on the docks, to sail across the North Atlantic into Hudson Bay. It was too late to conduct explorations that same summer, so Middleton headed for Fort Prince of Wales (at present-day Churchill, Manitoba) where he hoped there might be some advantage offered by the Hudson's Bay Company post, notwithstanding his strained relationship with Chief Factor James Isham. Ten of Middleton's men died of scurvy that winter. Others, severely frostbitten, lost their toes to amputation. Middleton freely dispensed alcohol to gain favour with his own men, as well as some of the HBC men and the post Indians. The next year, Isham reported to the HBC Committee in London that Middleton had been "a Very Troublesome Guess [guest]."

On July 1, 1742, the *Furnace* and the *Discovery* were laboriously cut free from the ice and set sail to head north up the west coast of Hudson Bay. Middleton was taking no chance of being too late this year. Rounding a headland, which Middleton named Cape Dobbs after his main promoter, the two ships were threatened by shifting ice at the mouth of a large inlet.* Carried by the swirling currents, his ships at risk of damage

---

* Conditions in mid-July are similar today, in that navigation through this entrance remains very hazardous during the prolonged period of breakup in this area.

by the ice, Middleton found his way into what appeared to be an endless passage he named after Sir Charles Wager, First Lord of the Admiralty. Effectively trapped inside by the ice jam at the inlet's mouth, Middleton ordered the ships' boats over the side to pursue exploration of this most promising inland sea. The strength of the flood tide racing into Wager Inlet suggested to Middleton that there must indeed be a way through to another ocean if one were to sail west from this ice-bound passage. His boats explored the interior, under the command of Lieutenant John Rankin (hence Rankin Inlet, somewhat farther south on the Hudson Bay coast), who described the harrowing experience of being swept by the tide in and out of the inlet's mouth surrounded by huge chunks of ice. Rankin ultimately reported back that at its farthest extent, a small waterfall emptied into the inlet, bearing semi-fresh water. At this, Middleton correctly concluded that Wager Inlet was a bay, not a strait.

The maps of the eighteenth and nineteenth centuries showed the indentation in different ways, penetrating inland to varied extents, and named it variously Wager Inlet, Wager River, Wager Water, and simply "the Wager." In the end, map-makers settled on Wager Bay.

In early August the ice cleared enough for Middleton to break free and sail farther north, toward what he named Repulse Bay, where again he believed the sought-for passage might be found. But on August 6, he wrote in his ship's log that "to our great Disappointment we saw the Land from the Low Beach quite round to the Westward of the North which met the Western Shore and makes a very deep Bay. Thus our Hopes of a Passage that way were all over."[3] He turned his ship's head for home and sailed for England, convinced that there was no passage to the Pacific from the west coast of Hudson Bay.

Arthur Dobbs did not accept this conclusion, however, and aimed his vitriol now against Middleton, accusing him of incompetence, of falsifying his reports, and of conspiracy with his former employer, the Hudson's Bay Company. Dobbs argued that there must be a passage because Middleton had seen whales in Wager Inlet of a sort not previously seen in Hudson Bay, which must therefore have come from the Pacific Ocean. Dobbs also bribed Lieutenant Rankin to perjure himself and declare that Middleton had indeed falsified his findings. Dobbs's campaign effectively ended Middleton's career, though the record shows that not only was Middleton correct about Wager Bay, he ought to be further credited for his extremely accurate maps of the Hudson Bay coast.

Not one to give up easily, Dobbs engaged William Moor to lead a private expedition back to Wager Inlet. Although Moor had written unequivocally in his journal in mid-August 1742 that "there is no Passage into the other Ocean between Churchill and the Latitd 67°N," and then back in England wrote to his older cousin about the "cock-and-bull story" being disseminated by Dobbs, he apparently changed his mind. Perhaps when Dobbs offered him command of the new private expedition, along with a piece of the action, saying Moor was "very sober and carefull [sic] and will also be an Adventurer [subscriber] himself," that tipped the balance. Temporarily, at least, Moor switched sides in the controversy.

In May 1746 two ships departed from England under William Moor's command, the *Dobbs Galley* and the smaller *California*. Moor imagined winning the twenty thousand pound prize put up the year before by Parliament for "discovery of the Northwest Passage." As a mariner and explorer, or as an expedition leader, Moor was not the equal of his older cousin Middleton. However, in the summer of 1747 he sailed farther into Wager Inlet, far enough to report that "we had the Mortification to see clearly, that our hitherto imagined Strait ended in two small unnavigable Rivers." With that, he limped home to face the wrath of Dobbs who, inevitably perhaps, turned on him immediately.

———

We know that Middleton's expedition encountered Inuit on the shores of Ukkusiksalik, but little more about the event. This was almost certainly the first contact between Ukkusiksalingmiut ("the people of Ukkusiksalik") and *qablunaat* (white men), however fleeting. It was a hundred years before there was more contact for the Ukkusiksalingmiut, and much the same for most of their broader cultural group, the Aivilingmiut. Edward Parry spent the winter of 1821–22 frozen in near Repulse Bay, where he had substantial contact with local Aivilingmiut, including a woman named Iligliuk, who provided Parry with one of the earliest documented Inuit-drawn maps. In the summer of 1836, Captain George Back, fresh from his successful descent — and subsequent ascent, all in a single summer — of the Back River two years before, was sent by the admiralty in the HMS *Terror* to find Wager Inlet and use it as a jumping-off point for an overland expedition to the mouth of his previous expedition's river. The *Terror* did not make it to Wager Inlet, became stuck in ice close to Repulse Bay, and just barely limped back to Ireland the following year. Another HBC man, a hardy Orkneyman named John Rae, stayed among the Aivilingmiut in Repulse Bay during 1846–47. He learned from them, and as a result became one of the most capable Arctic explorers of his time. Then the American Charles Francis Hall arrived along this same coast in 1864 and stayed for several years. His was the next ship to sail into the mouth of Wager Inlet. He documented a wealth of local knowledge during his time with the Aivilingmiut, and his published record confirms that Inuit lived and hunted in Ukkusiksalik at that time.

FURTHER READING

William Barr and Glyndwr Williams, eds., *Voyages in Search of a Northwest Passage 1741–1747* (London: Hakluyt Society, 1994).

Charles F. Hall, *Narrative of the Second Arctic Expedition Made by Charles F. Hall: His Voyage to Repulse Bay, Sledge Journeys to the Straits of Fury and Hecla and to King William's Land, and Residence Among the Eskimos During the Years 1864–69*, edited by J.E. Nourse (Washington: U.S. Government Printing Office, 1879).

R.L. Richards, *Dr John Rae* (Whitby: Caedmon of Whitby, 1985).

Glyndwr Williams, *Arctic Labyrinth: The Quest for the Northwest Passage* (London: Allen Lane, 2009).

Glyndwr Williams, *The British Search for the Northwest Passage in the Eighteenth Century* (London: Longmans, 1962).

Bryce Wilson et al., eds., *No Ordinary Journey: John Rae — Arctic Explorer 1813–1893* (Montreal and Kingston: McGill-Queen's University Press, 1993).

PART TWO

INUIT UNIPKAUSINGIT
THE PEOPLE'S STORY

Previous page:
Some of the informants of the Ukkusiksalik story-collection project gathered at a field camp in 1996.

INTRODUCTION

With one exception, all of the people in this section recounted their stories during a lengthy Parks Canada oral-history project in the early 1990s. The exception is Marc Tungilik, whom I was fortunate to meet and interview only weeks before he passed away, shortly after my first trip to Wager Bay in 1986. I never forgot his words: "People are always happy to go to a plentiful land — that is how I felt about going to Ukkusiksalik." The tiny ivory carvings he gave me that day are among my treasures, but his inspiration to return to Ukkusiksalik may well have been even more valuable.

My 1986 experiences led to an ongoing involvement in Ukkusiksalik in many ways, most important of which was the invitation from Parks Canada to conduct the extensive work of gathering the elders' memories of the area in which they had lived before their shift into communities. This fundamental transition from life on the land to town-based living swept across the North in the 1950s and 60s, largely as a result of government intervention. The change in lifestyle was dramatic, so these stories offer a unique glimpse back in time to a way of life that has disappeared forever.

I sought out everyone in the surrounding communities who had previously lived in Ukkusiksalik and offered them this opportunity to document their knowledge.

The stories here, in each case in the informant's own voice, are distilled versions of their lengthy, sometimes rambling, and sometimes disjointed but always fascinating accounts, related during several interview sessions with each person.

Although I had a list of subjects for exploration in the interviews, the informants themselves were also given free rein to tell whatever stories they wished and to offer whatever knowledge about Ukkusiksalik they wanted to record for posterity. The original recordings and transcriptions are all held by Parks Canada. The interviews were conducted in the informants' home communities — Repulse Bay, Coral Harbour, Chesterfield Inlet, and Rankin Inlet — by me, with the aid of very capable interpreters, often over successive days. I spent many weeks in each of these communities between 1991 and 1993. In every case, I returned to visit the informant again at least twice to clarify details and to ensure that each person was comfortable with what he or she had recorded (on tape).

Most of the informants included here were elders at the time of the interviews and have since passed away. There was, however, a handful of younger people who were not yet adults when the shift into community life occurred, who offered their own reminiscences of growing up in Ukkusiksalik. Their stories provide an additional perspective on the place.

After this process was complete, in 1996 several of the elders involved travelled to Ukkusiksalik in order to show me the places they had lived and to record the additional memories which were inevitably stirred by this emotional reconnection to the land after an absence of several years or even decades.

The first-person accounts in the following section are direct translations of the elders' words, edited and condensed in order to provide an appropriate glimpse into each of these remarkable lives.

———

A note on names: older Inuit referred to in these stories normally had just one name, given at birth. Inuit did not traditionally use the Western convention of a given name plus a family name. Women did not take their husband's name. The use of "Christian" names began with the arrival of missionaries, so Victor Tungilik (for example) was called Tungilik by his parents when he was born, and then later baptized with the name Victor. But among Inuit he was always called Tungilik and everyone knew he was the son of Soroniq. None of this was written down before the missionaries arrived.

Families were known simply by the father's name, even though the family members did not actually carry his name. So when they say "Soroniq was there" it may be implied that the family of Soroniq was with him.

LEONIE SAMMURTOK,
1902–97
CHESTERFIELD INLET

My husband always said it was really dangerous to go into Ukkusiksalik.

Before I was born, my parents used to live up in Ukkusiksalik. My mother — my real mother — and my father lived in that area before I was born. My mother's name was Betty Tautu and my father's name was Johnny Tamanguluk. They used to live around the Repulse Bay area before I was born, and they hunted in the Ukkusiksalik area for muskox. I don't know how long they lived and hunted in Ukkusiksalik.

When I was born, they lived in Aivilik, in Maluksitaq, on the other side of Repulse Bay. I don't know what year I was born — my parents were not worried about the year. There were no trading posts in Repulse Bay at the time [so, it was before 1921].

I don't remember moving from Aivilik to Qatiktalik [Cape Fullerton]. I started to remember things after I got to Qatiktalik. I remember there were two policemen in Qatiktalik. Inuit called them Kayukuluk ["dear brown-haired one"] and the other one Keekiaksik ["big nail" to imply that he was a big boss]. That's what they were called in Inuktitut. I remember my father going on patrol with Keekiaksik to Repulse Bay and back. I remember because I was tired of my father being gone for so long.

My father never told any stories about Ukkusiksalik. I don't know if the RCMP established a post in Ukkusiksalik when I was young. Maybe.

I don't remember when ships were travelling with sails only. I heard about the whalers back then, around Qatiktalik and up the coast to Repulse Bay, but I don't remember whether I saw them.

The buildings were built in Ukkusiksalik when I was an adult, after I had my first child, Nutaratnaq, when my husband was piloting a ship for the Hudson's Bay Company. My husband, Sammurtok, and my brother Kusugak, and two other men, Kadjuk and Iqungajuq, were working on that ship, when they started building the post in Ukkusiksalik. Iqungajuq has a [adopted] daughter in Coral Harbour [Tuinnaq Kanayuk Bruce], but she is actually the daughter of the Bay manager at Ukkusiksalik.

The *Nascopie* used to come in to Chesterfield Inlet to bring supplies for communities like Repulse Bay and Coral Harbour. Then a smaller ship would take the supplies to Repulse Bay and Baker Lake. The smaller ship would stay in Baker Lake. It would just get frozen in, at Baker Lake. These three men were working, bringing supplies from here on that smaller ship.

There was one winter that Iqungajuq was the manager for the year. And the following year a white man came in who managed the store with him. I think for one year the Inuit manager was alone there and then the second year the *qablunaaq* came. He stayed working for the Bay even after *qablunaat* came. The manager would leave and somebody else would come in to replace him but Iqungajuq was always there. He stayed on even after they left. He had a house there. If he needed supplies for his post, Iqungajuq had a smaller boat, not as big as a Peterhead,* that he would use to get supplies from either Repulse Bay or Chesterfield to trade at his post.

My husband said there was quite a strong current in the entrance and it was really hard to navigate that current, it's so powerful. My husband said it was way too far into the bay, where they established the post. They put the post in so far inland so that people could get to them easier, when they were hunting or had traps inland. The Hudson's Bay Company had competition back then. They were trying to be accessible to everybody. It was easier for them to trade from here than anywhere else. They wouldn't be so far from one group of people. The main competition was called Ningikliit [Revillon

---

* The Peterhead boat, referring to a style of boat that originated in Peterhead, Scotland, became a popular vessel in the Arctic, particularly among the more affluent Inuit.

Frères, a French trading company in direct competition with the HBC, eventually absorbed into the HBC in 1927].

Isumatakuluk was a white man; he worked for the competition to the Hudson's Bay. Isumatakuluk went up to Repulse Bay when my second son was born, when he was still an infant. He went to work up in Repulse Bay for the other store. The manager from the other store went to Baker Lake. Eventually they folded, and then everybody left from that company.

I heard that people would hunt seal through the ice at Ukkusiksalik. Whenever they came from inland to the coast, they would be hunting for seal anywhere there's ice along the coast.

My husband always said it was really dangerous to go into Ukkusiksalik. One time, in the spring, when my husband was living there with his parents as a very young man, they were travelling back into Ukkusiksalik. They were trying to go in, waiting for the current to start flowing inward rather than out. It was still flowing out. They saw this big piece of ice. So they were going to wait for it to pass through. They landed their boat on the floe edge but there were two big pieces of ice pushed up by the current. They watched for this ice that was coming through the passage, and when that big piece of ice hit one of the other two pieces of ice, they fell down and the boat was wrecked. My husband broke his leg when the mast fell on him. Ovinik's two wives were both killed in the accident and one of them had a child in her *amautiq*, and Puyatak, a brother. There were other people killed in that accident, too.

TUINNAQ KANAYUK BRUCE, 1925–2012 CORAL HARBOUR

We all went to Ukkusiksalik the autumn after I was born.

I was born in 1925 near Naujaat, Repulse Bay. My mother was Toota. My real father was an HBC man, Jimmy Thom. Later, my Inuit father was Iqungajuq. First of all, Iqungajuq and Toota were husband and wife living near Naujaat; they had one child. Kupak and Niaqukittuq was another couple. These two couples, Iqungajuq and Toota, and Kupak and Niaqukittuq, were close. Then Kupak, the husband of Niaqukittuq, died. So Iqungajuq went to get Niaqukittuq. That's how Toota and Iqungajuq separated. So Toota was then with Jimmy Thom. Inuit used to call him Tunusuq. That means "the back of the head." He must have had a big head or something.

That's how I was born. I really don't like to talk about these two couples because some people might think wrong or they might think that I am trying to put Niaqukittuq and Iqungajuq down but I'm not. When Niaqukittuq's husband, Kupak, died that's when Iqungajuq went to get Niaqukittuq and they started living together and that's how Toota ended up with the *qablunaaq* Bay manager.

We all went to Ukkusiksalik the autumn after I was born: Toota and Jimmy Thom, Iqungajuq and Niaqukittuq, Iqungajuq's brothers: Samson was Ipkarnaq, Johnny was Siulluk, Tommy was Talituq. [The brothers had been given the English nicknames Samson, Johnny, and Tommy.] Siulluk got that name after he started having a hearing problem. He was a strong man.

Iqungajuq's mother went along. Those four brothers — Iqungajuq, Tommy, Samson, and Johnny — with their wives went to Ukkusiksalik in a small whaleboat with Jimmy Thom, to meet the ship from Chesterfield. They went ahead of the ship so that they could put up their camp before the ship came. The four brothers and their families waited for that ship in Ukkusiksalik. The ship from Chesterfield Inlet brought the wood to build houses. A *qablunaaq*, or half Inuk and half *qablunaaq*, Sam Voisey — the manager in either Arviat or Whale Cove — was sent there to help build the foundations of the buildings. They all went to Ukkusiksalik and started building the Hudson's Bay post at Tasiujaq.

After the ship unloaded at Tasiujaq, it went to Naujaat to pick up some supplies. Iqungajuq's mother had been left behind in Naujaat because she was scared to go on that small boat. So she went on the ship. The ship returned to Nuvuk&it* in Ukkusiksalik, where Iqungajuq and his brother met it, picked up the supplies and their mother, and returned to Tasiujaq. At the same time, they took Inugluq [another man who had been helping at the new post] to Nuvuk&it, so he got on the ship going back to Whale Cove.

My real father, Jimmy Thom, left from Ukkusiksalik a year later.** Even though Iqungajuq wasn't my real father, he brought me up really well when I was growing up.

---

* The ampersand symbol "&" is used to mark the so-called voiceless lateral fricative in writing Inuktitut. Designated ɬ in the International Phonetic Alphabet (IPA), the ampersand, combined with Inuktitut vowels, results in the approximate sounds: &i = "-shli-"; &a = "-shla-"; &u = "-shlu-".

** When Jimmy Thom left Tasiujaq in the late summer of 1926, he gave Toota an old British coin for his daughter Tuinnaq. It was a coin, he said, that he had inherited from an old lady in Britain, about the size of today's two-dollar coin, but the colour of a copper penny and with an image of St. George slaying the dragon on one side. He said that if Tuinnaq ever needed money, she could sell this coin and she would have enough money to live. She kept it for years, through moves to various camps and eventually into Coral Harbour. Many years later, in the early 1960s when her only son, Louie, was taken away by authorities to school in Churchill (against his parents' will), Tuinnaq sent the coin with the young boy, in case he needed money. She was so worried about him and loved him so much, she recounted many years later, that this was all she could think to do for him. Shortly after Louie Bruce arrived in Churchill, the coin was taken away from him by someone at the residential school, and the family never saw it again.

I remember I used to go to the *qablunaats'* house at Ukkusiksalik when I wanted them to give me a bath. I realized later on that those people weren't my father. I also remember when we first saw an airplane, one of those planes that had two wings, one at the bottom and one at the top. I don't remember why it came.

My adopted father, Iqungajuq, didn't always stay at the Hudson's Bay houses, but we lived in that area. When we were at the post we lived in a rough wooden house, probably made with scraps from the store and the manager's house. I remember one winter Iqungajuq must have asked for leave. He wanted to have a break. I remember that one winter when we didn't work for the Bay manager. That's the first time I remember when we lived in an iglu. We went to Tinittuqtuq, where Iqungajuq used to hunt. I remember when it was Christmas, the Bay manager sent me a little doll and candies.

I can't remember what really happened between Toota and Niaqukittuq. But I remember Niaqukittuq's mother, Qatani, came to the Ukkusiksalik post to tell Niaqukittuq that she should leave them, so Toota and Iqungajuq can live together again. That's how Niaqukittuq got separated from Iqungajuq. He didn't live with Niaqukittuq after that. People knew Niaqukittuq's mother as a wise person. Qatani told Niaqukittuq that she was adopted by Iqungajuq and Toota. The rest of the family [in order of age from oldest to youngest] was my sister, Avaqsaq (a.k.a. Niveaksok); me; Leo Napayok; my brother, Tatty; and then [a younger brother] Tattuinee. Leo Napayok was a child of Iqungajuq and Niaqukittuq. He died this year [1991]. Iqungajuq had two children from Niaqukittuq, but the other one died. Leo Napayok was just a little bit older than Tatty.

I remember two other HBC men: Buster Brown, whom we called Ikumalirijialuk ["he who works with engines"], and Sammy. Brown lived in the middle house, with his tractor. The others [Sam Voisey and the clerk, H. McHardy] lived in the manager's house. Brown had a machine like a tractor, to go [overland] to Back River. I remember these people leaving. There are lots of hills in that area, so they used to put it backwards to climb up the hills. Because the hills are too steep, it would almost fall down.

We used to take walks up along the hills behind the post. My brother, Tatty, and I saw a place where somebody must have carved out a piece of soapstone to make a *qulliq*. That big piece of soapstone is still there. Somebody tried to carve it out but never got it out.

Just over the hill behind the post, there is a little lake with some small fish. In spring, some little creeks started flowing. It was really fun to live there.

When we were children, we would fish for those small, ugly fish that come out from under the rocks. We used to look for siksiks [ground squirrels]. We used to pick berries. We never used to be bored, even though there weren't that many people living in that area.

My parents adopted a polar bear cub and we used to play with that cub. One time we were playing with the cub in the water, and we started throwing rocks, not really at the bear. It ran away. When we got home, he ended up with another family that lived a little bit farther away. But they brought it back to us. As it grew, he was always living with us, in the house. He didn't seem to understand when we talked to him, but somehow my mother told him to go away because she was worried that he might attack people, or that people might be scared of him. I really don't know how it understood my mother when she told him to go away, and he never came back. My mother didn't want him killed by the people, so she sent him away.

There were just a few of us living there and we were related to each other. We didn't really compete against each other. Not many people used to go there. There weren't any strangers at that time. As I grew older, once in a long while people would come. People came now and then but they never used to spend much time at the post.

There were other families living at the post some of the time. Tommy and Johnny and Samson, and their families, would come in the summertime and put up their tents and live with us for a while, then go back to their hunting area when winter came, to trap for foxes. They used to go to Nuvuk&it to hunt seals for the dogs.

Those four brothers, the three brothers of Iqungajuq, were the main people in this area. Tommy and Samson moved away when Samson was starting to have pains in his stomach, because there weren't nurses or doctors in Tasiujaq. So Tommy brought Samson to live in Chesterfield Inlet. So Iqungajuq and Siulluk were the only brothers left in Tasiujaq area. When Samson died, Tommy had to go all the way up to Tasiujaq to tell his brothers that Samson died.

There was another person with us, Sutoqsi. When he was a little boy, his mother went out to find some wood for a fire but she never came back and they never found her. Because Sutoqsi was too small to look after himself,

Iqungajuq and Toota started looking after him. This was before Iqungajuq and Toota had any children, way before I was born. When Sutoqsi grew up he was hunting for rabbit but never came back. When they found him, he was already dead. We don't really know what happened to him. They found his tracks. We figure he must have been running away from something. He went behind some rocks and he fired three shots, but we don't know what he was shooting at. Samson and Sutoqsi died in that same year.

I remember one time people came from the Back River. Those people had those wooden snow goggles that they made and I was wondering what kind of people they were. That was the first time I saw people like that. They seemed like different people. Their dialect was different from ours. How they dressed was different from us. I also remember when Iqungajuq went up there to their camp [at Back River] he brought back a fish almost as big as me.

Iqungajuq had some kind of a diary. He used to write down every day what happened on that day. But in 1945, we had to go to Repulse Bay, and we never got back to Ukkusiksalik. We left everything behind in Ukkusiksalik and we never went back to get them, including that diary. I still think about that diary. If I had kept that diary, I would know everything that happened then.

I remember they used to have square dances at the post. One year at Christmas, they had a big dance and big meal and everybody enjoyed the celebration. The music was [supplied] by Tommy on an accordion. Tommy was really good at the accordion and he spoke English really well because when he had an injury on his arm, he was down south for a long time [where he learned English in the hospital]. Even though he had an injured arm, he was really good at playing accordion. I remember getting a rocking horse; either it was a present for me or maybe Agulaq [a man who worked around the trading post occasionally] just fixed it up for me. I remember that rocking horse.

The only way out from this lake at Tasiujaq was a little river called Sarvaq. It follows the tide [reverses direction]. One time, after the ship we called *Umiajuarnaq* brought supplies for the store, it was trying to go out and it got stuck, I was on that ship when it got stuck. It touched the bottom. There were two big pieces of wood from the bottom of the ship that broke off. The ship didn't get wrecked, just the two pieces came off. When that river is flowing down it gets very strong, so the ship got pushed out of the river and it went on its way again.

I am not sure if [after that] they brought the supplies to Iglujuarnaaq. There was this little building there, that's why they called that place Iglujuarnaaq [which means "place with a little building"]. I remember there were some supplies in that little building. We used to spend some time in that area. We would camp in the spring, but we never spent the winter there.

It seems that ever since that ship got stuck in that river, they had to go get their own supplies for the store. I remember there was a calendar in our house and I remember 1933. Qauluniqsaq, "the one with lighter hair," and Qiniqniqsaq, "the one with darker hair," were the last two [HBC traders] that left in 1933.

I have heard — I might be wrong, but I have heard — that there weren't enough foxes and not enough people were going there to buy from that post, not enough trappers to get foxes for the post. That ship came to Ukkusiksalik and those HBC people came to us in their little boat from the post. When my family and I were at Qamanaaluk fishing, some people came to us, with Amotee (David Aglukark's grandfather) interpreting, to ask Iqungajuq if he could take over.* I think that same summer the ship got stuck in that river at Sarvaq, on its way out the last time. Iqungajuq didn't want to take over because he didn't know what to do. He really didn't want to take over but they told him just to write down everything that is sold. They persuaded him.

Those *qablunaat* really wanted to send Tatty down south for schooling. But my parents didn't want to send him away because he was the only son of the family. The *qablunaat* wanted him to get ready to take over when Iqungajuq quit being manager.

When that ship stopped going to Ukkusiksalik, Iqungajuq used to go to Chesterfield Inlet or Naujaat (Repulse Bay) by Peterhead boat to get supplies for the post. One time he went to Naujaat by dog team in winter to get more supplies. I don't remember how many times he went to Naujaat or Chesterfield Inlet to get more supplies. Chesterfield was farther away than Naujaat, so he started getting supplies from Naujaat. In springtime he

---

* Iqungajuq did take over operation of the post on behalf of the HBC (see chapter 35, "An Inuk Manager for the HBC Post").

would go on the dog team and pick up supplies from Naujaat. But it was in summertime that he would go by boat and then I would trade [at the Tasiujaq post].

In Ukkusiksalik, only Siulluk, Tommy, and Iqungajuq had little boats with sails and motors, smaller than a Peterhead, like a whaler's boat. They were just open boats with no deck. They fixed it up and put a deck and a motor. So those were the only people that could come to trade from other parts of Ukkusiksalik. Those people that couldn't come by boat they would come in the winter by dog team. The people from Back River came down by dog team in winter also. Once in a long, long while they would come in summer. They would walk overland to the post.

When summer came nobody really traded because they would have to walk to the post. If anyone did come in summertime when Iqungajuq was away getting supplies by Peterhead, I would do the trading for him. I would use small pieces of wood as money [HBC wooden tokens].* I would write down in Inuktitut things that were traded. I didn't like trading because some people weren't happy. People traded for bullets, flour, tobacco, lard, ingredients for making bannock, things like that. They weren't expensive at that time. I had to write it all down in Inuktitut. I learned to write and read by myself. When I was a little girl, I memorized a song, and someone gave me words to that song written out in syllabics, so I started reading it by what I had memorized. I learned to read by myself.

There are a few times I remember at Ukkusiksalik.

Four brothers, Kreelak, Kapik, Taparti, and Kaput were surviving on fish but they were going hungry. So Siksaaq, their father, went to the post to buy some food. Siksaaq's family owed too much to the post in Naujaat, so they couldn't buy from the store in Tasiujaq. Iqungajuq's family had to supply some food for Siksaaq. We were doing it out of love. It was all from our own supplies. We gave a little bit of food to them. He was going back to his family, walking. He got to Kapik in Qamanaaluk, and after Kapik's, he left to walk to Kreelak. He was going back to Kreelak's family and at that time Kreelak was with his mother, Siksaaq's wife. But on his way to Kreelak's camp, he never got there. He was found the following spring or summer.

---

* The HBC trader would give people so many tokens as payment for their skins, and those tokens could then be exchanged for the trade goods.

He was not found until the snow melted and we figure that he had built an iglu. Some say he was attacked by a polar bear. Either he was pulled out of the iglu by a bear or he had a knife and tried to fight the bear with the knife. He had four sons, but since the brothers didn't have dogs they gave up, because they had to walk to look for their father. There was a fifth son, Okpik, who also died while they were in that area. He drifted away when he was trying to get a seal when the wind was blowing.

There used to be lots of wolves in the fall because the cubs are born in the spring and they grow during the summer. So there are lots in the fall. They started howling and we could hear them. Tatty and I would go across the lake and put up some traps. Iqungajuq had some meat cached in that area [south side of Tasiujaq], so we would put up some traps there. We would go there on a small *qamutik* [sled] with two dogs. One of us would run and one of us went on the *qamutik* because the *qamutik* was small. When we got to the other side of the lake there were lots of wolf tracks, and our dogs were sensing there was something there. I didn't realize there was a little hill above that meat cache. They went over the hill and I didn't realize they were there. We got scared so we just left without putting up the traps. As soon as we got home, our father, Iqungajuq, went back with us to where we were going to trap. He brought a rifle with him and he set it up there in that spot where the tracks were so it would go off on its own. He put the meat on the ground. He tied it with some rope. And he ran the rope across under the rifle. He put some meat in front of the rifle. He tied the meat with a rope and he ran the rope behind the rifle and tied it to the trigger of the rifle, so when the wolf pulled on the meat the rifle would go off. The next day they went back, and the wolf was shot right in the forehead.

There were also other animals. There were caribou, rabbits, ptarmigan, and wolves. Those wolves would tear up the foxes that were trapped and people didn't really like that.

We didn't go hungry. But we were short of food sometimes, when Iqungajuq went to get some supplies for the post. We really couldn't store food in summer. There's lots of Arctic char in summer, but we got tired of fish. At one time in Iglujuarnaaq, Iqungajuq had gone to get some supplies and he had left us a boat with a motor — my sister and I hunted for seals in summer. Tatty was youngest, so he was driving the boat. My sister and I did the shooting.

We weren't allowed to hunt muskox, because there weren't that many muskox at that time. Kreelak and his family would hunt muskox but I don't remember seeing a muskox because we weren't supposed to hunt them. I never saw a live muskox. I saw some skins or meat from animals that were hunted. Kreelak and his brothers were hunting quite a few muskox even though they weren't supposed to. They were hunting muskox in spring, and that same year their father died. We heard rumours that some people weren't happy because they weren't allowed to hunt muskox.

While Iqungajuq was managing the post, some *qablunaat* came to visit the post. RCMP came once in a while by dog team in winter. I'm not sure why they came but I think one time they were sort of investigating the deaths of those two men, Siksaaq and Sutuqsi. They stayed with us; there were other buildings besides our house but we couldn't spare wood or coal for heat. So they stayed with us. They were friendly. I never used to be scared of *qablunaat* when I was a little girl. I probably thought they were my father.

One time Kupanuaq [the name Inuit gave to Tom Manning, the British-Canadian explorer, biologist, geographer, author, and Arctic travel-ler] and his assistant, came to our camp but they stayed at another house, not our house. They were both *qablunaat*. They weren't RCMP. They tried to go to Back River with Iqungajuq but they came back because the snow was too deep. The same Kupanuaq was the guy who brought some caribou from Coats Island to Southampton Island.*

I remember my mother telling me the story about the ship being wrecked when it was really windy. The man that owned that ship was called Angakkuq by Inuit. He was a *qablunaaq* but the reason we called him Angakkuq [mean-ing "shaman"] was because Inuit saw him as a person who knew a lot of things. He was on that ship.

Iqungajuq's Peterhead boat wasn't in very good condition. One time, we were waiting in Naujaat for the supply ship to come, but it didn't come until very late in the fall. It was almost winter so we had to head back to Tasiujaq. Iqungajuq got half of the supplies from Naujaat; we got a little bit of flour and lard and fuel from Naujaat, left over from the Naujaat post. We started heading back to Ukkusiksalik.

---

* This was done as part of a federal government project, led by Tom Manning, to populate Southampton Island with caribou.

At Umiijarvik, it was already icing up. The ice was getting thick so we couldn't go on. It was really cold, very late in the fall. Our boat didn't get wrecked because we landed before it got wrecked. My parents got scared that it might sink because the ice was scraping on the sides of the boat. So we landed on shore and got our supplies on land. There were only my parents, my brother, Tatty, and his wife — they were young then — myself and another guy that was the same age as Tatty, plus Tattuinee and Susie.

When we got to shore, Iqungajuq built a shelter from ice. It wasn't too cold, just before winter came. It was really nice to live in that ice house for a while because we could see through. When winter came we built an iglu and moved into it. Our parents knew where the fish were. If they weren't with us, we wouldn't have survived. Our boat wasn't wrecked, so we had the supplies we got from Naujaat. But we didn't have water so we drank tomato juice. We had to stay in that area where we were beached and we spent part of the winter there.

I was really mad at the Hudson's Bay people because they were the reason. I think they should have looked after us more because they knew that [the] Peterhead's motor wasn't running well.

Some trappers came so we sold some stuff to them. We had left our dog team in Ukkusiksalik but they weren't being fed, so they starved and we didn't have a dog team anymore. Somehow, in the winter — I don't remember whose dog team we used — with somebody's dog team we went to Naujaat. We couldn't go back to Ukkusiksalik so we went to Naujaat.

My mother, Toota, really wanted to go back to the post because she was thinking the *qablunaat* might think that the Inuit don't really try hard to do things that they are told to do. Iqungajuq and Toota sort of disagreed.

When we left Tasiujaq at that time, we were going to go back but we didn't, so I am not sure what happened to the supplies. We left everything behind because we were going to go back. Tatty and another man went back to the post that winter but I am not sure what they brought back because they went on a dog team, so they couldn't bring that much back. Maybe some papers or something.

We had left our dogs behind; Agulaq was going to look after them. Three brothers — Tavok, Kingumuk, and Qabluittuq — all lived in the same area as Agulaq, around Nuvuk&it. Agulaq got married to Sutoqsi's wife after Sutoqsi was lost while hunting. We had a plan. Tatty was going to go get the dogs so he could bring them back to us. We were planning to go back by dog team when Tatty came with the dogs. But the dogs were dead because they had starved. Agulaq was an old man. He was too old to look after them properly. When we were going to Naujaat, Siulluk left for Chesterfield Inlet at the same time. If Siulluk had looked after the dogs instead of Agulaq, they would have survived.

Tatty was quite young then. He was just riding with Angutinguaq on a single dog team because he was planning to get our dogs and come back to get the family and go back to Tasiujaq. Agulaq had adopted Angutinguaq as his son. I think they brought a few things but not much, because it was winter and it was quite far from where we were camping at Umiijarvik.

I recently got a letter from Archie Hunter, remembering me as a little child. His Inuktitut name was Titiraqtikulu. He was probably the assistant to Jimmy Thom when he was the manager. In Naujaat, he [Archie Hunter] was called Titiraqtikulu [which means "the little one who writes" i.e., the junior clerk]. Whoever was the assistant to a Bay manager was called Titiraqtikulu. He moved to Ukkusiksalik to be manager at the post in Tasiujaq but even though he wasn't a junior clerk any more, they just called him Titiraqtikulu, even though he was a manager.

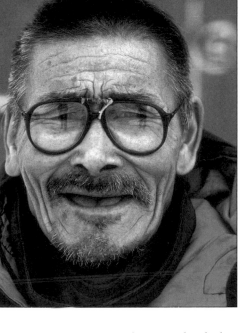

SIX

MARIANO AUPILARJUQ, 1920–2012 RANKIN INLET

This is our land, this is our home, which means that it actually ties up with our lives and we become one.

S ince I'm becoming an elder person now, I finally begin to understand that the land and the human being have something in common. As people living in the North, this is our land, this is our home, which means that it actually ties up with our lives and we become one. I never thought of it this way until just recently, when I became an elder person. Sometimes the land will produce, meaning that it will have a lot of wildlife, and some years we may not have any.

Even though people used to live around Ukkusiksalik for the longest time, not all of them survived. Because of that, it's so important to document the names of the areas around Ukkusiksalik, so people will remember that people used to live there, and that some survived and some didn't.

That is my introduction to my father's song. It's not a made-up story, it's a song from my father about what actually happened with regard to Ukkusiksalik. I can talk about it from the beginning to the time that he got to Ukkusiksalik, all the way from the western Arctic.

Although the Inuit didn't have pen and paper like the *qablunaat*, I guess we do have a natural pen and paper in our heads. Even when it's from ancient history, we don't forget it.

I'm just going to begin to sing from when they left Repulse Bay all the way to Ukkusiksalik, crossing over by dog team, and that's where I'll stop.... [*Sings father's song.*]

That's the song my father made when he was leaving Repulse Bay on our route to Ukkusiksalik. I can explain what the song is all about.

I mentioned earlier that for Inuit, the living person and the land are actually tied up together because without one, the other doesn't survive and vice versa. You have to protect land in order to receive from the land. If you start mistreating the land, then it won't support you.

Inuit, in our times, had laws, even though the laws weren't similar to the laws we have today. It was the law of the Inuit that in order to survive, you have to respect the land and protect it. The land is so important for us to survive and live on — that's why we treat it as part of ourselves.

When my father started to make the song, it didn't just come out from his head. He had to do the actual things described. For instance, when he left Repulse Bay he had to pick a title of the song. It's called "Ukkusiksalik." He mentioned something about Ikaariarvik, a place in Ukkusiksalik that is part of the whirlpool you have to cross to get to the other side [if you're] coming from the Repulse Bay area. Ikaariarvik, meaning "place from which you cross," is near the entrance to Ukkusiksalik from Roes Welcome Sound. This is about having to respect the land because it's part of you. In the spring you have to wait here until a certain time when you can cross. There are stories that people did not make it.

Before you crossed to the other side, to respect the Inuit law, if a person had any bad feelings toward another person, you'd have to confess, with your voice, without hiding it. You actually have to talk about it. "I'm sorry I did this to you before" or "I'm sorry that I stole your rifle." Any bad thing has to be dropped before you cross, because if you don't do that, then you'd never make it to the other side. That's why there are stories about people having accidents. That's the meaning of respecting the land.

In those days, when we didn't know anything about Christianity, before the *qablunaat* started introducing it to us, shamanism was more like our religion — having to believe and respect the land. The Inuit custom was to leave everything behind, to confess among other people that you have been a bad person, that you did things you aren't supposed to do to another person. You had to confess to the people around you, before crossing the mouth of the river. Respect for the land and respect for the people is just as one.

The land can only survive if it's protected by Inuit, and a living person can only survive if they respect the tradition of the land.

Before the missionaries came, and there were no doctors, nobody like that, when I was a boy, we learned these things from our parents and our grandparents. We were told to do this by our parents; don't just go ahead and forget about it and do our own thing. Today, people just do whatever they want, instead of listening to their parents. Myself, today, I still respect what my ancestors have told me. Although we don't have pen and paper to write it, it's still on my mind very clearly: to respect the land and respect what it can do to us. My ancestors believed in the important parts of the land. There was very strong meaning from the land — when you respect it, it will respect you. Those are some of the words of my father's song, describing what he did and how he crossed.

He didn't have an outboard motor. He had an *umiaq* [a large boat] that you have to row. He sings about rowing for a number of days just to get to the other side. His breath was tiring.

That's almost the end of the song. I don't want to go beyond that because I don't want to mislead in the story of my ancestors. The wording of his song I still respect because he talks about his journey.

I wasn't even born yet, or I must have been just a baby. My father tells this story through his song. The reason I talk about it is to respect the elders. I do know it actually took place, and I know the land, and the laws of Inuit are real, having to respect the land. That's why I would pass it on to younger generations. The story I remember is just from what my father tells in the song.

I was born in the Pelly Bay area. The only way I can estimate the date is, in Repulse Bay there used to be two outposts: the one existing now, where the Roman Catholic mission is, and before that, the first one was put up. That's around the time I was born. I can't recall the year, but before the first post was put up.

Much later, afterward, my father and myself lived south of Ukkusiksalik, but it's so long ago I can't remember. I was told that we lived in the area south of Ukkusiksalik, but I can't recall because I was only a small boy.

At the time, there was a man that died there because he didn't follow the laws of the Inuit at Ukkusiksalik, not to eat berries or pick up the leaves, the stuff that they used to smoke. If you have never been here, don't do this for the first year. But he went ahead anyway, even before the year was over.

He died there. That person, Kuujuaq, wasn't married, although he was a grown-up man already. He was always with us. He was in the same iglu before he passed away. Although he was told [not to], without letting other people know, he was doing this anyway, eating berries and smoking little leaves. I guess he became a little bit crazy the first year. I don't know how long he was like that. We didn't count weeks, but it was for quite a long time. Just before he passed away, in the iglu, I guess the demon was trying to make us understand that he was doing this. He was even picking up little rocks, trying to chew them. He didn't tell us verbally but he was already a little crazy. When my mother asked him, "Kuujuaq, what are you doing?" he said, "I'm picking berries and eating leaves." That's the only answer he used to give us.

We never understood why Kuujuaq was doing all this because he was unable to talk anymore. But when I say we respect the land, that means respect the traditional customs of the Inuit. If you are told "Don't do this in the first year," you don't. The following year, you can. If it's not your first time, or if you've been there long enough already, it's all right, but not in the first year. That's what I mean by respecting the laws of the Inuit, and the land itself.

I don't think anybody can say when all that actually began. When I said respect your elders, all elders respected the eldest, and we can go on and on and on. We respected the Inuit customs and laws long before Christianity. Our ancestors respected the land, and as a result we survived. When we say that the land belongs to the Inuit, we are saying that from the bottom of our hearts, it belongs to the Inuit! We have to respect the laws and the beauty of the land.

Not so long ago, when I was already married and had children, we went to Ukkusiksalik by boat, around Bennett Bay, right at the corner. That's the only other time I travelled to Ukkusiksalik.

I'm not trying to say let's go back to ancient history, back to the traditional laws. That's not what I'm trying to say. When I talk about this history of the Inuit or when I talk about the land, they are not made-up stories. When you respect the eldest, the history of our ancestors will still be within you. When I talk about the ancient history, I'm not trying to say that I'm a disbeliever. I believe that there is a Lord and I believe there is a demon. But if you look at yourself being in the middle, the shamanism and today's religion are similar.

FRANCIS KAPUT, 1930–
RANKIN INLET

Ever since I started to remember, my parents were always on the go.

I was born in 1930 around Ukkusiksalik, in the Qamanaaluk area, beside the river to the northwest of Tasiujaq. From my older brothers and other people I know, they told me that I was born close to the mouth, close to Tasiujaq.

When my father, Siksaaq, was a younger person, he lived around the Nattilik, Pelly Bay area, all that area northwest of Repulse Bay. My older brothers were born toward Repulse area, and north of Repulse Bay, but younger people like myself were born around Ukkusiksalik. My father lived around Ukkusiksalik area even before the HBC post. There was abundant wildlife — caribou, fish, and mainly polar bears.

We left Qamanaaluk for Chesterfield Inlet in the early 1930s, shortly after I was born. About nine or ten years later, we moved back to Ukkusiksalik, around 1939 or 1940. We came back from Chesterfield Inlet because my older brothers and my older sisters were still living around the Ukkusiksalik area. We travelled by the ocean and cut across from Chesterfield Inlet area by land, on foot, to go back and live with my brothers and sisters.

Ever since I started to remember, my parents were always on the go. In the summertime, they never stayed along the coast. They were in the mainland; they'd always travel on foot and with dogs. The dogs would help carry some of the belongings. We carried our belongings on our backs, packing them. On the way, we were trying to collect caribou hide for clothing for winter. After they were dried, we would roll the skins up and cache them, to pick them up on the way back.

We travelled by dog team from Chesterfield Inlet along the coast, until the ice broke up, and from Kimnik [south of Ukkusiksalik along the Hudson Bay coast], we started walking through the mainland toward Ukkusiksalik. It was around early August when we started walking. When we left the coast from Kimnik toward Qamanaaluk, we spent a lot of time hunting caribou and drying the skins. The only wildlife we came across on the land were the caribou and sometimes ptarmigan. On our way to Qamanaaluk from Kimnik, we never actually looked for caribou itself but we got caribou that were on our trail. Once we got caribou, we would stay, make camp, and when the caribou that we had caught were gone, then we continued on the route to Qamanaaluk. We actually never went somewhere just to caribou hunt but there were caribou all along the way. I recall that my parents, every time that they saw caribou, they made camp there until the meat was gone. Sometimes they were caching the caribou meat. My parents also wanted caribou hide for clothing for the winter. I remember some of the caribou caches that we made; we never went back to them because later on we went back by another route.

We took our time going back, so it was toward the end of September, or the beginning of October, when we arrived in Qamanaaluk. At Tasiujaq, we got my brother Kreelak. He and his family were looking after the dogs at the Hudson's Bay post, because the manager, Iqungajuq, had gone to Repulse Bay to resupply the post.

After that we lived northwest of Qamanaaluk. My father was always helping the Hudson's Bay post manager. He used to tell us that he was one of the men that helped to build the post itself. He used to help unload the ships when they came in to resupply the post. There are rapids you can actually go right through to Tasiujaq. There's another little house close to the mouth, where they used to unload after the ship got grounded.

Every spring my father took the HBC men out to the coast to get some seals for dog food. People knew that my father was capable of travelling along the coast safely.

Then, one time when my father went out hunting, somewhere north of Qamanaaluk, he never came back. He got lost. He was by himself, on foot. He always had a rifle then. He must have because he was out hunting. They kept looking for him, but it was almost a year before they found him. I can't exactly pinpoint where he was found. It was Mikitok and Mikitok's father that found him. When he went out hunting, it was full winter. He had stayed in an iglu, but the summer came and he was just lying on the ground when they finally found him. He wasn't very far from his caribou skin bedding. From the stories I heard, he must have been carving something. There were pieces of wood lying around and he had a piece of wood in his hand when they found him.

He didn't die of starvation or illness. Nobody attacked him or anything like that. There were medicines and shamans during those times. I remember when we walked from Chesterfield Inlet toward Qamanaaluk, the first night when we got to my brother Kreelak, early in the morning, I heard [my father] speak when he was getting ready to go out hunting. "I'm tired of being around Ukkusiksalik and tired of these demons, the shamans trying to get at me. Next time I see this person I'm just going to give up and not even fight back." It was Udlut's wife's brother that was always after him. I guess he was a shaman. That's what my father was telling my older brother. I guess that's what got him, a demon or shaman. I guess he never fought back, like he told my brother that winter. After he told my brother what he planned to do, that's when he disappeared.

Courtesy of Francis Kaput

I assume that, because I heard him saying that he was tired of these demons and shamans trying to get at him and that if they tried again, he was just not going to fight back. My mother knew that some day this would happen.

We left Qamanaaluk that fall after my father was found. It was almost

Siksaaq, father of Kreelak, Kapik, Okpik, Kaput, and Taparti.

wintertime. We were on foot. My brothers were the only ones that went to the post to get resupplied. I myself never went there. We took the load through the land, around the south of Ukkusiksalik, to Bennett Bay on the other side. The following summer we hunted around there. In the fall we went to hunt for caribou. Then we went to Nuvuk&it by dog team. It was around 1940 or '41 when we lived in Nuvuk&it area. My brother-in-law to-be came from Chesterfield Inlet area to pick up my sister because they were promised to be married. When he got to Nuvuk&it, we were there, and we went back to Chesterfield Inlet with him. Ever since then, we lived around Chesterfield Inlet.

I know one old story that actually happened. The reason I know this is because my father was one of the people that almost perished when they were going to Chesterfield Inlet to get resupplied by boat. They had the two boats. They had an accident near the mouth of Ukkusiksalik, and there were a number of people who perished in that accident. My father was one of the people that was almost a victim, but he was lucky enough to survive that accident. John Ayaruaq was one of them, when he was a boy.*

I can honestly say that Ukkusiksalik is a very historic area. People always lived in that area, long, long before our time.

---

* Ayaruaq recorded the story of this accident (see chapter 32, "A Fatal Accident").

EIGHT

MARY NUVAK, 1908–99
CHESTERFIELD INLET

People had to move to survive, so that's what they did.

I was born at Qatiktalik [Cape Fullerton] in April 1908. My parents brought me here to Chesterfield Inlet because I was going to be adopted by someone here. The first Bay manager was living here then. The RCMP post was still at Cape Fullerton then. I just remember from being told. I don't actually remember. Later on, when I was growing up, I was told that there were police and a doctor there.

Before I was adopted, my adoptive parents were living in Ukkusiksalik, before they moved here. The man's name was Aguatik and the woman's name was Nanaouk. When they left Ukkusiksalik they went inland toward Baker Lake, in that area. Then they moved here when the Hudson's Bay post was established here. Inuit used to travel to survive. They had to travel. So, when they heard that the Hudson's Bay Company was going to open a post here, that's when they moved here.

They didn't tell me stories about living in Ukkusiksalik. I was too young to notice. They did live up there and when they moved here, my father Aguatik started working for the Bay. He worked here for a while until he got blind. But he knew the area up toward Baker Lake and Ukkusiksalik. He travelled that route a lot, up and down the coast to Marble Island.

The reason the HBC opened the post up in Ukkusiksalik was for fox skins. They wanted to be accessible to trappers. That's what they were going after. They had competition, so they wanted more people to trade with them. That was the main reason they opened that post. They wanted to make sure they got the business.

The managers in Ukkusiksalik came from here [Chesterfield Inlet] at first. I saw these people. They were taken by the smaller ship from here to Ukkusiksalik. They came from here, and they were transferred up to Ukkusiksalik. I remember the people that were going to build the new post. I can remember one who was a former policeman, and one of his prisoners escaped, so he quit the force and went to work for the Hudson's Bay Company. His name was Mr. Brown, Pukiqtali'naaq ["little policeman," although Brown was a big man]. The other one that I remember was Mr. Joe, Makutu'naaq ["the small, young one"]. I don't know the other two managers' names. There were two others. When the post there closed, there was an Inuk running the post.

After the *Nascopie* unloaded at Chesterfield Inlet, the smaller ship delivered supplies up to Baker Lake, Ukkusiksalik, Repulse Bay, and Coral Harbour. That ship was called *schooner-galaaq*, meaning it was a smaller ship, but it wasn't really that small.

I've never actually been there, but I heard about people trading with the post for fox furs. That's the reason why the post was established. People came from Repulse Bay and people who were living in Ukkusiksalik were trading at the post. So, there were people that came from all over to bring their fox skins, to trade them with the manager of the Hudson's Bay Company at Ukkusiksalik.

There were police patrols going up there. They went up by boat and by dog team. They would go up to Repulse Bay, but I don't know if they went to Ukkusiksalik a lot. They went a lot to Cape Fullerton because there were two policemen there. I'm not sure if the police went to Ukkusiksalik a lot but they went up to Repulse Bay.

I remember the first bishop for this diocese. He and the other priests here travelled to Ukkusiksalik, to conduct baptisms, stuff like that. The priests travelled a lot. They travelled up to Ukkusiksalik. I'm not sure if a priest lived there.

People were nomadic. They travelled to survive, to hunt, so it wasn't all the time that people lived there. People had to move to survive, so that's what they did — they moved. It was not like today, when we live in one community. Back then, they had to travel.

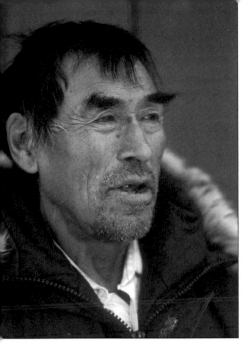

OCTAVE SIVANIQTOQ, 1924–98 REPULSE BAY

Just when I was just born, that's when they started using rifles.
Before that, they were using bow and arrows only.

I was born near Igloolik, Amittuq, in 1924. I do not know exactly which month or day. My birth certificate says January first, but that is completely off from what I heard in stories about me. I suspect I was born cither [at the] end of July or beginning of August. I heard from Igloolik people that there were a lot of mosquitoes around and the caribou had just finished shedding their hairs and starting to grow new ones, so I suspect around the beginning of August.

My father was Manilaq and my mother was Navak. Both my father and mother are from Nattilik. I heard from on old lady called Kinikuluk that my dad was born in a place called Sinik and my mother in Iluiyuk, around Nattilik area. If it was not an island, in the old days, it was called *iluiyuk* because it looks more solid than an island, [but it is] not an island, it is a complete land, the mainland.

The original set of people used to call the Kivalliq people *Iluiliqmiut* because they are on the mainland. We are losing some of our own language.

My parents stayed in Igloolik for about two years, then they moved to Repulse Bay for a while. We did not stay there very long and then, from Repulse, they moved down to Ukkusiksalik. At that time, I could start crawling around and could probably start walking. I was the oldest. I was the only child at that time. My grandparents, my father's mother and my stepgrandfather, were with us when we moved from Igloolik down to this area. My father was just going with his parents when they were moving around.

I never really heard who was there in Ukkusiksalik already when we first went there, but as I was growing up I knew some people there, not all that many. When I start to remember later on in life, I think they were staying there with us because we went out together all the time. We were always in the same area. Whenever we went caribou hunting in summer, we got together again, to go caribou hunting inland. In winter and fall I know that we got together again for seal hunting. I was growing up with another boy, Taparti; he lives in Rankin Inlet. Taparti's father was Siksaaq, and his mother was Amalutitaq. He had some older brothers, too. The oldest brother was Kreelak, then Kapik, and Okpik. That is all I know from the oldest to Taparti. He also had a younger brother and two sisters. Siksaaq's family mostly stayed around the main part of Ukkusiksalik.

All these people were from Nattilik area, and they all moved down to Ukkusiksalik. Siksaaq and my parents and my grandparents are from Nattilik.

Another family I recall is Soroniq. Soroniq is also from Nattilik. He moved from Igloolik with us. When we moved to Ukkusiksalik, he followed us. He stayed out in the main body of Ukkusiksalik. His son is Victor Tungilik, here in Repulse Bay. (There is no connection to Marc Tungilik. It is just coincidence that Victor is named Tungilik. Marc Tungilik is from Nattilik area and he came down here when he was a grown man, at a later year, so they are not related to each other.) We are almost the same age. Victor is just a little bit younger. His [Victor Tungilik's] wife was Irkirouk. Her real name is Irkirouk, but they used to pronounce it Irkiroukinjuq because she was so small.

There was another family that was there from the Repulse Bay area, Iqungajuq and his brothers. He had an older son and two daughters. His brothers Ipkarnaq, Talituq (a.k.a. Tommy Taqaugaq), and Siulluk were there — I don't know how many children Taqaugaq or Siulluk had.

All four of them were brothers, but Siulluk was the stepbrother of the other three. They all moved to Tasiujaq once they heard about the trading post there. They were within the bay, but as soon as they heard there was going to be a trading post, they all moved to Tasiujaq.

Taqaugaq was the captain of the group. He was the person that was bringing supplies in there and taking out these traders to wherever they wanted to go. I remember one time, Taqaugaq was bringing the supplies by sailboat, when they did not have any motors, and he was close to Qakiaq in Ukkusiksalik. He was caught in a very bad gale-force wind, so he anchored to wait for the wind to die down. The anchor rope broke and his boat went onto the shore, where it was destroyed. All the supplies were destroyed by the water. We used to walk from Ak&ungirtarvik along the shore, and we could see the anchor and the rope in the water.

When they started using the boats that have a single hand-cranked engine, he broke his arm starting one of them. When that happened, he stopped being a captain and stopped working at the post. Taqaugaq told me the story when I was young. After he broke his arm, he was called Talituq, which means he had no more arm. It never really healed the normal way. One of the traders had to sew up the muscles back to the bone, and it just kept working. It seems like he had two elbows after he broke his arm. Every time, when his arm started moving, it could make a complete circle. But he still kept going hunting; he was considered one of the best hunters there. He used to make an iglu with his broken arm. It acted like a normal arm except it has two elbows instead of one, and was more flexible than his other arm.

I do not remember how many people moved from the other Utkuhiksalik [near Back River] to this Ukkusiksalik [Wager Bay].* People from that other Utkuhiksalik were always going back and forth, and some of them moved down to this Ukkusiksalik. People did not stay in this Ukkusiksalik all their lives. They were always on the move. So people here were considered "Ukkusiksalingmiut." But people from the other Utkuhiksalik, near Back River, they spent all their lives there and they are called Utkuhiksalingmiut. I believe that was because there was no trading post at the other Utkuhiksalik, and they used to come down here to trade. When we lived in Ukkusiksalik here, we were not as hungry as the other people.

My parents moved down to this Ukkusiksalik, and there was a group that went down before them. When we were still living up there, near Igloolik,

---

* As often happens in the Arctic, there are two (or more) places with the same name, simply because places are often named after a characteristic. The two different spellings here reflect the local dialects. See the map on page 17.

the others moved down to Ukkusiksalik because there wasn't enough game to support them.

Three people — Qamukkaaq, Kimaliarjuk, and Iglunaliq — all moved down to Ukkusiksalik after they were adults and then moved on. Kimaliarjuk went down to the Rankin Inlet area, and the other two moved back to the other Utkuhiksalik area, near Spence Bay. Qamukkaaq stayed in Ukkusiksalik almost all his life. He went there in his early adulthood and stayed there until he was very old, then he moved back to the other Utkuhiksalik. Shortly after that, he passed away.

In winter in Ukkusiksalik, my parents were around the middle of the bay. That's where we were based in winter. But in summer, we were always on the move — around the bay, or inland for caribou hunting, but constantly on the move. In spring, my grandparents used to go down to Masivak to go fishing and Piqsimaniq later on in the spring, and later still they would go to Qaurnak.

Others, too, were always on the go. They were not stationary in one place all the time. They were always on the move trying to find game, so they would go after Arctic char when the fish were going up the rivers. In winter, they would seal hunt near Tikirajuaq, where they did most of their seal hunting in the winter, and also right beside Nuvuk&it [Savage Islands]. They would go down to the floe edge, too.

There is no current at all within that area, so they always hunted seals there. The narrow place is where the currents are strongest, not the mouth, but right where Piqsimaniq river comes in. That is where they would do their fishing.

The four places I just mentioned — Piqsimaniq, Masivak, Qaurnak, and Kuugarjuk — those were the major fishing areas at that time. Kuugarjuk was the only place that didn't have as many fish as the others. In summer, when the fish are going upriver, Qaurnak is the place where a lot of fish used to be. Also Qamanaaluk and Tasiujaq River [the reversing falls, where the water flows in opposite directions, depending on the tide, between the main body of Wager Bay and Tasiujaq], but they couldn't put a fish weir there because the river is too strong. That is the only place I know for sure that there is a lot of fish, where I was told that they didn't fish too much because they couldn't put in a fish weir. I think that that river [Tasiujaq] is always open all through the winter because of the flow.

The fishing was all done at the weir using a *kakivak* [fish spear]. They were not using nets at that time. What we did was make a weir first, so that the fish won't escape, and then use the *kakivak*. We used fishing hooks. Not these modern types, but the ones we made out of bone. When I was still living down there, we used to use metal hooks, a hook that we happened to get from the trading post. There is a small hip bone that looks almost like a hook, and we would just take it out without breaking it and that is what we were using before. I also experienced that we were not using these twines, not the rope type, not the nylon twines; we used the caribou sinew and we braided them together to make a line. Once the caribou sinew is braided together, it is not going to snap, no matter how hard you try, compared to what we have now. It will stretch, stretch, stretch but it won't snap.

There were fish weirs way, way inland at one time. The sea was that much inland; that is where they had to put the fish weirs before. Near Masivak there was another one, too, that was a little bit closer to the shore but still at a good distance inland. I know for sure that there were fish weirs which they had used before.

The whole winter and the whole spring, we were using harpoons to catch seal. We couldn't get too many bullets for our rifles. One person could catch so many seals at one breathing hole in just a short time, with harpoon. Each breathing hole is different. If you happen to see a lot of seal together in one breathing hole and if you are close to it, you could catch ten seals in half a day. It depends on the seals, too. In a group of hunters, one person could catch ten seals from one breathing hole and the person next to him could catch nothing, or maybe one, in the whole day. So, it all depends where the favourite spot is for the seal. One person says he is catching a lot of seals and the next person is catching nothing, and he wishes that the seals would come his way instead and still, nothing. I have said that before. One time I took a lot of seal and the other people were not catching anything at all, or hardly catching anything, and I was feeling good about myself that I caught all these seals. It does not apply only to seals. It also applies to fish and to foxes. There are certain people who can catch a lot of seals and catch a lot of foxes and a lot of fish, and there are people who just can't catch anything at all.

Just when I was born, that's when they started using rifles. Before that, they were using bow and arrows only. I was growing up with rifles and boats, the whaler boats, when we were just changing. I just missed by a few years the people who were hunting with *qajaq* and bow and arrow. It happened pretty quickly. I was taught by my parents how to hunt this way, too, in case I ever ran out of bullets. There is another way of surviving, instead of just depending on rifles. Like what I was talking about seal hunting, at the breathing holes — we are still doing it up to now.

I didn't catch those people who were hunting for caribou using only bow and arrows from a *qajaq*. But I heard about them. This was a different generation. I never really saw this happening when I was still living in Ukkusiksalik. I heard about people trying to catch caribou from their *qajaq* but I never really saw it. The lake called Nadluarjuq is where they kept their *qajaq*, so that when the caribou are crossing that lake, that's when they mostly hunted the caribou in summer.

When I was growing up, we had guns. When we went caribou hunting, we were just using guns and we would go as a group. We divided the caribou amongst ourselves. We would have a leader, to decide where he was going to take us for caribou hunting. There were times when people went straight to a herd of caribou, and other times when a person would go and see nothing the whole day. We didn't actually choose a leader, but we would make the oldest person a leader, whether he was going with us or not.

When you look at modern life right now, it was just the same with *qablunaat* and Inuit. There are people with a lot of money and there are people with a little bit of money and there are people with no money at all. People with a good job, in-between jobs, and no job. At that time, it was pretty much the same because there were people with lots of food, a little bit of food, and no food at all. So, there were different types of groups.

The leader planned before we went, saying that this person will get so much meat, and this person will get so much, and this one will get so much. We had to listen to the oldest person when he said something like that. We respected our elders a lot more than we do now. Before a caribou hunt, one person would be told by the elder to get just so many caribou and then he would have to get only that much caribou. The next person will get so many, and the next person will get so many.

For example, if there were three people who went on a polar bear hunt, each person could be told to get only one bear. The first person who caught one will get one. I could catch two, but I can't keep the second polar bear to myself. I would have to give it to the third person. That is what we were told. The oldest person, even if he is not on the hunt, will tell us to listen. Out of respect, we listened to our elders.

Suppose we were trying to stay at Piqsimaniq during the whole summer, including the fall, just to catch fish. If the elder people knew, or had a gut feeling, that there was not going to be enough fish in that area, in Piqsimaniq, we would move to another river and stay there the whole summer.

In summer, if we didn't have a boat, we would walk across the land. Our dogs would help to carry things. We would spend nights on the way, but we would try to get there. If the game is very scarce around one area, and we could not go across Ukkusiksalik without a boat, we had no choice but to stay in that area and try to survive.

The boats we were using at that time were those whalers' boats, the ones with the sail and oars only.

I can talk about some of the places around Ukkusiksalik. There is a small island called Ibjuriktuq [the northernmost of the Savage Islands] because of the soil, where the grass grew the most. That's why it was called Ibjuriktuq. Qikiqtaarjuk [the middle of the Savage Islands] means "biggest island." Iriptaqtuuq means "clean." The reason is it called Iriptaqtuuq is because if you climb, you will notice that there is a white spot there. It seems like it is really clean, even from a distance. That's why they call it the clean area. If you are looking at it from inland outwards, on top of a hill, you will see that it is white, and it looks so clean. Uttuyasuaq [about ten kilometres west of Iriptaqtuuq] is a very deep cliff in a valley; the name means it looks like a vagina. Kingarsuaq has the highest hill of the whole area. Somewhere along that shore there is a small river and it is called Kiirqvik. At Ak&ungirtarvik, two big stones were put together, side by side, so people could put a rope across there to do tricks. Those are some of the major places and hunting grounds that I know.

In winter, we used an iglu only. When my father died and I had a step-father, we were not living as good as before, so my mother used to make sealskin tents. When we were in Ukkusiksalik we never used a *qarmaq* [sod house], but when we moved here, to Repulse Bay, that's when we started using a *qarmaq* made of rock and sod. Probably the reason why we didn't use a *qarmaq* there is because as soon as the ice formed, we started moving around. In winter, we were always on the go, all the time. The people from Repulse and also Igloolik used *qarmat* [sod houses] because there were more people based there, whereas in Ukkusiksalik, even when we were moving around, I never saw one. After I was an adult is when they actually started building *qarmat* in Piqsimaniq, not before.

My parents would sometimes go to Tasiujaq to trade. By the time I was an adult, the *qablunaat* traders had moved out and Iqungajuq had taken over the trading post. He wrote everything down, so all the records were written in Inuktitut when he was a trader. His daughter, Tuinnaq Bruce, used to do the records for him, too, in the later years. Robert Tatty was born in Tasiujaq; he was actually raised around the trading post. By the time he left Ukkusiksalik, he had a wife. He looks like a very, very old person but he is actually younger than me.

I was with my father and my mother twice on trips to the Tasiujaq trading post before he passed away. I can't really remember these trips. I was around four or five years old when my father passed away. When we went to the trading post, I remember one very big person — I figured he was *qablunaaq*, but he was an Inuk from the Baker Lake area. I was scared of him. He had a very big nose. My father was sitting at his side. I also remember a person named Angangra, and the other name he used was Ikumaq. There were two people fighting, not really fighting but playing rough. They were trying to take our *kamiit* [plural of *kamik*, meaning "boot"] off and tickle our feet. The second trip we made is when I saw that big person from the Baker Lake area.

Iqungajuq had a little house behind the warehouse. That is where we were staying. We went there in summer, just when the supply ship was coming in.

I remember the supply ship coming for the post at Tasiujaq. It was very big, with a lot of smoke coming out. We were all waiting at Tikirajuaq. There was a whole bunch of people there, waiting for the supply ship to come in. People came from all over Ukkusiksalik. I remember seeing the supply ship coming in. The ship anchored a fair good distance from Tikirajuaq. They unloaded everything by Peterhead [boat] first to that small warehouse called Iglujuarnaaq. The little house there is not insulated, as it was not used for living quarters. It was just used during the sealing, and as soon as the sealing was over, they left that place alone. It was like a warehouse. The ships went there to unload. I actually remember just one ship because I was too young. I was there at Iglujuarnaaq when they were unloading the ship into the warehouse. They used those whaling boats — loaded the whaling boats and towed them in by the Peterhead. When they were brought to the shore, they would unload from the whaling boats to the building. As soon as the ship was emptied, it left. There were a lot of people unloading at that time. From there, the supplies were brought by Peterhead to Tasiujaq.

Iqungajuq spent a long time as the post manager. They were sending him supplies at the beginning but they stopped. So he bought a Peterhead [boat] to go down to Chesterfield Inlet to get supplies. Later, since that took too long, he started going to Repulse Bay to get supplies. He did this for a long time. The Peterhead's motor wasn't running well later on, so then he stopped altogether. Also, because there were hardly any foxes around. So he just stopped altogether.

When I was a young adult I used to trade with Iqungajuq. Only when it was a hard time, later, we changed to Repulse Bay. Probably because he was inexperienced, Iqungajuq at that time had the same prices for all the foxes. Whether it was a bad fox or a good fox, they were all the same price. In wintertime he couldn't tell whether the prices had gone up or down. The only time he actually knew the prices was when he went to get the supplies in summer from Repulse Bay or Chesterfield Inlet. Then he was told, "This is the price of a fox skin." He would use the same price throughout the whole winter. I also remember that one winter the manager from Repulse Bay went down to Tasiujaq to notify Iqungajuq about the prices of foxes or the prices of the goods, whether up or down. He travelled with a man named Kagutaq from Repulse Bay down to Tasiujaq.

People from Ukkusiksalik area did their trading mostly at Tasiujaq. They used to go up to Repulse at very odd times if they needed something that was not at Tasiujaq, but we did our trading with Iqungajuq most of the time. They used to bring mail by dog team from Chesterfield Inlet to Repulse Bay, so all the mail would go to Repulse from Chesterfield, instead of stopping at Tasiujaq.

When my father passed away, we moved down to Chesterfield Inlet, but I don't remember how long it was. It seems like it was a very long time that I was in Chesterfield Inlet. We went down there using a dog team and came back to Ukkusiksalik using the same dog team. So I figure it must have been a year or two, but I am not sure. It seems to me a very long time. I think I was there a long time but I realize that it was not all that long. After I moved down to Chesterfield Inlet, then we moved back to Ukkusiksalik. We spent two years there and then finally moved to Repulse Bay.

I went back to Ukkusiksalik before I got married, as a young adult. I was there for about three years in Ukkusiksalik, just before I got married. The trading post was gone at that time when I moved back, so we had to do our trading in Repulse Bay. Later on, when I got married, my wife and I went down to Ukkusiksalik but it was just for one winter and one summer, and then we moved back to Repulse Bay for good.

I know two people who lived in Ukkusiksalik much of their lives, Tatty and his sister, Tuinnaq. Those are the only two older people who have really lived there.

While I was there nobody even mentioned the white whales and I never saw any whales. But before that, at an earlier time, I heard stories that there were some bowhead whales in Ukkusiksalik. The only whalers that I heard of were down at Qatiktalik [Cape Fullerton]. They used to have a trading post there, and that is where the major whaling station was. Before there was a trading post at Repulse Bay, there were a couple of whalers who wintered in the Harbour Islands; that is where people got boats and rifles. That is where they were trading their goods before the trading post came.

We traded only with foxes, no polar bear, and no sealskins. I never traded with those. If a person caught a polar bear, that person kept the skin. The sealskin trade started just recently. As a matter of fact, it was about 1954 when they actually started trading with sealskins. When I was in Ukkusiksalik, we never traded with sealskins at all. It was only foxes and wolves. So it's just recently, maybe even later than 1954, that they actually start trading sealskin.

People would make two trips to the trading post each year by dog team. People from the other Utkuhiksalik used to trade at Tasiujaq also, probably because there was nobody stationed in Spence Bay or Gjoa Haven. Those people used to trade there. That's the only people that I am aware of. We didn't go to trade too much, because most of us spent the winter around Nuvuk&it. It is so far from there. It all depends on foxes, too. If they could catch a lot of fox then they would trade quite a bit, but if they don't get a lot of fox, then they hardly go trading.

There was no priest stationed in Ukkusiksalik at all. The priest came from Repulse Bay to go to Ukkusiksalik, instead of being stationed there. The house in Nuvuk&it was the warehouse in Tikirajuaq previously. I was part of that operation when we took it apart there and put it up at Nuvuk&it.

It was smaller when we put it up! The RCMP told us to go ahead and take the house, but the priest said you are not going to be using it, so the priest told me to move it down there for him.

When I was in my late twenties, I was working for the RCMP, stationed out of Chesterfield Inlet. Then I was told that my wages were too small and they didn't have enough money to give me at that time. So what they did was they asked the headquarters in Winnipeg, or some place, if they had heard about this building that had belonged to the Hudson's Bay Company. They asked the Hudson's Bay Company if I could have that building, and they said yes. So I was told to get that building.

When I was going to get it, Father Didier found out and he told me that I was not to use that building, that he was going to take it himself. I gave this building to the priest. We took it apart and even helped him bring it down to Nuvuk&it. A man named Anawak helped. He used a bigger boat [but not as big as a Peterhead] and I was using a freighter canoe when we moved the building. My canoe was towed by the bigger boat when we were going down. Father Didier used it only in winter, for a short time. Before that, priests used to go to Ukkusiksalik but they didn't go to Tasiujaq. They stayed amongst the Inuit around the main area.

People didn't mind the building being there because they liked the priest to come in there once in a while, so they didn't mind it at all. The priest would just use it once in a while, in winter, but they were just happy that the building was there. It wasn't used by Inuit at all. It was just there for the priest and as an emergency base, such as if a family had nothing to eat at all. There was always something that he left behind, tea or biscuits or whatever. In case of a really bad emergency or if there was no food at all, a family could go there.

Father Didier was not the only priest who went there. It wasn't very long that the priests were going there. There were other priests that went there, too, so it was used now and then by priests. I don't remember how long it was being used but only in winter. It was not used at all in summer because there was nobody living in the Nuvuk&it area the whole summer. They all moved around to other places, be it Tasiujaq or around the main part of Ukkusiksalik. So, nobody was there in summer. But in winter they all moved to the floe edge for seal hunting. And the priest would be there for about two weeks, three at the most, each time when there was a priest.

There was Father Didier and another one whose nickname was Iksirajualaq, but I don't know what his real name was, and then Father Laveille. Those were the priests that would go there. When they stopped using this building, it was given back to the Inuit. Father Didier just gave it back to the Inuit.

The RCMP patrols used to stop at Nuvuk&it when they were passing through. I never noticed the RCMP going to Tasiujaq but I saw them at Nuvuk&it on their way to Repulse Bay from Chesterfield Inlet. This was the passing point. They just spent the night there and then they would continue on to Repulse Bay. I never knew of any post for the RCMP there. Even in summertime, the RCMP never went to Tasiujaq by Peterhead boat.

There is a story of an old ship in the whirlpool. As the story goes, there were whaling ships around the Cape Fullerton area, and the captain of one ship was told about the whirlpool, so he went to investigate. They made sure the ship was watertight. They checked the hull in all places. Then the captain got all the crew inside the ship, all of them, all watertight, and he himself was just at the mast. When they went to the whirlpool, the ship was pulled down, right down to the bed of the sea. It wasn't very deep, so it went down to a certain point where it just stopped, and the ship was inside the water at the whirlpool and the captain was on top of the mast. They were there until the whirlpool started turning the other way, and the ship went out. They went back afloat and then the captain knocked on the mast and the crew was happy to get out of there.

The name Ukkusiksalik means there must be some soapstone around the area somewhere. I know of one place where someone found some soapstone, just north of Piqsimaniq. I noticed that the soapstone was taken out of there in two or three different places, beside some big boulders. Those are the only places that I know of that Inuit have found soapstone.

I like Ukkusiksalik so much because the game was always within easy reach: belugas, caribou, wolves, fish, seal, and polar bears. You've got everything there. Before the government stepped in, that's where I would have preferred to stay. It is a good spot for hunting.

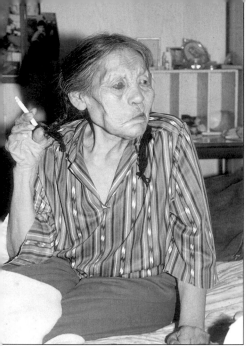

HELEN NAITOK, 1915–92
CHESTERFIELD INLET

I used to travel anywhere with my father. I remember how much he loved me.

I was born in the winter, but I don't know what year. I was born around Gjoa Haven [probably near the Back River]. We were living around Gjoa Haven, not right in Gjoa Haven but around the area, maybe on the mainland. People from Gjoa Haven came to get things from my father.

After we left the Gjoa Haven area we went to a river called Itimnajuq. We made dried fish and then hunted for caribou in the fall when the fur is thick, for clothing. This particular place is on a hill. If you're going to put up a tent on it, you can't have children because it's too much of a cliff. There is a waterfall there, too. So many parents would tell us not to play along the riverbank because it was dangerous. We were camped in the river valley where there was less current. We caught fish with *kakivak*, and gathered them all into one big weir that we built.

I used to travel anywhere with my father. I remember how much he loved me. I went with my father hunting; he would always take me along. We travelled where there were caribou. I never liked seal meat; the meat was too dark — it didn't appeal to me. When my mother caught a small fish, she would cut it up and feed it to the children. It was hard to get meat then; we ate what we could get.

My father's name was Kimaliadjuk. My mother's name was Amagunuak. I named one of my daughter's children Amagunuak. I had one brother,

Ookootak; one of my sons is named after him. Maybe I had a younger sister, too, but I'm not sure. We were related to Nugjugalik. [Nugjugalik was Octave Sivaniqtoq's half-sister, same father.]

We moved to Ukkusiksalik in the spring, with my uncle. He was married but his wife couldn't conceive, so they adopted a young boy that had lost both parents. We spent the summer there with them. Maybe that same year, in the winter, we came down to Chesterfield Inlet from Ukkusiksalik with Kreelak, and my aunt Aknalukteetak. I don't remember how old I was when I was living up there. I was raised by my father, so he was the one I wasn't afraid of.

I remember one time my father had a bad infection in his leg. There was something wrong with a wound and it infected the leg. I'm not sure what happened to cause the infection in the leg. He couldn't walk anymore. He was trying to drain the puss out. It was in the summer this happened. He was sitting on the caribou skin that we would sleep on as a mattress. I could see this stuff coming out of his leg, and I heard him yelling in pain. I remember that very well.

My grandmother said, "If I die, my son will start walking again." I believe it when elders say that; these are very powerful statements and sometimes they work. After she died, my father started to walk again. I was too young to remember a lot of it but I remember him walking again.

In Tasiujaq, Sivaniqtoq's father and two others also died. I'm not sure what these people died of. It might have been bad seal meat.

Joe was the Bay manager at the post there [J.L. Ford, HBC manager at Tasiujaq, 1929–31]. His son was Jerome Tattuinee in Rankin Inlet. There was another *qablunaaq* there also, but I don't remember the name. When we first arrived at the post, the manager gave us food to eat. That was what was happening. I remember when we came down to here the manager gave us food so that we had something to eat. That happened at Baker Lake, too.

When we got to the post, the manager did some trading but my father didn't. They gave him free supplies, in those big brown sacks that they put potatoes in. They filled them with the supplies. We also traded fox and wolf and other skins at the post. My favourites were candies, chocolates, gum. I really enjoyed that! They tasted so good.

I never liked cigarettes back then but later my husband started to buy things for me. He bought me cigarettes. At first I didn't like them, but eventually I started to get the taste and have been smoking since then.

I remember the supply ship that brought supplies for the HBC post and the police.

We travelled to pick up my father's equipment, which was between here and Baker Lake. We went to Baker Lake for Christmas celebrations one year. Father Rio had a nice voice and we liked him very much. At first we were staying with Hicks, the manager, but ended up staying at the priest's place.

When we came down here from Ukkusiksalik the first time, I was very young, I had no kids. I had my first child close to Baker Lake. I named that son after my father. So, whenever my son asked me to go hunting, I was always happy. When I went back to Ukkusiksalik later, I had two kids, and we spent three winters there. One of Kopak's older brothers shot himself when we were on our way back to Ukkusiksalik in the spring. My second child, Ramona, was five months old. I remember that because my legs were paralyzed, so I couldn't walk for a while. At that time, there was Iqungajuq and Tuinnaq and Avaqsaq at the post.

I remember my father played jokes with them, but they grew up together and that's what they did to their friends. One time when I was pregnant, my father was wrestling with one of them and ended up on the bottom, so I pulled the other guy's leg to get him off my father. They all said, "Don't wrestle with him when his daughter is around."

I remember one time a man named Anakak was visiting at my father's place and he started assaulting his wife. I tried to stop him from beating up his wife, and eventually he stopped. After that, I never returned to Ukkusiksalik.

FELIX KOPAK, 1918–2005 REPULSE BAY

At that time, we didn't have a compass at all.
Our ancestors could navigate using the stars.

I was born in the springtime, perhaps in June or July, in Maluksituq [on the Rae Peninsula, at the mouth of Lyon Inlet near Repulse Bay]. I know this from Uktuq's mother, Utuguvinyak. She knew when I was born. She said I was born at a time when spring thaw had begun and there was water on the sea ice. Tigumiaq [brother of informant Arsene Putulik] was born one year to the day after I was born, so they used to call us *ikimutit*, which means born at the same time. When a person reached exactly one year old, they used to say the person *nalliutijuq*. There was no such thing as holidays or special celebrations. Now that language has changed, like everything has changed, that means "Happy Birthday" instead. They say I was born in 1918. Now I have many, many grandchildren, and a few more that are going to appear very soon. My house is never silent for one moment.

I was adopted at four or five years old. My adopted father was Irqijut, and my mother was Tigvariaq. With my adopted parents, we went to Ukkusiksalik. It took us three or four days, by way of Mattuq, travelling by dog team. They dressed me in new caribou-skin clothing to keep me warm. I remember when we got to the shore of Ukkusiksalik, my stepfather walked on the sea ice, trying to catch a seal, since at that time we didn't have any meat for the dogs. Then we went across Ukkusiksalik to the other [south] side and we stayed with Qingatoq; I believe Ataq and Alooniq were there also. They were all related to each other. These families were at Masivak, directly across from Nuvuk&it. My stepfather mentioned the reason why it is called Masivak is because char go upstream in that river.*

In the winter we lived in an iglu, and for the summer, at that time, we had a canvas tent. But I remember my stepmother made a sealskin tent, and we used it as well.

Qingatoq had a boat. I remember the men sinking it in a crack on the ice, so the boat would get soaked. We stayed with those families through the whole spring and all through the summer. We were going after fish, and the only way we were catching them was with a stone weir in the river, because we did not have any nets. The men also caught whales and bearded seals from the boat.

[The men] made their own bullets. I remember they had bullets, some about three inches long, and the others half that size. They had a block of lead which they would heat in a frying pan over a fire made by collecting *qiuqta* [arctic heather]. They poured the molten lead into a [bullet mould] to make tips for the bullets. They had primers for the cartridges and they had powder. They always saved the brass cartridges. They weren't as fortunate as we are today.

Qingatoq's family, with the boat, eventually left us there toward fall. We started heading inland, but we ran out of food and got hungry, so we went back to Masivak to get extra food. We went inland again; we were hungry most of the time. Then we went to Iriptaqtuuq, where we found some other families: Uliq, Ataq, and Nuvak [late husband of Mary Nuvak]. They fed us and we weren't hungry then. I know we spent a winter there and then we moved back to Masivak. But at that time we did not remember to keep track of months or days.

In early spring, when the days are getting longer and it's a little bit warmer, we travelled up to Tasiujaq by dog team to trade. There were five of us with one dog team: my two stepsisters, my step-parents, and myself. We overnighted twice on the way. We were at Tasiujaq two days or more when I got very sick, so we ended up spending longer there. We were staying at

_____

* The name Masivak refers to the smell of the fish, see chapter 37, page 216.

Iqungajuq's house. The manager was named Ikumalirijialuk [Buster Brown]. I do not know his white name.

I was very sick and I almost died. Ikumalirijialuk gave me medicine and took care of me that time. I was so sick that I could not see. I became blind. The only thing I could do was that I could hear. I was very sick. I remember he [Ikumalirijialuk] came to Iqungajuq's place where we were staying, at Tasiujaq, and he rubbed a white liquid substance on my skin, something that was really stinky. I remember this medicine. I know it very well. It looks something like Vicks VapoRub, but in liquid form. It's white, very sticky, very thick, and very stinky. I was given a tablespoon of that medicine mixed with molasses, and he told me to swallow it very quickly. All the way down to my stomach it was burning and it hurt very much. After I swallowed the medicine I was given a glass of water, which I drank so that I could rinse everything down to my stomach. That first night I felt a lot better, but on the fourth day is when I got really well and was finally able to get up and go outside. Our life at the time was not like the modern, religious life we've got now. Before I took that medicine he asked me if I was worrying about any of my family members and then he gave me the medicine. That's how I got better. I remember seeing Iqungajuq, Siksaaq, and Kreelak at the post.[*]

In those days we used fox skin to trade. Sometimes we used to trade with meat that we had. We nowadays use a poor excuse for a fox skin [i.e., dollar bills]. What the traders used as money was a piece of wood about a half-inch thick by four inches long, sometimes cut in half. That is what we used as currency. This is how they used to trade, first of all, for bullets, then for powder and the other stuff you needed for the rifle, and they used to get tea and biscuits and sometimes sugar. What I remember as tobacco was about eighteen inches long and about four inches around in the middle and sort of narrow to the ends and coloured black. That was the first tobacco I remember. The other one was smaller and in a spiral; it was considered a better quality tobacco. The big, dark ones, if they were to be sold today, would cost about $200. I am not sure what they used to be worth, but you could trade for those large tobaccos for less than half of what one fox skin was worth. Maybe today, that would be worth about five dollars. If a trapper

---

* If Ikumalirijialuk (Buster Brown) was the post manager, this was 1926, when Kopak was eight years old.

went to trade with ten or twenty fox skins, he would come back with the *qamutik* loaded two or three feet high. I remember they used to trade for pilot biscuits in a box, and the same size box for cookies. That is how we used to buy them. They used to buy one hundred pounds of flour. That's how they used to buy it, when they bought flour. Those were very happy occasions.

The fox price used to vary from year to year. In a good year, you could buy a hundred pounds of flour with one fox. In a bad year, you would buy it with two skins.

At the trading post, I remember three buildings: the staff house, the "Native house," and the store. On the hill behind, there was a mound where we went on top and slid down on the *qamutik*. It was quite scary to go sliding on that. They say there is another building at Sarvaq, near the reversing falls, but I myself never saw that building.

At the time we lived there, there was no RCMP there and I was never aware of any missionaries visiting the area, either Anglican or RC.

I remember four camps around Ukkusiksalik at the time: three families and their sons at Iriptaqtuuq, about thirty kilometres west of Masivak, which is where my family was. After we moved to Iriptaqtuuq, there was no longer anybody living at Masivak. Then there was Qaurnak, a little bit west of the Sila Lodge site.* We were related to the Qaurnak group — I believe it was just one family. The final one was around the post at Tasiujaq, maybe three families plus the traders. Iqungajuq was there, and Kreelak, and also Siulluk. When their parents were still alive, they were there as well.

All these camps went to Tasiujaq to trade. When I was a child, a family did not have a permanent land they stayed on. They walked from one area to another in search of more game. We spent a full year around Ukkusiksalik and then we went to Umiijarvik, roughly halfway between the mouth of Ukkusiksalik and Repulse Bay, where we found the families of Pudjuk, Anawak, and Anawak's parents. I believe my stepfather wanted to go back to his relatives. In those times, they would move to an area where they had relatives and spend some time there and go back to the original relatives, travelling back and forth amongst relatives.

In those days, when I was a child, there were times when game was plentiful, and other times there would be nothing. It fluctuated. At the time,

---

* Sila Lodge is an Inuit-owned naturalist lodge for tourists, opened in 1987.

animals were our only livelihood, so what we did was hunt all the time. Our elders used to tell us when the game got scarce, it was not that they were going extinct, it was just that they had gathered in another place, be it seal or caribou or what have you. They were not here because they were in another place. The ones before us used to say that if the animals are not in the immediate area, that does not mean that this land is not good. They used to say that the animals will come back to this place again, sometime in the future.

I know in Ukkusiksalik that families living there used to go after wildlife and were constantly on the move to a good hunting site. I know families used to go from one area to another, constantly on the move, when I was a child.

Inuit used to go inland to hunt caribou. They could not bring along all the belongings they had at the coast. A *qajaq* can be used after the ice forms to keep a crossing open for the caribou. They would use the *qajaq* but I have never heard of a *qajaq* being used in the fall in the sea, just in the lakes, where the caribou cross.

Where caribou cross a river or lake, the hunters would build stone lines. Since caribou are scared of wolves, the hunters would howl like a wolf, to scare them, and make them swim across. The stones keep the caribou from going in another direction. These were put near a lake, and it's not that you are going to hunt right there. There is a person on the other side of the lake who is going to wait for the caribou to come on shore, to come to him. The stones guide the caribou into the water. These are fixed in an area where caribou constantly go through. It is just to make sure that they stay on that path. Inuit try every possible hunting method they can. That was the only way.

If the caribou were coming toward the hunters, you would not hunt the first caribou. You would wait until it passed, and then you could hunt all the other ones following because they are going to follow the leader. You do not go after the leader; they will want to follow the leader and keep going, so you will end up with more caribou that way. Inuit consider the land surrounding Ukkusiksalik a very good hunting area.

Our ancestors and the people I used to know in the old days, they used to be able to predict what the weather would be like, although they didn't have any modern equipment to tell them. They used to look up to the sky and predict what the weather would be. Suppose there were stars and the stars were really blinking, they would know that the weather would turn bad.

I know a little about stars, but some of the stars I don't know. The three stars in a row, which are very clearly visible, are called *Ullaktut* [Orion's Belt; the Inuktitut name means "runners"]. They're in a straight line on an angle in the sky, three stars in a row. In the traditional Inuit story, there are actually four stars, which are four brothers. A polar bear came and the brothers started running after the bear. The oldest brother was the first one and the youngest brother was the very last one. The oldest brother told the youngest brother that he dropped his mitt, that the polar bear was running away, so go get the mitt. They asked the youngest one to return, so you see the three stars in a row chasing a bear. I know the story of the three stars that are running. I don't know what the story means. During December, when the days are very short, they usually come up at an angle so they are pointing at another group of small stars bunched up together. When the days are getting longer in February, they move down toward the east. They point at a little group of stars called *Agiattat* [Pleiades; the Inuktitut name means "branches, or tines, on a caribou antler"]. There are legends for those particular stars also.

The brothers [of *Ullaktut*] are following two clusters of stars [Hyades and Pleiades]. They are both called *Agiattat*. They say the brightest one in the middle of that group of stars close together [Pleiades] is a polar bear. The stars around the bright star are dogs surrounding the polar bear. I don't know too much about stars; I just know the stars by the stories that are told about them.

Just below *Ullaktut* [Orion's Belt] there is a lone star that blinks red; it sort of twinkles. We call it *Kajujuq* [Sirius; the Inuktitut name means "reddish-brown"].*

I don't remember anyone using any of these for navigation. But there's a group of stars right up north that are together, with one that is the brightest toward the north — that's what people used. The one in the north is called *Nuuttuitut* [the North Star or Polaris], which means it never moves, it always stays in one place. *Nuuttuitut* never moves at all.

---

* More widely known, in the western regions of the Arctic, as *Kajuqtuq* (the red fox) and sometimes referred to by the extended name *Kajuqtuqlu Tiriganiaqlu* (the red fox and the white fox), it is said to be fighting over possession of a fox hole, which produces the flashing, prismatic red and white colours of Sirius. In the eastern Arctic, Sirius is called *Singuuriq*, "the flickering one."

They also used *Ublugiasujuk*, a big bright star that comes up in the east. My uncle, Nuviya, used to tell me that the star which is very low in the east is the one always to the sea. If you go toward it, you will end up at the sea. And on the other side will always be the direction of our prevailing northwest wind.

I have heard about *Tukturjuaq* [the Big Dipper], *Amarujjuk* [the constellation Cassiopeia], and *Nanurjuk* [the star Aldebaran]. I know exactly where the *Tukturjuaq* is; that means "the spirit of the caribou," because it looks like a caribou. But I don't know exactly where *Amarujjuk* or *Nanurjuk* are. *Amarujjuk* means "the spirit of the wolf," because it looks almost like a wolf. *Nanurjuk* means "the spirit of the polar bear."

At that time we didn't have a compass at all. Our ancestors could navigate using the stars.

If you want to find out more about the stars, Ukusitoq, Sivaniqtoq, and Angotiajuq [three men living in Naujaat, Repulse Bay at the time] were all taught on the stars, so they know. They could tell exactly the names of the stars. Their ancestors knew more about these stars.

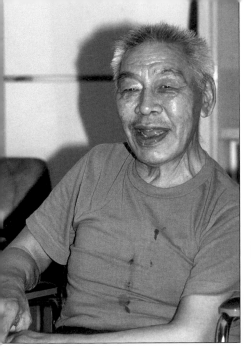

GUY AMAROK, 1932–95
CHESTERFIELD INLET

The story was that he was taken by the evil spirits.

My parents used to travel along the north side of the main body of Ukkusiksalik. They had a camp I remember near Douglas Harbour — it might have been one of those islands [Nuvuk&it] — when I was a very young child. Then we moved up the inlet to where there were houses [Tasiujaq]. That's where we travelled to. When we came up from Chesterfield Inlet, we went to the old Wager Post, then moved up the river into Qamanaaluk. That I remember very well. I was roughly six years old, maybe a little more. I remember the people from Repulse Bay would come down overland, in through Douglas Harbour, into Ukkusiksalik.

I was born in 1932, somewhere between Chesterfield Inlet and Baker Lake. My father was Kreelak. I remember moving up to Ukkusiksalik by Peterhead in the summer. I was old enough. I remember Iqungajuq, an Inuk, who was the post manager at the time. He had a wife there with him. And I remember that they had a house and the store and the warehouse when we first moved up.

When we came up in the summer, we spent the summer at the post with Iqungajuq's family. In the winter, we moved up to where other people were living, at a place called Kugajuk. I was young, but what my father did was wrap me in caribou skin so I could stay warm, and tied me down to the *qamutik.* That's how we travelled. I don't know exactly how far inland [*he points to an area approximately a hundred kilometres northwest of Qamanaaluk on the map*] but I remember we were eating muskox for food. There were muskox in that area. We travelled by dog team from the post up to where the Inuit were. We slept one night out on the land on the way. We were travelling very fast by dog team, so we slept one night and then reached the other Inuit the next day.

At Kugajuk, I remember these people's names: Qamukkaaq, Iksatitak, Ukayuitok, and Pisuyuitok. Iksatitak was driving his dog team through fog and he went over a cliff and he was paralyzed by the accident. Ukayuitok wasn't very old then; he was a young man then. Qamukkaaq has two children in Rankin Inlet, two daughters that live in Rankin Inlet.

We lived in this area during that winter only. In the summer, we hiked back to the post at Tasiujaq. It was right in the summer because I remember there were lots of mosquitoes. It was maybe during 1936 or 1937 that we spent that winter at Kugajuk.

When we were coming back in the spring from Kugajuk, we passed the area where my father's older brother Kapik had been with my grandmother and my grandfather Siksaaq. My grandfather got lost and was not found at the time. They found him dead later that same year. He had built an iglu, but his body was on the floor of the iglu and his feet were on his bed. He was pulled partly off the bed, with his feet still up on the high part [sleeping platform] and his body on the floor. He was pulled down and killed by spirits. There was nobody else in that area, other than himself. The story was that he was taken by the evil spirits. People looked for him for a long, long time. That spring, when we were going back to the trading post, I fell off the sled beside an esker.* As soon as I fell off I started to cry. I remember the landscape, the esker and the slope and this flat valley, all very well. I was too young, so I couldn't run to keep up with the sled. I remember seeing this animal, sort of like a raven, coming at me. You see ravens today that are small, but this was bigger. I tried to run away from it, and I saw my mother coming to pick me up. Then I looked up and this thing wasn't there anymore. I was the only one who saw this thing. It was like a spirit that

---

* An esker is a long, winding ridge of stratified sand and gravel deposited by a sub-glacial river during the last ice age. Many of these are evident across the tundra.

went after me. It was close to there that Siksaaq's body had been found. My grandfather was an *angakkuq* [shaman]. It looks like he was killed by another *angakkuq*, another spirit. That's what it looked like, but that's how he died. Back then, people died of accidents or people died of getting murdered or people died of carelessness or just pure negligence, those kinds of things. People didn't die too often from disease like they do now. [*Amarok breaks into chanting song as he tells this story.*]

We spent the summer and fall at the post, with my father's younger brother, Okpik. There were no *qablunaat* at the post, just an Inuk as manager. We lived in part of a building in one of the porches. It was probably the manager's house. There was another family that lived in part of the building with us. I remember that my parents and myself and Anawak's family were living in the porch and the post manager had his room with his wife in that building. We were living in the original trader's house and there was another building, either a warehouse or a store. Off to the side there was an outhouse. The reason why I remember the outhouse was there was one wolf that kept coming back, and the manager's dogs would get into fights with it, but never killed it. They would gang up on the wolf but they would never kill the wolf.

I remember there was some kind of stove in the house, either a wood-burning oven or a space heater. I remember going into the store quite often. I remember that there was no heat in the store, and all they could sell was food that could freeze but not perish because it was frozen. Those were the kinds of foods that I remember being traded. My father was trading fox skins during the winter for tea, tobacco, sugar, biscuits, flour, porridge — that is the food that I remember. The post didn't have the food that we have today, which is perishable when it freezes.

The only thing traded then was fox skins. We didn't trade muskox skin. We used it in the fall when there was no snow and you can't freeze anything. We used it as a sled; we tied it together and it's very slippery, so we used it for dragging. Later, after the Rankin Inlet [nickel] mine opened, that's when we started selling sealskin and other skins.

My father hunted caribou around Tasiujaq and to the west, inland. In the summer we didn't have a canoe, so we hunted only caribou in the summer. In the winter we hunted seal.

In winter we moved from the post down to the islands [Nuvuk&it]. There were other people who had come from Repulse Bay when we moved there. These people were Puujuut, Uliq, and Ataq. These three were men, and Itimanik, who was my aunt. Ataq and Itimanik were married. We spent the winter with them. I heard when they were coming in through the entrance, there was a boat lost because of the current in the whirlpool. We spent the whole winter at Nuvuk&it. In the winter, we lived in an iglu. In the summer, we had canvas tents. Before we made the move up to Ukkusiksalik, I heard about people living in caribou tents and sealskin tents, around Chesterfield Inlet.

I remember a priest there at Nuvuk&it. This priest was living with the people. He lived with Inuit, but he had his own iglu. I remember every morning at seven, we had to go to church. The services were held at a family's iglu, the biggest iglu in the camp. The only time that I ever remember coming to a real church was in Chesterfield Inlet. Today, it's not every morning that church is conducted. It's either Sunday or on special days. They called him Father Vilea. He died here after he came down from Ukkusiksalik, when he was walking on the sea ice. He might have gone through the ice.

I remember playing ball. We used a piece of stick, any kind of wood, for a bat. In the winter, snow would build up on the outer layers of the parka and we had to use a stick to knock off the ice. So we used that for a bat. We had a caribou skin for a ball, which somebody sewed together to make it kind of round, round enough to use for a ball. That's what we used for playing ball. The bats we used were not like the ones they use on TV, where they are totally smooth and shiny. We just used any piece of wood. Another game I played quite often, I would pretend to hunt caribou. I used caribou antlers, lined them up on the snow, and I would throw something as my weapon. If I hit the caribou antlers that I had lined up, that would be my hunting game.

For toys in the spring, we used bone and rock; we didn't have real toys. I remember my father built me a bow and arrow out of caribou antlers. That was one of my toys. I hunted ptarmigan with it because they don't fly off very quickly. You can get really close to one. So I hunted ptarmigan with that bow and arrow.

I remember one time in the late spring, the snow had melted on the land and over the ice, but one night it got really cold and the ice on the lake at Qamanaaluk melted and then froze over. Then there's water and then ice, water, and then very thin ice. When we were walking on top of this thin ice, we would go through. By the time we reached the other side, we were soaking wet. I remember that very well. I don't know why we were crossing it when it was like that.

We also lived over near Iriptaqtuuq at one point. I remember one particular area when the tide changed, when the tide went out, it turns into an inlet or a little bay. It turns into a river and then fish would get trapped in there. I remember people were catching fish, but it's really so silty, it was dirty.

We lived in Ukkusiksalik for two or maybe three winters, but not longer than that. Then we moved back down to Chesterfield Inlet. I don't remember what age I was then.

Long before we were there, I heard there were some whalers coming into Ukkusiksalik. One story I heard, from before I was born, there was a wooden ship with sails that came in, and it was shipwrecked. I don't know where it was. That's one story I heard about the whalers being in there. The place where it was wrecked, there used to be a little shack that was probably used by the whalers. That's where that wreck happened. After that ship got wrecked, people used the ship for firewood.

JOHN TATTY, 1946–
RANKIN INLET

My father always remembered Ukkusiksalik when he was a kid there.

I didn't know anything about Ukkusiksalik except what I heard growing up from my parents [Robert and Annie Tatty], until I went there as an adult. I got a job up in Repulse Bay in 1974. I was there for one year. When I quit that job and started heading back to Rankin Inlet by Ski-Doo, I went to Ukkusiksalik then for the first time. I went by sea ice from Repulse and then cut overland down to Nuvuk&it. There's a little shack, which used to belong to the church, and we spent a couple of nights there. This was close to the seal hunting. I'm not sure how long that building has been there. It was moved from Iglujuarnaaq, meaning "a little building." It used to belong to the Hudson's Bay Company. There are pieces of equipment there [that] used to be Buster Brown's. There's a good-size anchor there, too. After the HBC was finished with the building, when nobody was using it, the Catholic church moved it — actually, the people moved it with a dog team — down to Nuvuk&it, close to where there's always open water, where there are seals.

When I was there, there were other people from Repulse Bay there hunting. They came down the day after me. There was open water near those islands at Nuvuk&it, about two miles from that old church building. We got polar bears, seals, lots of seals. I didn't have enough gas to go up to the old HBC post. It's a very long way from Nuvuk&it. So I stayed there another day and then had to get down to Rankin. We didn't have a radio, so nobody knew where we were, so we had to get down to Rankin as soon as possible, before somebody came looking for us!

I left the other people from Repulse there. They were going to look for more polar bears. Two guys already got a polar bear and another guy still had to get a polar bear, so I left them. I think they stayed there for a couple of days more.

There used to be no polar bear, or hardly any polar bear. It changed to where you might see maybe four or five polar bear in a day at Ukkusiksalik. Before my father was born, and when he remembered as a boy, there was no polar bear. You saw them just once in a while. Before that, way before he was born, there used to be lots of polar bear. So, there was no polar bears in that area. The old saying is that there was a woman, her son got killed by polar bear, and she cursed the place that there would be no polar bear. So, there was no polar bear for a long time. But when I got there in 1975, there was lots of polar bear. There were lots of tracks everywhere. My father hardly believed it. I don't know when they started coming back, when that curse went off.

My aunts told me the polar bear went out on the ice, near the mouth of Ukkusiksalik. There's lots of current there. You have to watch the ice. You see the ice really move with the current, very strong current, and a whirl-pool. You go very fast in a boat. It's better to wait until it's slowed down. The currents take turns [reverse with the tide]. So they say you don't see the bears for a long time. They used to think there's a hole somewhere on the bottom. I don't think so. I went there a few times. Some people were afraid of that because it went so fast. A long time ago they used to say that there's a hole in the bottom of the sea. There was an accident down there one time.

There was another accident at Bennett Bay, when they were hunting seal. One man went out to get a seal, and he broke a paddle, and it was getting windy. The boat filled up with water and he was lost.

The next time I was there was when my parents moved back in 1979 to the old post and stayed there for a couple of years. I went there the year after them and spent the winter up there.

My parents used the building in the middle at the back, which used to be the garage for the tractor. I was in the one that used to be the store. My father told me he was born in the old trader's house.

I heard [about] two guys with machines, a D2 Cat [a D2 Caterpillar tractor] and another tractor. The machines were tied together and tried to pull each other, to find out which one was stronger. I'm not sure what happened to these two. I think the HBC men left the tractors up near Gjoa Haven to do something. I'm not sure.

My father did quite a bit of work on the house then. They had to put in some insulation, get a generator in, put in an oil stove. He asked the Hudson's Bay Company if he could get those buildings. He got an okay from Hudson's Bay Company.

It was pretty good living there but hard on the snowmobiles. I took two new machines one winter. A lot of travelling, mostly chasing wolf. Pretty rough country up there. Going up hill. Lots of rocks.

Every time wolf came around, if I got them, seemed to be no wolf for a while, then they came back. Sometimes you can tell it's the same track. But if three wolves came, you can see the tracks. I didn't get them right away. When I got them, I thought there would be no more wolves, but a week later, there were more. I didn't go far from the post to hunt wolves. I never went far enough out to sleep. I never went out overnight. I always came back. Maybe the farthest was forty miles. There were more wolves to the north of Qamanaaluk and Tasiujaq than to the south. That winter I got around thirty wolves, at $400 or $500 for a pelt.

We didn't see any muskox at all but lots of caribou. And lots of good char. No problem with food that winter.

When I was up there for the winter, it was a good feeling. We left for the kids; they got no school there. And the women, they like the running water and flush toilets. I think if we had our way, me and my father, we would probably be still out there. But the kids have to go to school. I think women don't like the land as much as men. It's too rough for them, I think.

My father always remembers Ukkusiksalik when he was a kid there with his sister [Tuinnaq Kanayuk Bruce]. He always talks about her. I think it is always a good time when you're a kid, when you think back.

My mother was more from Repulse Bay area. Her father was Suvisuk; that's my name, too. Her family used to go down to Douglas Harbour or Piqsimaniq, but not for too long. When they got married, they stayed around Tasiujaq.

I was born near Ukkusiksalik, and shortly after I was born, my family moved down to Duke of York Bay. My parents always talked about Ukkusiksalik.

ARSENE PUTULIK, 1935–97 REPULSE BAY

My father walked in front of the dogs the whole trip,
from Naujaat to Ukkusiksalik.

I was born in Chesterfield Inlet at the hospital run by the nuns. I don't know what year it was. My parents were both from the Pelly Bay area, Nattilingmiut ["people of the Nattilik region"]. As soon as I was born, my mother took me, they got on the ship, and we came to Repulse Bay. The captain of the ship, *Umiajuarnaq*, was Angilak. I believe he was a Roman Catholic missionary. The men working on the ship were Nuvak (late husband of Mary Nuvak) and my father.

Much later, shortly after I got a wife, when there was no longer anybody at Tasiujaq, we were in Ukkusiksalik briefly. I don't know which year. My wife was also from the Pelly Bay area. She was my father's older brother's daughter. We moved to Ukkusiksalik with my father. I never used to separate from my father, along with my younger brothers. There was my father, Paul Akkurdjuk; my stepmother, Eitoq; my wife, Celina Putulik; my brother Anthonese Mablik and his wife, Suzanne; my brothers Pilimon Tigumiaq and Francois Nanuraq; my stepbrother Antoin Siatsiak; and my stepsister, Annie Qupanuq.

We started from Itiglikuluk, near Repulse Bay. From Itiglikuluk, we brought a boat to the floe edge by dog team. It was a wooden whale boat, about twenty-seven feet long. We used to sail it. My father and his two brothers, with their father, all together, they bought the boat with fox skins. By boat, we went to Sublu through the channel to Ijuriqtuq and across to Umiijarvik, ended up in Umiijarvik, stayed there until midsummer when all the ice moved away from Ukkusiksalik. We made it to Ukkusiksalik after all the ice was gone, probably in late July.

Although my father had been there before, he didn't quite know where the good anchoring places were. But he knew that a man named Saniqtaq was there with his younger brother Tavok. So we kept going, looking for them. We found them in the mouth of a river. The name of the river, I believe, was Kuugarjuk. When we got to Kuugarjuk, my father asked Saniqtaq if he knew of a place where there is good anchorage. Saniqtaq replied that although he has never had a boat the size that my father had, he could have a look at Tinittuqtuq. He said if my father sees the area, he will know whether it is good or bad for his boat. So we went on to Tinittuqtuq, to a good place to keep a boat. We made camp not directly at the mouth of the river, but just a little south of it, just past the mouth of the river.

After we got to Tinittuqtuq, we went to Tasiujaq by boat, looking for caribou. When we got there, there was no caribou along the coast. There were lots of wolves along the coast. So we went out of Tasiujaq, across to the other side of Ukkusiksalik, where we got caribou. We then returned to Tinittuqtuq.

Then my father and my brother Pilimon and Saniqtaq went back to Repulse Bay by boat in August. The rest of the family stayed at Tinittuqtuq while the three men went up to Repulse Bay to trade. I am not sure what they were going to use to trade. Perhaps they were thinking that the family allowance might be available then. Mablik and I stayed behind to hunt for the families. We waited for them through the rest of the summer, but winter came before they ever returned. We didn't have any communication with Repulse Bay then, so we had no idea where they were.

What happened was, they got to Repulse Bay, but the ice came into the bay and they could not leave. I told my brother Mablik that once the ice on the lakes got thick enough, we should go to Repulse Bay to find out what had happened to them. Then I started gathering food so that we could leave the families with a lot of food if we go. We did our hunting by foot, and we got back with enough food to leave the family, but doing all that walking, we were tired. As we were resting in preparation for the trip, people saw the dog team coming with Saniqtaq and my father. They would have made it to Ukkusiksalik earlier, but Saniqtaq had had TB before, so had bad lungs. They were given three dogs for Saniqtaq to ride on. Saniqtaq would walk alongside the sled at times, but would be on the *qamutik* a lot. But my father walked all the way from Repulse Bay to Ukkusiksalik. Saniqtaq had travelled once to Ukkusiksalik before, but he didn't know exactly which route to go. But he would advise my father which direction he should be walking. So my father walked in front of the dogs the whole trip.

After the lake ice was thick enough, about mid-November, and the trapping season opened, my father advised us to go to Repulse Bay to pick up my brother. So we got together with my father and Saniqtaq, and I asked them about the trip to Repulse Bay. I was told what to do and what not to do. At that time, my father told me if the evenings are nice and I am going to travel at night to the north, to remember *Tukturjuaq* [the Big Dipper], which will always remain on the north side. If I lost my way, it will always be on the north side. So, in the evening, when I started making an iglu, if the evening was clear and I could see stars, I would leave a stick there at night, so when I wake up in the morning and start packing to travel, getting everything ready, then I would go to the little stick, which I put the night before. I knew where my north was and kept travelling that way. This was how I travelled toward Repulse Bay.

I knew *Nuuttuitut*, the North Star. It doesn't move. *Tukturjuaq*, the Big Dipper, goes around it. *Ullaktut* is Orion's Belt. The legend says the three stars side by side in a straight line are three brothers who are running after a polar bear. There is a cluster of stars higher in the sky, called *Agiattat*. The brightest star in the middle is the polar bear and the ones surrounding it are the dogs.

My father also told me about *uqalurait*, snowdrifts from the north wind. But it was too early in the fall for snowdrifts, so he advised me to make sure I remember where *Tukturjuaq* was. It's not right on the horizon — it's up higher — but when it first appears, they are on your *uangnaq* [where the prevailing winds come from].

When I was taking too long to Repulse Bay, I started worrying that I was travelling too much northward, that I was going to miss Repulse Bay altogether. My father told me what the land should look like. I was worried that I wasn't coming across the river Sipujatuq, which I should have crossed, so I didn't know where I was. My father had told me that if I knew where north was, there would be no problem going southeast, and I ended up near Qasigiaqtuq, across the bay from where the community is.

We stayed at Tinittuqtuq until the ice got thick enough, when we moved to Nuvuk&it, to be near seals so our dogs can live. When we got there, it was storming for a long time, so we were hungry. My father told me to go inland to Tinittuqtuq because we had caribou left there from the summer. I was to go get that meat, so we can live on it. He told me to take Mablik with me to go get the caribou. He said he was going to stay behind to try and catch seal near Nuvuk&it. The next day it wasn't storming so bad. We got up before daylight and we left very early in the morning to go to Tinittuqtuq. Shortly after we left Nuvuk&it, my dogs smelled something. I told my brother, I think my dogs smell caribou. So I walked from there to look for the caribou. And I saw the caribou and I got some of them. We went back to Nuvuk&it the same day we left. I got back to our camp, and the three men — my father, Saniqtaq, and Tavok — still weren't home. They were still hunting. They got back after dark, and their sleds were full of seal. It was a very happy occasion for us.

At Nuvuk&it, we hunted seals at the ice edge in the polynya.* We did not hunt seal through the breathing holes at all. That's why Nuvuk&it was a popular base, because it was close to the open water. The northern side of Ukkusiksalik was always frozen over completely, except at this polynya. Except for the families at Masivak, who didn't really move around much, people anywhere else around Ukkusiksalik used to go to Nuvuk&it for winter. The only source of heat available was from seal fat. So, you had to be at Nuvuk&it for the seal fat and in order to feed your dogs.

The elders around the area were Inusatuajuk, Tavok, Saniqtaq, and my father, Akkurdjuk. They made the decisions. Inusatuajuk, with his stepson, Kaunak, and his children, and Utaq, who was a little boy then, were living at Piqsimaniq. During the winter they came to Nuvuk&it, to make sure that they had food for the dogs.

I travelled up to Tasiujaq from Tinittuqtuq once by dog team, for caribou hunting, but there was no one living there. Some of the roofs were sagging

---

* A polynya is an area of water in the Arctic Ocean where the currents prevent the formation of ice even in the winter. The open water allows hunters to access seals.

already. At that time, I did not really go to the buildings. I had heard that they were haunted. I did not dare go directly to them. Travelling near them, it seemed that somebody might come out to greet you or something.

In the spring, we went back to Repulse Bay. My father had all the authority over where and when we moved. It was my father's idea to move. I have no idea what was in my father's mind. So, after that one winter in Ukkusiksalik, we went back to Repulse Bay by dog team. My father's boat was already there, because he had travelled in it the year before. Just those with my father and all of us kids went with my father. The rest of the families stayed in Ukkusiksalik. It was late spring.

Saniqtaq eventually came up to Repulse Bay that same spring. We all ended up in Beach Point [just south of Repulse Bay], our family and Saniqtaq's family together, with my dog team, my father's dog team, and Saniqtaq's dog teams. My father and I brought the boat down to Beach Point, hauling it on the ice with dogs. When we had the boat near the open water, my father told me to return to Repulse Bay with Saniqtaq. He said otherwise there would be too many dogs to put in the boat to get back to Repulse Bay after the ice left. So, leaving my father behind to wait for the ice to go out, Saniqtaq and I went to Repulse Bay in July. My father was to follow us after the ice had left.

I only went back to Ukkusiksalik once after that, many years later.

ANTHONESE MABLIK, 1940–2001 REPULSE BAY

People lived in Ukkusiksalik before I was born and before anyone today was born, long ago, probably in the Tuniit era.

We know for sure that people lived in Ukkusiksalik before I was born and before anyone today was born, long ago, probably in the Tuniit era. When you look at it closely, there are inuksuit [the plural of inuksuk] and other structures made by human hands that have been there for years and years, before any of us were there at all.

I was born November 1, 1940, in the Repulse Bay area at Tikiraq. My father's name is Akkurdjuk. I think he was from the Pelly Bay area, Nattilik. My mother, Tannaruluk, was from the same area.

I first went to Ukkusiksalik when I was seventeen years old, in spring, around May. We used to travel from one place to the other, to look for more game, for hunting and trapping. At that time, in the Repulse Bay area, food was getting scarce, so we moved down to Ukkusiksalik.

There were two dog teams, my father's and my older brother's, Arsene Putulik. There were about eight people: my father, Akkurdjuk; my stepmother, Eitoq; my brothers Arsene Putulik, Pilimon Tigumiaq, Antoin Siatsiak; plus my stepsister Annie Qupanuq and Arsene's wife, Celina, plus my wife, Suzanne. We got married earlier that spring. We were newlyweds on a honeymoon! We were married in church in Repulse Bay.

From Repulse Bay we went across the sea ice and stopped at Beach Point. Then we went along the shore; our next stop was at Qiniulik, then Ikalupilina. We stayed there at the islands. It was in early spring so the trip was very easy. There were no soft spots. It was fun. We didn't see many caribou but quite a few seals.

We stayed at Nuvuk&it for a while. There were two families there: Tavok and Saniqtaq. Our boat was already there. After the ice was gone we moved to Tinittuqtuq, a good place to anchor the boat. We stayed at Tinittuqtuq during the summer, although we used to go up to Tasiujaq for caribou hunting. The boat was a whaler with a sail and an inboard engine. It was called a *tuq-tuq-tuq* because of the sound.

I went to Tasiujaq in the summer by boat, but I never actually went to the buildings. I could see the buildings, but I never went there. I don't know why, but my father and also Saniqtaq told me not to go to those buildings. Those two were the boss; I had to listen to them. I was told that the place was haunted. I know I wasn't going to see any ghosts or anything, although it can happen.

One time I went on a caribou hunt with my younger brother, Tony Siatsiak, to a place called Umiijarvik. We were walking, and my younger brother saw a person with a tusk. He was so scared that he didn't know what he was doing any more. I myself saw nothing at that time, but my younger brother was so scared that I believed he had actually seen something.

We based the whole summer at Tinittuqtuq, staying in a canvas tent, trying to catch caribou. Tinittuqtuq is where my fond memory is, because there were both seals and caribou there. I caught a lot of them when I was there. The place itself is beautiful also. That's why I like it there. We didn't stay there long enough, only one year.

My older brother, Arsene Putulik, and I walked from Tinittuqtuq straight north, inland, looking for caribou. There were not very many caribou, just a few. Then, in the winter, we moved down to Nuvuk&it, because it's close to the floe edge, for hunting seal. We lived in an iglu there. We stayed there the whole winter. We used to get hungry all the time. There wasn't enough caribou or enough seal. We got very hungry during that year. In spring, sometime in May, we moved back to Repulse Bay.

We travelled by dog teams again; instead of two dog teams there were three dog teams, one for each family. I don't remember how long the trip took. We were travelling at nights, too. So I don't remember how many nights we stopped on the way back. We brought the boat back with us by dog team. We had large dog teams; I estimate about fifty or sixty dogs altogether. Not too many people had twenty per team; the normal was between six to twelve. Not many had fifteen dogs per team. We got all the dogs together to pull the boat up a hill.

When we came back from Ukkusiksalik, Inusatuajuk and his son, Utaq, were living with us. Utaq was very young. His older brother, Kaunak, stayed with Tavok and Saniqtaq as a group.

My parents never went back to Ukkusiksalik. Utaq and I went there again a few years later by dog team to go seal hunting in late April. After Tavok and Saniqtaq came to Repulse Bay, about a year later, we went down to Ukkusiksalik. Later on, my older brother and I went down by snowmobile to Ukkusiksalik for a seal hunt.

When Utaq and I went there, I was in my twenties. Utaq was younger than me, and he brought his son. We left our wives behind in Repulse Bay. We were at an *aukaniq* [polynya] where the flow of the water keeps it open. That time, there was a lot of seal, so much seal that we didn't have to use a boat to get them, just on the ice. We brought a boat with us, but we never used the boat at all. It seemed like [the seals] were ducks, birds, popping up and down, there were that many. They were right close to the edge of the ice, so we just used harpoons. There were so many that we were right close beside them. We had to pull it up very quickly because of the current. If we took our time the seal would go under the ice because there were very strong currents, so it was hard to pull up. As soon as we harpooned it, we pulled it right up quickly. We were at the *aukaniq* for two days. The first day we caught a hundred ringed seals. The next day we were going to catch a little bit more, but there were too many seals to skin, so we stopped after two days.

We brought only a certain amount of the seal meat back home. We couldn't carry it all. We cached them right in the ice, so if anybody went there from anywhere, they were just there to help themselves.

It was approximately two kilometres from Nuvuk&it to the open water, the polynya, which is about a hundred feet across. The polynya near Nuvuk&it was open during the winter months. Toward spring, about the time we left, in April, it was frozen over, instead of the other way around.

I am not sure if this happens every year, but when I was there, that's how it happened.

I saw three seals had been killed on the ice when they were basking, and I figured they were killed by a wolf. If they were killed by a bear, they would have been eaten, but they were just killed and not eaten at all. I noticed that there were quite a few wolves but I was just using a dog team, not a snowmobile, so I couldn't go chasing them.

When I went back there seal hunting later with my older brother Putulik, by snowmobile, in the very early days of snowmobiles, we went to the same *aukaniq*, but there were very few seals this time, not many at all, because that's the way Ukkusiksalik is.

It's the tradition of Ukkusiksalik that if there's people living there, the game will get scarce. Once there are no more people there, the animals will return. If people live there a long time, the game will go away, and when they are gone the game will come right back again. This is different from other places. What I think is that Ukkusiksalik is so narrow at the mouth and the bay itself, a lot of snow accumulates on the sea ice. The seals get scared and start going away. That's what I think, myself.

When there were too many people there, that's when the seals started to get scared away. So, when Tavok moved from Ukkusiksalik to Repulse Bay, we knew there would be a lot of seal soon, after nobody stayed there for a whole year. After Tavok left Nuvuk&it and moved to Repulse Bay, that's when we went to go seal hunting. We used all the seals, for food and dog food, and also we used the skin to buy some groceries. Utaq was going back to Igloolik with his wife. I had to get some seal meat for dog food and food for me and my wife. I was also using the skins to buy some groceries. We were not using money then, just trading tokens.

At that time, food and everything wasn't that expensive. I remember [that] for one good-quality skin you could average twenty-five pounds of flour. Smaller flour bags were cheaper. For one sealskin, you could get a bag of flour, a pound of lard and baking powder, and also a box of bullets. It's kind of hard to tell because the sealskin prices always went up and down. And it all depended on the quality of the sealskin. I figure at that time, five good-quality skins for a new rifle.

There is an unwritten rule of life: too many people scare the seals away. It is something that was true in the past and will probably be true in the future, too. Wildlife gets frightened away. That's why, in the past, we respected the policy to get enough to last you, no more, so that you won't waste the meat, and so there won't be many bones littered all over the place. So the land and the air will be clean at all times. This was respected by the younger people; the older people made sure they were going by this. If the oldest people figured there was enough to last them a whole year, they told the other people, that's enough, no more, and they will stop hunting. That is Inuit philosophy.

PETER KATOKRA, 1931–2005 REPULSE BAY

He did this according to Inuit tradition, using his Inuit power,
the Inuit knowledge he has.

People have always lived in Ukkusiksalik, before the white men or the trading post. Inuit lived where there was game. They didn't stay in one area. They moved according to where they could survive.

I was born in Pelly Bay [Kugaaruk] in November 1931. I am very old. I am already sixty-one years old. We moved here to Repulse Bay area when I was thirteen years old. My parents were born in Pelly Bay area with Nattilingmiut.

When I was aged fifteen or sixteen years old, we moved to Ukkusiksalik, and we lived there. There was my grandfather Akkiutaq; my grandmother Kinakuluk; my mother, Arnarqriaq; my father, Ulikataq; my uncle Marc Tungilik; my sister, Qiluk; my brother, Aquitaq; and my grandparents' adopted son, Iyakak. Also there, at that time, was Sivaniqtoq and his family, plus Tavok and his brother.

At that time, we did not get any government assistance of any kind. At times, Repulse Bay didn't always have enough game to live on, so we moved to Ukkusiksalik to be near game. In those days, it was hard to stay alive. You had to go from day to day with whatever you caught.

We walked inland to hunt caribou in the area north of Ukkusiksalik. My grandparents paddled into Ukkusiksalik, and told us that they were going to Piqsimaniq, to see if the caribou were there yet. My father and I walked back to our camp and we stayed there until the freeze-up, then my uncle and I went back to Repulse Bay by dog team to trade. Then we returned to our camp and then to Piqsimaniq.

The main reason we moved to Ukkusiksalik was to survive, to be able to hunt caribou. The immediate area around Repulse Bay didn't always have caribou, so caribou was our main reason to move to Ukkusiksalik. There is caribou in Ukkusiksalik year round, and there's also seal and fish there. We moved to Ukkusiksalik to have a better living, so that we could be happy. So, I now know where to hunt, for which game, at what time, and where in Ukkusiksalik. It's a very beautiful land.

Fishing was important. In the summer, people used stone weirs in rivers to trap the fish and then catch them with a *kakivak*. In fall, when the river hadn't frozen yet, they would go to the inlets along the river where there is no current and fish there with *kakivak*. After the lakes freeze up, they would fish there with *kakivak* as well, through the ice, using a lure made out of ivory, about an inch and a half long, with a little flipper, on the end of a string. You put that down a hole in the ice to attract the fish, and then use a *kakivak*. We also had very short nets we made ourselves by hand with string, a little bit thicker than thread, that we bought from the trading post. We were quite capable of making stuff. Although any game was hard to get with the lack of material, we were able to get by.

I was born long after the rifles came north. The only way we got caribou was with a rifle. On the sea ice, we hunted seal with a harpoon and a rifle.

At that time, when people were living here, there was hardly any polar bear. You very rarely got a polar bear in those days. After the people moved away, Ukkusiksalik started getting more polar bear.

I think there were about five families there. This was after most people left Ukkusiksalik. Before our time, there used to be a lot of families in that area. I believe they moved away because the trading post closed down. I am quite sure it was because of the trading post shutting down that people there left. Although there were not as many people there, there was always somebody in Ukkusiksalik. I know the last people were [the] Saniqtaq family and Tavok family. The reason they moved back here to Repulse Bay was because of sickness. Also, people were starting to gather here in Repulse Bay in the 1960s. Those two families, Tavok and Saniqtaq, always lived in

Ukkusiksalik; the time they moved to Repulse Bay was the only time they finally left Ukkusiksalik.

Our family and the Sivaniqtoq family were in Piqsimaniq. Piqsimaniq was popular because there's Arctic char there and it's close to caribou. Masivak [on the other side of the bay] is also popular for the same reasons; it's got Arctic char and is close to caribou. The Tavok and Saniqtaq families were in Tinittuqtuq. Tinittuqtuq is popular because it's close to caribou and also there is char there, but not as much as at Piqsimaniq and Masivak. They spent the winter there, and in the springtime they moved to Nuvuk&it. Nuvuk&it was a popular spot because it's close to the floe edge, where you can hunt seal. There was a little mission building at Nuvuk⁢ after we were there, Inuit in the area started using it. The building belonged to the Tasiujaq trading post, and they brought it to Nuvuk&it from Tikirajuaq.

The floe edge near Nuvuk&it is different from all the other floe edges because even if there's a strong north wind, the ice can come up at a fast pace toward you. One person almost drifted away because he didn't know about it being different. Joe Netar, a man who now lives in Rankin Inlet, fell in and the ice was going to crush him. His hunting partner, Saniqtaq, yelled to the open space and the ice stopped. They say this is what happened. He did this according to Inuit tradition, I believe, using his Inuit power or the Inuit knowledge he has.

The name Piqsimaniq is because of the bend in the river. It is coming here and then all of a sudden heads this way. I do not know why Masivak is called Masivak. Qaurnak is named after this mountain; *qauq* means forehead, and when you look at the mountain from a distance, you can see it is very smooth, just like looking at a forehead. Tinittuqtuq is called that because, in Inuktitut, *tininiq* is the tide, "where it goes down," and there is a lot of tide there. Just west of Tinittuqtuq, on the other side of the peninsula, is an island call Aibrujat. Although I am Inuk, I admire that island. The name comes from *aiviq*, because it looks like a walrus. "Aibrujat" means a small walrus. The group of islands out there in the bay, like a point or peninsula, is called Nuvuk. The one farthest out, sticking out because of all these islands, it sticks farthest out in the sea. One of the two islands is called Ibjuriktuq.

The area is called Ukkusiksalik because of the soapstone there. I can't point out on the map where the soapstone is. In other places, soapstone is very hard to find, even very small pieces of soapstone are hard to find.

Ukkusiksalik has more soapstone than other places. Sivaniqtoq is one person who knows exactly where the soapstone is. He knows more about the area that I do.

When we were in Piqsimaniq, we lived in an iglu in winter and a canvas tent in summer. We had a dog team and my grandparents had a paddle canoe, with wooden ribs, bought from the Repulse Bay trading post. I never went up to the trading post at Tasiujaq. I do not believe the buildings were used at that time. We were very scared of touching the white man's belongings. So, our parents were scared to even go there. Long after we moved to Repulse Bay, when Robert Tatty lived there, I went to the trading post.

The way we were taught — we still honour this — was that what does not belong to you does not belong to you. I remember once, here in Repulse Bay, when I was about seventeen or eighteen years old, I am not sure what year it was, a trading manager came to our home and told us to move out. I myself wasn't scared but my parents were extremely scared because he's a white man. In those days Inuit used to be scared for no reason at all. When we were children, if a policeman came we would stand in one spot until he left. Nowadays, the kids don't even notice when the RCMP come around. Our life is totally changed today.

I heard of a person who killed a man named Amaroalik somewhere in the Repulse Bay area. I have heard a little bit of that story but I cannot tell the whole, complete story, the way it happened. It was sometime after the whalers came, when Inuit started using rifles, in the period 1890 to 1920. I don't know what happened.

After the time at Piqsimaniq, around June of the next year, we went from Piqsimaniq by dog team down toward the mouth of Ukkusiksalik and along the coast to Repulse Bay. The main reason we went back to Repulse Bay was my brother and my sister were sick most of the time. There was a trading post and Roman Catholic mission in Repulse Bay, and from those two places you were able to get a little bit of medicine for the sick. After we moved out of Ukkusiksalik, maybe two years or so, suddenly a number of families moved into Ukkusiksalik.

JACKIE NANORDLUK, 1937–99 REPULSE BAY

There was a time when my grandfather drifted away.

Thinking back now, my father lived in Ukkusiksalik. I can't say how many winters or how many summers he lived there. He used to say "Tuma Qotoq" was his real name, but people call him Siutinuaq. My nephew Andreasi Siutinuar was named after his grandfather, my father, Siutinuaq.

Both of my parents were from the Pelly Bay area and we grew up in that area. Although our parents didn't have snowmobiles to travel with, they were able to travel from place to place. My father even has a song which mentions Ukkusiksalik. The song is in a deep Pelly Bay dialect. I don't know all the words to the song, but he mentions Ukkusiksalik and then going on to Chesterfield Inlet. [About] the song, he stated, "The song and the words couldn't come up to me until I started travelling, then the words for my song started following me and came to me" while he was travelling. In the song, he mentions the mouth of Ukkusiksalik, where they were going by boat. It says it was extremely dangerous in the mouth of Ukkusiksalik with all the ice moving back and forth.

I am the youngest of my brothers. I was born in Pelly Bay on October 10, 1937. I am already an old man. A lot of people who are younger than me look like old people.

My older brother, Mariano Aupilarjuq, in Rankin Inlet, would know more about our father's trip.

There was also a time when my grandfather drifted away. This is how my father told me. It was on a trip from Chesterfield Inlet to Repulse Bay. They got to Piqiuluk, a place on this side of Chesterfield Inlet, in my great-grandfather's boat. I don't know whether they fell asleep while sailing, but a storm came up when they were travelling. They were on the opposite side of the ice, which was drifting away, out to the sea. They were on the outside and the ice started to drift out toward the middle of Hudson Bay. My father was about the same age as my grandfather Hoviq. Those two were young men. Their job was to secure the sail on the boat. One of them knew that on a windy day, you have to make a good knot to make it secure. The other method is just putting a loop so that if you have to take it off, you can do it in a hurry. They tried to stay on top of the ice but it got too rough, and they decided they were going to sail. That knot came loose, which was holding the mast secured, causing the mast to fall. That was the main reason they had no control over the boat. They eventually ended up on the east side of Chesterfield Inlet on an island called Piqiuluk.

I cannot recall what year it was the first time I went to Ukkusiksalik. But I know I went there with Peter Katokra. That was the time we went to get Andreasi Siutinuar. He was staying with his grandfather and grandmother. I was around sixteen years old, or close to twenty. Andreasi was about ten or eleven years old. Katokra lived there at one point, so he knew the route to Ukkusiksalik. I was just along on the dog team for the trip. I was just a passenger. I was too young to have a team of my own.

My brothers and I went to Beach Point, where you went to hunt for seal at the floe edge. I ended up staying behind when my brothers went back to Repulse Bay. I believe Peter got the message that he was to go get Andreasi in Ukkusiksalik, so we left from Beach Point and overnighted once, and the next day we got to the place we were going. Marc Tungilik's family was staying there. We went from Piqsimaniq to Nuvuk&it and across to Masivak, where we had a good sleep. From there, since it was springtime, with the spring thaw, we immediately started heading back to Repulse Bay.

I went back to Ukkusiksalik quite some time after that, after we got snowmobiles, fairly recently. I don't know exactly what year. I went on that trip because Louis Pilakapsi and John Tatty were going to Ukkusiksalik and we were going to meet there. I went to the trading post to bring naphtha and gasoline for the Tattys. I had never been to Tasiujaq before Tattys were there.

That old building at Nuvuk&it was given to me by Yvo Airut, the Yamaha dealer in Rankin Inlet. It was given to him by word of mouth by the Roman Catholics since they were not going to go there. When Yvo got it, he fixed it up, made it look very nice. Then people started going there. People from Coral Harbour, from Chesterfield Inlet, from Repulse Bay, and from Rankin Inlet started using it. It is now very messy. There are also a lot of drums on the outside. The building was in nice shape. But sometimes people leave meat or blubber inside, which thaws in there, so the floor needs to be fixed up again. Damage was caused by polar bears going in there, breaking the doors and window to get inside and doing damage inside the building. I will go there whenever possible and stay there to do some hunting.

I have never been to Ukkusiksalik in the summer, only in winter. I have seen soapstone around Ukkusiksalik, although not a good quality. *Ukkusik* is a soapstone pot. There were no metal pots in the old days.

ANDREASI SIUTINUAR, 1947–2005 REPULSE BAY

There were times when we went hungry.

I was born in Qaraak, Lyon Inlet, on August 21, 1947. My mother was born in Igloolik area and my father, Louie Oksukittoq, is from the Pelly Bay area. My grandfather was Inusatuajuk. When I was a child, my mother had to leave for hospital when she had tuberculosis. The TB crew took me on the plane to Ukkusiksalik to stay with my grandparents, who were living in Ukkusiksalik. The plane came to get my parents. The TB crew went to Ukkusiksalik to pick up all the families there, to come to Repulse Bay to get their X-ray. On their trip back, I was taken on the plane with my grandparents to Ukkusiksalik. I was about six years old, about 1953.

We landed at Masivak, where my grandparents were staying. I know we were at Masivak and then we moved. I started hearing about Iriptaqtuuq. We stayed there, then moved back to Masivak in the winter. We used to move around in Ukkusiksalik. I know one time we went to Nuvuk&it in the spring, and the Tavoks came to Nuvuk&it at that time. In early spring we would gather at Nuvuk&it, due to the seals and the floe edge being close. But there used to be Saniqtaq and his family in Piqsimaniq, also Marc Tungilik and that family. They would move in different areas at different times, but come early spring we would end up getting together for the seal hunt. I also know that Sivaniqtoq was there. I don't know who else was with him, but they lived around the area as well.

My grandfather was at Piqsimaniq, and he had a *qarmaq* [sod house] there. The one that belonged to my grandfather was made out of stone. The other one, on the other side, the one close to a little lake, which belonged to Angugatsiaq [Marc Tungilik's wife], is made out of sod. We also had an iglu there.

There were times when we went hungry. Sometimes there was hardly any game. Piqsimaniq was a good place for Arctic char, and it was close to caribou. I remember we were briefly at Kuugarjuk and then we went to Qaurnak, again for the char, and also it's closer to caribou. We spent much of the summer in Qaurnak for that purpose. From Qaurnak we went to Qamarvik, toward Chesterfield Inlet, for caribou. In summer we travelled around in a freighter canoe, about twenty-two feet long, paddling and using a sail. We moved around to good char rivers and to hunt seal for dog meat for the winter, and trapping foxes. For those purposes we used to travel around. It seems as though that's a lot of travelling, but it's not. We just stayed in one area until the game got scarce, then we immediately moved to the next area, perhaps in a few days. In the winter, we were closer to the floe edge and the seal. Also, you have a better route to Repulse Bay from Nuvuk&it for trading.

After two summers in Ukkusiksalik that time, my mother was going to come back from down south. So Jackie Nanordluk and Peter Katokra came by dog team to get me from Masivak. They spent about three days in Masivak with us and then they started taking me back to Repulse Bay. Along the route they stopped and cut my hair off completely, to the skin, because they found out I had lots of lice on my head. They also took my sleeping bag and turned it inside out to beat the lice off it.

When we left Masivak we camped on the land, and I think we slept three times before we arrived at Mattuq, opposite Repulse Bay. We got to the coast between Repulse Bay and Ukkusiksalik on the third day. Peter Katokra knew the route before because his uncle, Marc Tungilik, was living there. At the time, I didn't know the names of places where we made camp along the way. But looking back at the route, I can recognize some of the places we camped. It was maybe about five travelling days to Repulse Bay.

About five years or so after, I was back in Repulse Bay, after leaving my grandparents in Ukkusiksalik, and they came to Repulse Bay on their way to Igloolik. I know my grandmother was originally from Igloolik. I don't know where my grandfather was from.

After snowmobiles got introduced in the 1960s, we used to go to Ukkusiksalik to hunt for wolf and polar bear. We used to come back to Repulse Bay for about three days, then go right back to Ukkusiksalik to check our traps again.

Sometimes on my hunting trips, we would use the old post at Tasiujaq as a base camp. It was a nice place to camp while you're out wolf hunting, and a good place for putting fishing nets. I remember the old trader's house was in the worst condition. The old store wasn't too good, either. The best was the middle one, the "Native house." I knew in my mind that they originally belonged to the Hudson's Bay Company.

There is a place just north of Tasiujaq where they used to get soapstone to carve a pot or a *qulliq*. You can see where someone took a piece off to make a *qulliq*. It's exactly the right shape. That must be how Ukkusiksalik got its name.

I have travelled all around Ukkusiksalik. After people weren't hunting there so much anymore, I tried to set up a camp with my family so that my children could understand the hardships of trying to live on the land. When we got to Ukkusiksalik that time, we first stayed at Nuvuk&it for about a month and then we went to the mainland and stayed at Piqsimaniq for about two months. This was just before the Tatty family moved to Tasiujaq. There was a whole lot more wildlife. That's the reason I wanted to be in Ukkusiksalik. After Robert Tatty moved to Tasiujaq, we took supplies for his family.

I remember one time, when I was young, my grandfather went on foot to check his traps. Later, we heard footsteps coming. We had ice for a window in the iglu, and he came through the window and said, "I got a polar bear." That was the only time I remember him catching a polar bear. At the time, you had to walk inland to get your caribou. There weren't too many seals and there weren't too many foxes. Now Ukkusiksalik is totally different. It has a lot of wildlife. I believe this is because there is nobody there anymore. That's the reason why it has changed. I believe there wasn't as many fish there either. I also remember only one time they were chasing beluga whales in Iriptaqtuuq. When my family went there, we saw lots of wildlife. We saw enough seals, enough caribou, and enough char.

Nunavut Gov/Donna Barnett

NINETEEN

LOUIS PILAKAPSI, 1937–2000 RANKIN INLET

I really love being in Ukkusiksalik because I remember growing up there.

I wasn't actually born in Ukkusiksalik, but from when I was a child around the age of twelve, I sort of grew up there because we lived in Ukkusiksalik for approximately four years after my twelfth birthday. I was born in 1937, so we moved to Ukkusiksalik in 1949. My grandfather was Matthew Kingyuk. My father was Joseph Pitowyuk. We were living in Repulse Bay area. The hunting around Repulse Bay in those days was very limited; there was hardly any wildlife, especially caribou. So, my grandparents and my parents decided to move to where the caribou was more plentiful and that's the reason we moved to Ukkusiksalik. We travelled there by dog team.

I remember travelling to Ukkusiksalik from Repulse Bay toward the spring of that year. Travelling by sea ice wasn't all that bad, but when we tried to go overland from the sea ice to get to Ukkusiksalik, that was the hardest part. There were a lot of animals there compared to where we had just lived.

When we first moved to Ukkusiksalik, we lived in Nuvuk&it in the fall, and we moved to Tinittuqtuq in the summer because there is a river there and the fishing was really good. There were other people around Ukkusiksalik, not all in one location. I recall Ikpanaaq's family, Kaititaq's family, Tavok's family. Most of the families were in the main body of Ukkusiksalik. In summer we moved farther up to the Qamanaaluk area and then caught fish with a *kakivak*. My parents and my grandparents used to tell me not to get so many fish, only to take what we needed, but I used to get all kinds of fish because I really, really loved using *kakivak*.

People today think of Bennett Bay — "Qaurnak" in Inuktitut — as my area because that's where my family mainly stayed in the spring. There are lots of Arctic char in that area.

When we moved to Ukkusiksalik, the HBC trading post was already abandoned, but my parents still did trapping. Once they got plenty of fox pelts, they used to take them up to Repulse Bay to sell them. Not just once a year but anytime they had a lot of fur to trade: fox, sealskins, and sometimes bear skins. When I was a child, I remember seeing just one polar bear, although we lived in Ukkusiksalik about four years. There are lots of bears now.

I recall that the RCMP made occasional visits. When we lived in Nuvuk&it, RCMP used to come around Ukkusiksalik from Chesterfield Inlet.

We didn't stay in one location all the time. We followed the animals when they moved. We never actually stayed at the old trading post but to the northwest, in the Qamanaaluk area, somewhere around the southern part of it. I'm not exactly sure where Joseph Netar had the camp, but I know that we were with his family at Qamanaaluk. They mainly lived around that area because they wanted to be where the animals were. There were some other families up there also.

When I lived around Ukkusiksalik as a teenager, I really enjoyed hunting. I was able to hunt caribou and trap foxes myself. One of the more thrilling trips that I ever did by myself was in the spring when I was about fourteen. I had to get my sister, Eva, from Joseph Netar's family, which was quite a distance. I never really thought then, but that trip was quite long.

My grandfather passed away at Tinittuqtuq. His grave was just north of Sila Lodge, where there is a little lake and it's really sandy. They buried him in the sandy area, and the wind blew it off. After that, we were at Tasiujaq, hunting caribou in the summer. A man named Qajajuaq [Joe Curley] came in his Peterhead longliner *Tuudlik* from Coral Harbour, to hunt caribou around the Tasiujaq area. We were with Qajajuaq for more than a week, hunting caribou. When that family was going back to Coral Harbour, they didn't want to leave my family just by ourselves in the fall. So we went back to Coral in *Tuudlik* with Qajajuaq's family. That's when we moved to Coral Harbour. We only stayed around Ukkusiksalik those four years.

I really love being in Ukkusiksalik because I remember growing up there. I get some emotional feelings when I recognize the areas where we normally played and hunted before. All those memories come back to me, and it's a really great feeling.

MARC TUNGILIK, 1905–86 REPULSE BAY

I once made a false tooth for a Roman Catholic priest out of a polar bear's tooth.

I was born in the Pelly Bay area, in 1905 I think, and I grew up near Spence Bay, Pelly Bay, and Holman Island. I moved to Repulse Bay in the mid-1940s because my uncle, Akkiutaq, was living there. There was a lot of game here then, especially seals. The only houses I can remember were the HBC and the other trading company, Revillon Frères. Later, with my family, I moved down to Ukkusiksalik.

I started carving ivory when I was still up in Pelly Bay. I am one of a kind; it's impossible for other carvers to make them so small. When I see something, it's usually far away, so that's why I make them very tiny. Back then, the HBC here would trade a package of tea and a package of tobacco for one small carving. Later, when money arrived, they paid me one dollar for a carving. I supported two families with my carving. I once made a false tooth for an Roman Catholic priest out of a polar bear's tooth.

In Ukkusiksalik, in the 1950s, we lived mostly around Piqsimaniq. We used a *qarmaq* that must still be there. We lived there because the caribou hunting was good around there and there were lots of char in the river. Tavok's family and Inusatuajuk's family were there too, at Piqsimaniq.

Life was not exciting, just a matter of everyday survival, hunting caribou by walking inland, and seal from a little homemade rowboat, and catching Arctic char when they came up the river. We had a stone weir and we caught the fish in there with our *kakivak*.

People are always happy to go to a plentiful land — that is how I felt about going to Ukkusiksalik.

THERESIE TUNGILIK,*
1951–
RANKIN INLET

*My father used to make me wooden dolls. But the barrettes he
made were ivory — those I really want to have back.*

I was born in 1951, far away from Ukkusiksalik, on the sea ice,
because my parents were living at the Harbour Islands near Repulse Bay.
They were trying to get to the community, travelling by dog team, so I would
be born in a community. But I was born on the way, out on the sea ice,
between Repulse Bay and the Harbour Islands. I lived around Ukkusiksalik
during the following years, but I wasn't born there.

I remember a time when we were travelling by dog team. It was getting
dark, so we stopped for the night. I saw my father building an iglu, getting all
frosty on his moustache from hurrying. Finally, he finished the top and we got
in there and I remember being too small to climb on the bed. I pushed a can
of Klim dried milk, climbed on it, and I was able to get up onto the bed. I was
on my own feet. My mother had a baby on her back and she was busy trying
to put the bedding right away onto the bed. That child died at the age of
two. I just remember a very skinny little boy. He was two years younger, and
the next one would be four years. So, I was about two, or slightly over two.

---

* Theresie Tungilik is the daughter of Marc Tungilik, previous chapter. Her
mother was Angugatsiaq.

I don't remember names, as young as I was. But I can envision what environment we were in. I could see very high, high mountains and steep cliffs at times. When we travelled on farther, and we had stopped, it wasn't as hilly as where we were before. So I don't know what direction we were travelling in at the time of this memory. That's my earliest memory.

I remember the time my younger sister, Marie, was born in 1955. My mother told my stepsister and me to go pick berries. I think my stepsister knew she was in labour because Angugasak was eight years older than I. It was already August. We took the water pail, and she said, don't come back until you fill up that pail with berries. So we collected berries. We filled it up and came back and there was blood all over the tent. After my father had delivered my sister, he tied up the cord but cut it too short, so he had to retie it again. In the meantime, the baby's blood was gushing out. I guess with the lack of blood she had in her, every time she cried, she turned blue, so my mother thought she was not going to last very long. She wanted to make sure the baby was baptized before she died. She thought women don't baptize, but she knew the procedures of baptism, so taught my father and he did the baptism on a Sunday afternoon. After that, my sister never cried herself blue anymore. It was odd.

I remember my mother telling me that we used to live mostly around Ukkusiksalik when the Hudson's Bay Company and the missionaries would allow only working people to live in the settlements. So we lived near Ukkusiksalik. In the winter it was extremely cold, so they would be a little bit more away from that area. In the summer it was just gorgeous all the time. I remember having very windy days when our tent would blow down, in really, really strong winds. There would also be times when it was so hot, it was just wonderful. I used to collect bugs in my hands, even bugs you don't see down here in Rankin Inlet; Ukkusiksalik is inland and much warmer. I remember one sunny day I was out searching for insects and I found a large hairless, green caterpillar. I could feel its legs crawling in my hand, but it fell and I couldn't find it again. I wanted to show everyone how beautiful it looked. My mother would have screamed if it came near her. My mother was petrified of bugs, so I would chase her around and she would run away from me.

I remember great big cliffs of sand, going down before the beach, hitting the water, too. I have always had that in my memory, but I don't know exactly where it is now. That place is somewhere around Ukkusiksalik, I think.

I recall my parents telling stories of their past lives, when we were growing up, but we were often told, "Don't listen to us. Go play with your own age group; we're adults and we're entertaining ourselves."

I remember the time, when there was a lot of tuberculosis going around, some people came in a small float plane who were taking X-rays. Because of the little community we were, maybe there were two or three families living in that area, the plane was overcrowded. So they attached my father's homemade boat, put the children in the plane and put the adults in the boat, and it puttered all the way up to Repulse Bay, just for the X-rays. I guess they didn't want to make a second trip. I don't know why. But that's how they did it. I remember looking out the window to see if my mother was all right.

They took us back down the same way, I think. But I remember more of it when they were taking us from our camp to Repulse Bay, because it was right in the middle of summer. When we got to Repulse Bay, the people there said, "Oh, there's so many mosquitoes." It was seventy-five percent less mosquitoes than where we were staying [in Ukkusiksalik].

I remember Piqsimaniq, where we left from in Ukkusiksalik. I remember my father calling it by that name. I remember Tavok and his family and Inusatuajuk, Laurent Utaq's [in Repulse Bay] father. I remember Inusatuajuk used to have the most dogs. That was considered rich.

I only remember canvas tents. I don't think I lived in a *qarmaq*. The other families there were not living too close, where you could just walk over. You could see their tent, so occasionally we would visit at times. But we were not close together like today's houses are, nothing like that. We had our own little areas. I can't remember if they were on the same side of the river, or the opposite side. When another family came by to visit, then we would play together, but I guess I wasn't wandering off as a child.

My father used to make me dolls. And my mother would help me make the clothing for them with leftover materials and sometimes leftover skins. They were wooden dolls, about four to six inches long, with no arms at all, so it would be easier to make clothing for them. But the barrettes he made were ivory — those I really want to have back. He decorated them by engraving and then melting plastic combs with different colours in there. My father also made me ivory ulus [the Inuit woman's knife], ivory knives and forks and spoons. When we played, it was usually more or less just running around outside or playing dolls. We would also use the land itself. We would fix up rocks so that it looked like our own home and use the cliff part as shelves. Often, we would take any canned food and save those [empty cans] just for playing. We would use mud for making bannock.

I was so young. I remember one time, we were travelling — on our way to Repulse Bay, I think it was — in that little boat my father had made. Evening was coming soon. There were lots and lots of mosquitoes. As soon as the boat hit the shore, our dog had four pups. She got off the boat and starting digging right away. But two pups died when they were swarmed by the mosquitoes. She was able to save the other two by burrowing them in the ground.

Another year, we were trying to get back to Repulse Bay before winter struck, in that same little boat. My father went blind. My stepbrother was too young to know the way. I could see my mother praying day in and day out, even while she was busy doing this and that. After several sleeps, I don't know how long, my father got his sight back just in time for us to travel. We were lucky enough to make it before the water was really, really cold. I felt so lucky that we were able to get there. At the time, I wasn't worried, but I knew my mother was worried.

I remember when my mother wanted to give me a bath in the iglu. She had one of those really round metal tubs and a Primus stove to heat the water. I remember seeing lots of heat and asking her what it was. She said it was for my bath, and I said "No, *ikkii* [cold]," so somehow she convinced me by saying that if you have so much dirt on you, you will get sick. She ended up convincing me and I took a bath.

We used to see lots of mirages, like two or three families' dog teams, with really high *qamutiit*, with lots of stuff on their *qamutiit*, coming toward us, and we'd be all happy. Then, as soon as they passed a pressure ice [ridge], we couldn't see them after that. We saw these mirages a lot, especially in the spring.

My parents were very religious. Every Sunday they made sure they prayed before doing anything. One time, just one other family was having a prayer with us on Sunday morning, when we heard a plane land just behind the hill where we got our water. They didn't stop praying to go see the plane. We heard it land and we never heard it take off. They did the whole prayer thing, and after saying our Sunday prayer, we went up the hill to see the plane. There was nothing on the hill. It's just a mirage, they said. They didn't get all spooked or anything about it. But I've never experienced anything else like that in any other place.

Ukkusiksalik was a very good hunting area. Soon after my aunt, and her family, went to Repulse Bay to marry my uncle, my cousin said, "Boy, your father looks like he just goes out in a storm and brings back food." When he went out hunting, he always came back with game. I think he really liked the Ukkusiksalik area because there was lots of Arctic char, good-tasting fish, and plenty of game.

There were lots of caribou. I remember my father and stepbrother would go out in the summer. They took dogs. They had sealskin sacks on them, so they could help carry the load. We would climb up the hill to the inuksuk looking for them to arrive home. When they were coming home, you could see them walking along with the dogs, carrying the food. Then our neighbours would come by and eat and celebrate because there was lots.

My father was trapping, he was hunting, and he was carving. He also provided for another family by carving. His older brother, Ulikataq (Peter Katokra's father), had his own family, but he couldn't carve like his younger brother, so he got my father to carve for him.

I recall when he would make soapstone carvings, because I guess it was faster and easier for him. In those days, when he would carve, they were bigger in size from what he later did after he got his eye operation [in later life, Tungilik was famous for his miniature ivory carvings]. As I recall his ivory carvings, they would be more like my ulus and my barrettes. I guess he did some ivory carving while he was still up in Pelly Bay with his first wife. So he did both. Most of the carvings he did while we were living at Piqsimaniq were soapstone that he was intending to trade. Sometimes he would say, "These are so heavy to carry," because he had to take them on the dogsled up to Repulse Bay and he had to pack them well, too. So he would use caribou skin to wrap them, and that's how they survived the dog-team trip.

I think he got the soapstone out of the ground himself. I was less than seven years old, so these things didn't occur to me then, like, "Where's my dad getting the soapstone from?" It was just a natural, everyday thing that he would come home either with meat or soapstone or a little bit of both if he was hunting in that area.

Mostly he carved land animals and people doing things. My father saw a windup musical box and he copied it as a carving. He actually made the little gears and everything. I don't know who has it, but I would like to know.

One of our old neighbours at Piqsimaniq, Kakiarmiut (a.k.a. Paul Sannertanut), reminded me how well my father supported his family, partly with carvings. He asked me if I still had the small ivory toy kettle, teacups, and stove that we used to play with. But they're long gone. He also reminded me about the ivory barrettes which my dad made, decorated with different colours, but sadly, I lost some and I traded some of them for religious pictures.

Mariano Aupilarjuq told me that my father was his inspiration to start carving. Aupilarjuq once told me, "I have seen so many carvings in my lifetime but none like your father's." He described a man whipping his dogs on a dog team, with the whip made out of ivory, and he said, "I don't know how he made that ivory so thin and yet curl in the end." He said that was the most amazing carving that he had ever seen. He said it is very hard to make curves, and also ivory tends to break when it gets thin. He said it looked like a real whip but it was made of ivory.

Aupilarjuq said the first time he really got envious of this success was when my father was coming to Repulse Bay from Ukkusiksalik with all his furs and his carvings. He bought so much stuff from the Bay that he couldn't take it all on his *qamutik*. He had to leave some behind. Aupilarjuq said, "That's the kind of man I would like to be, to be able to provide for my family well."

They both grew up in the Pelly Bay area. My father was born in Spence Bay and grew up in Pelly Bay. Aupilarjuq was born in Pelly Bay.

One year when we were living in Ukkusiksalik, the animals weren't around much. There were hardly any caribou. There had been a blizzard for days and days. So my father planned to go to Repulse Bay with his carvings, to sell them and bring back some food. But because of the blizzard they were delayed. My mother said we didn't have food for three days.

I remember waiting impatiently for my father to come back from the store. It is like he went out shopping to Repulse Bay with his dog team. So, a good three-day trip out and a good three-day trip back. I remember my stepsister, my mother, and I stayed up nights sometimes, wondering if they would come in during the night. I remember it was just getting dark and we could hear dogs barking and we knew they were arriving. Such joy! All this food they brought. He brought surprises for me, too. He brought those safety pins — I didn't have a clue what they were. I thought they were for your hair or whatever. It was fun to be young. I remember we had what looked like a huge explorer's box, a big wooden box. It was so high. I remember [that] in spring we filled that box with eggs. We used to have eggs upon eggs for days. Then we didn't collect any more after we filled that up or else they started going bad. But I remember practising cooking eggs because we had so many, different kinds, different sizes, but I don't know whose eggs they were.

My father made his own fishing nets, and he would repair them a lot. He had a netting needle — he used to make his own, with a piece of wood, depending on the size of the mesh he wanted. He was pretty fast. He said the net was a lot easier than using a weir. I recall seeing weirs, but they were from an earlier time. In the summer, he would catch fish and cache them for the winter. He wasn't very interested in fishing in the winter because he could catch bigger animals. I recall him chiselling on the ice, with a long scoop for getting the ice chips, and making a shelter for my mother where she would fish by jigging [dropping a hook and line through a hole in the ice, and then gently bobbing it up and down to attract fish down below]. In the spring, he would hardly do any fishing at all. He would be out at the floe edge, seal hunting, which was one of his favourite pastimes.

I remember, in the spring, travelling by dog team. I would get sun-blind easily, so my father always ended up making wooden sunglasses with little slats for the eyes. The seal holes were quite big then because the water was already starting to go up onto the surface, from it being such a wonderful spring. I recall the dogs were wearing slippers to help prevent them from cutting their feet on the sharp ice that you only get in the spring. My mother and father, Angugasak, and Leo, they all had their own harpoons. But there I sat on the big *qamutik*, and our dogs sat to rest, while everybody took off to look for their own *aglu* [seal's breathing hole]. They had stopped right next to a seal's *aglu*. Just as everybody was getting far away, the seal popped up right beside me. I thought, oh no, the dogs are going to follow it and I'm going to go right underneath the ice with the dogs because I was told to hang on to the *qamutik*. I remember having that fear; that was so funny.

My father also hunted for seal at the coast. One time he caught a seal at the floe edge, before he made his little boat. So he swam and got it ashore on the ice. The seal meat was for the dogs and for us. Sometimes my father could cache it, just in case, for the dogs. The skins were for clothing. Most of our clothes were made from the animals that were caught. Caribou was the most useful because it covered you from head to toe. We didn't have rubber boots at the time. Sealskin boots kept your feet warm and dry. The seal blubber was also used for the *qulliq*. That was lots of work — you had to pound out the oil from the fat.

My mother was using a *qulliq* right up to the time she passed away in 1985. Every summer she would set up camp at North Pole River [near Repulse Bay] so she could live the way she used to long ago. That's what she enjoyed the most, what both my parents enjoyed the most. So, as soon as school was out, they left town to go to another place.

The old Primus stove she had, we probably bought at the Hudson's Bay store. I remember we used to be able to bring ammunition shells and get a little bit of money. I remember my parents had this great big noisy stove. I thought it was part of the plane engine or something. They would use it only occasionally, but it would heat up the iglu really fast.

My mother had all the scraping and softening instruments, which my father made for her. She also had stuff that her own father had made for her. She was a real treasure keeper. I recall her laying down the skins; she used wooden pegs to hold down the edges while the skins dried. She made sure they weren't getting wet. She would leave some space between the ground and the skin itself, making sure they weren't touching. She would be so busy with the skins when it was the proper time to prepare the skins for clothing. Because I went away to school at Chesterfield Inlet, I never got the chance to do the traditional sewing she wanted to teach me. As a kid at school, I thought that was an old-fashioned thing to do. Now I regret that.

I never saw an RCMP officer there in Ukkusiksalik, but I remember the missionaries coming to visit occasionally, maybe once or twice a year. They stayed for just a few days, then they had to travel all the way back again. They knew how to provide for themselves. They were well taught, so they knew how to make their own iglu and hunt for food for their dogs and stuff like that. They didn't need a guide. Once they knew their route, they did it on their own. The missionaries helped out, too, like having flour and biscuits.

Father Didier was the one who arranged for my parents to be married to each other. He travelled to come and visit us by his own dog team. I remember rejoicing then because he would bring me some Christmas candy and butter. Those two things I remember the most. Otherwise I don't remember much. Other priests, like Father Guy Mary-Rousselière from Repulse Bay — we used to call him Ataata Mari — also used to visit. I remember when he came to visit one time, he brought me a windup toy mouse and we had it running around the floor of the iglu. My mom thought it wasn't a funny toy. The visits were probably for religious purpose, really, but for me it wasn't about that.

I recall one time my stepbrother and his wife lost a child. Weeks or months later, I went for a walk and found this little pile of rocks and I starting undoing it and found the baby's clothes. I took them back to my mother and said, look what I found. I feel bad, but then again, I was just a child.

Every time I think of Ukkusiksalik, I see beautiful, hilly landscape and fast rivers flowing and really huge waves splashing against a very rugged edge on the land. Living close to the coast, I have vivid images of the waves crashing against a rocky shore. Then, it could be so calm. The land was beautiful all the time. I remember the grass would turn green, so very green. I remember the time when the season started changing to fall time.

I also remember living in Repulse Bay. My father built a house there, so we called it, but if you think back it probably was just a little shack. That was when my third sibling had already been born.

I remember when my parents said that we would have to go to Repulse Bay because I was going away to Chesterfield Inlet to go to school. I knew this had been discussed on and off, so I was pretty anxious to be going. We travelled in that little wooden boat my father made: my father and mother, a baby on her back; my stepsister, Angugasak; Leo, myself. So, at this time, my sister Marie had been born already.

My family had to go to Repulse Bay first, so I could go with the other children. That plane had already picked up Pelly Bay, Hall Beach, and Igloolik students. They passed through Repulse and picked us up. We flew on to Chesterfield. It was so different for me, to get on that plane. I was so proud to be going to school. I didn't go to school till I was seven. So by the time I got to Chesterfield Inlet [1958], it seemed there were so many houses there. The mission, the residence, the hospital, the school, and the

Department of Transport area were the main buildings. Trying to sleep that first night was awful. The air was dry. I couldn't sleep. That was the first time I didn't sleep in caribou bedding — it was sheets, and it was too hot. I really had a hard time sleeping that first night. But I got used to it after.

My parents said I was very talkative when I was a little girl, so I would demand a story if they put me to bed earlier than usual. They would end up telling me stories, and sometimes they would run out of stories to tell or were too busy to tell stories. But if my mother was sewing, she could listen and talk at the same time, so she would say, you tell a story. So I told stories, making it sound real, but a lot of the time making it absolutely ridiculous and funny.

I haven't been to Ukkusiksalik since I was seven. I had a good life there. Not too many kids my own age lived the way I did. It was so much happiness, with so much family involvement. When I think back to Ukkusiksalik, it brings me back to my childhood memories. It's precious. I feel like saying it's mine.

ELIZABETH AGLUKKA, 1950– REPULSE BAY

We were the last family in Ukkusiksalik.

I was born in Ukkusiksalik in 1950 at Tinittuqtuq. My parents were Jean Tavok and Theresa Angasivik. My mother was from the Pelly Bay area and my father was from around Ukkusiksalik. Before he was married, he went back and forth in the area between Chesterfield Inlet and Repulse Bay. After he got married he stayed in Ukkusiksalik. He was older than my mother; I think he was born in 1912. I lived in Ukkusiksalik until I was eighteen. My family moved to Repulse Bay in 1968. My father was in poor health, so we were scared that he might die while we were alone there.

Before I was born, my father used to go to the trading post at Tasiujaq when it was operating, to trade and to hunt around that area. But he never worked for the *qablunaaq* at the trading post.

There was a pattern to our life in Ukkusiksalik. We camped in different areas at different times of the season. At the time, there was my father; my mother; my brother, Matthew Niuvituaq; me; my sister, Lucy Kinakuluk; and my youngest sister, Pilagi Kavik, who was born in 1962. All of us four children were born in Ukkusiksalik. My father's older brother was there with us, with his wife and his two sons.

I was born at Tinittuqtuq. When winter came we moved to Nuvuk&it, about December, because the floe edge was close by, so there was seal. We stayed there until spring, maybe June, when the ice starts melting and there is water on top of the ice. Then we moved to Qakiaq, because it was on the mainland. You wait for the ice to go away so you can get around the point and get to Piqsimaniq. In August, we moved to Piqsimaniq for the char and caribou. At some time when I was very small, we went back to Tinittuqtuq again one summer.

We used an iglu in winter and canvas tents in the summer. In the early fall we would use a *qarmaq*, sod house, until the snow was good for an iglu. A *qarmaq* was a structure of rock and sod, with the rock on the inside as a wall, covered with sod on the outside, and a roof of either a canvas tent or caribou skins. The clothing we had was totally out of caribou skin. Summer or winter, we had nothing but caribou clothing.

People went to Ukkusiksalik because they could hunt any type of animal there. When my father came to Repulse Bay to trade, we would have *qablunaaq* food, tea, tobacco, and flour. Sometimes our supply lasted long enough until the next time my father went to Repulse Bay again. Other times, we ran out of *qablunaaq* supplies. He bought a rifle from time to time, but in those days a rifle used to last for a very long time. He needed bullets. My father had a freighter canoe with a sail, no motor, which he got from the trading post in Repulse Bay. My mother had a kettle, a bucket, cups, and a clock from the trading post. Those were the main things she had.

My father used to carve when we were in Piqsimaniq. There is soapstone near Piqsimaniq, to the northwest. I don't know the exact spot. I am sure the area is called Ukkusiksalik because there is *ukkusiksaaq* [soapstone] there. The main purpose, before turning it into money, was for making a *qulliq*, the stone lamp, and *ukkusik*, a pot.

The main thing that my father did when we were in Ukkusiksalik was gathering food all the time, to make sure we had enough meat and fish. He was constantly hunting. Also for our clothing, and to make sure the dogs had enough to eat. As well, my father was constantly trapping foxes and also sealskin because there was a demand for those. He took the sealskin and fox pelts to the trading post in Repulse Bay. He usually went twice a year, by dog team, in about December because in November the ice is still too thin, and in May before the spring thaw.

He would be gone anywhere from seven to ten days for a complete round trip. In those days, the dogs were in very good condition, better and stronger, as long as they were not hungry. It used to vary in the spring; it could take him only four days for a round trip. He didn't like having too many dogs. He used to have about nine or ten dogs. One time he went to Repulse Bay with just one dog, with my cousin Pie Sannertanut, the son of Saniqtaq, and, I believe, also Kaunak, with one dog. All the dogs had rabies and we ended up having only one dog.

In those days, he travelled with Kaunak. When Inusatuajuk and Satpisu were living there, at times he would travel with them, but after they moved away he would travel with my brother. When Inusatuajuk's family was living there, there were two separate dog teams. But later on, when my brother travelled with him, they went together with just one dog team. They would travel on the *qamutik*. The only time they would get off the *qamutik* would be going up steep hills. But when they had only one dog, they had to help drag the *qamutik* as well.

My sister and my brother and I carried water, and I helped my mother with skins and with whatever else I could help, like the easier stuff with the skins. We collected *qiuqta* [arctic heather] to burn in the fire and helped out in all sorts of things. Plus, we had lots of games. In the summer we made little tent rings as a pretend place made out of rocks, and we had things like food and different types of rocks as human figures. Since we were children, the tent rings were small, not the regular, big-tent ring size. And in wintertime we played *ajagaq* [a traditional Inuit game of skill] and the ball game and string games, and we would play "close your eyes and try to point at persons." We played hide and seek and *inugaq*, the game with knuckles of seal flipper in a bag and tossing them on the ground.

I do not really remember other families living there because they moved out of Ukkusiksalik when I was small, but I have heard that other people were living there when the trading post was still open. I remember Arsene Putulik and his father, Akkurdjuk, were there, but they did not stay with us. They stayed in Ukkusiksalik for one winter during that time, when I was nine or ten years old.

When I was about seven or eight years old, Felix Kopak's family came through our camp in the spring, travelling by dog team. They did not even stay overnight with us, because the spring was coming and they were trying to get to Rankin Inlet before the thaw. The next year, I believe, the Kusugak family came through, too, going in the same direction.

The Roman Catholic priest used to come to us once a year by dog team from Repulse Bay. He stayed about two weeks. We would have services with the priest and he would teach us while he was there. There was a mission building at Nuvuk&it where the priest would stay. During those years, the only person that used it was the priest. He came regularly, but toward the time we moved to Repulse Bay, the visits slowed down a bit.

When we were in Nuvuk&it, a policeman came to us. He came in by plane and stayed about half an hour. I didn't know why they visited at that time, but from the stories after that, I eventually found out they came in to look for someone who was also there, but had left. His name was Amaroalik. I'm not comfortable saying why they were looking for Amaroalik, although I know about it. I think I was seven years old. I was extremely scared because in those days we used to be scared of RCMP. I remember when the plane landed, we started walking toward it. As soon as the RCMP got on the land, he started running toward us and fell on a crack and although I was scared, I really laughed. He then got up and proceeded to come to us to find out whether the man he was looking for was with us.

I believe, maybe in 1959, we ended up being the only family living there, until we moved in 1968. We were the last family in Ukkusiksalik. My father didn't like a crowded place. He preferred to be in an area where there was good hunting and the immediate area of Repulse Bay didn't really have all the wildlife that he needed to hunt.

A lot of people have died in Ukkusiksalik. My uncle's son, as an adult, died in Tinittuqtuq and was buried there. The father of Joe Netar was also buried at Tinittuqtuq. Angugatsiaq's son [who died as a baby] is buried at Piqsimaniq. My father's father is buried on the island that is next to Nuvuk&it. They are not buried the way we do it nowadays, with a coffin. We used to bury them by putting caribou skin around the body. I would be happier if they all remained in the spot they are now and not be disturbed.

TWENTY-THREE

GENEALOGY ASSOCIATED
WITH THE HBC POST

The intent here is to display graphically the current understanding of the relationships and ancestral connections among people associated with the old HBC Post at Tasiujaq. It may be imperfect — in some
cases, contradictory information has been recorded — but this is an attempt
to present what appears to be the most likely correct account, based on the
information gathered from the informants.

The man at the centre of so much of the history of the HBC post at
Tasiujaq is Iqungajuq, also known as "Wager Dick" or "Native Dick." Family
Tree 1 shows his ancestry and that of his two wives, Toota and Niaqukittuq,
as well as the two women's children, all of whom were either fathered by or
adopted by Iqungajuq, as indicated.

Note: In the family tree diagrams below, (m) indicates that the person is male, and (f) indicates that the person is female.

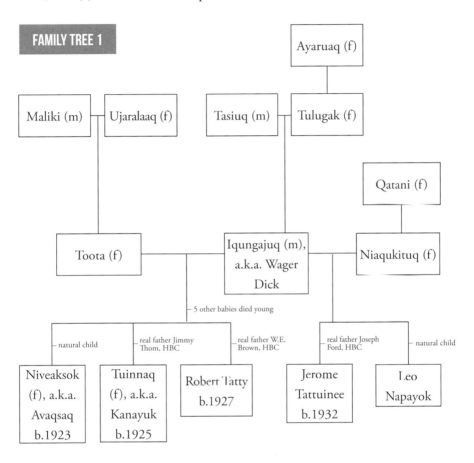

FAMILY TREE 1

Ayaruaq (f)

Maliki (m) — Ujaralaaq (f)   Tasiuq (m) — Tulugak (f)

Qatani (f)

Toota (f) — Iqungajuq (m), a.k.a. Wager Dick — Niaqukituq (f)

5 other babies died young

natural child | real father Jimmy Thom, HBC | real father W.E. Brown, HBC | real father Joseph Ford, HBC | natural child

Niveaksok (f), a.k.a. Avaqsaq b.1923 | Tuinnaq (f), a.k.a. Kanayuk b.1925 | Robert Tatty b.1927 | Jerome Tattuinee b.1932 | Leo Napayok

According to Tuinnaq Kanayuk Bruce's oral testimony, the mother of Iqungajuq and his three brothers (Ipkarnaq [also Samson], Siulluk [also Deaf Johnny], Talituq [also Tommy Taqaugaq]) was named Arnnagruluk (also Tulugak).

Maliki (Toota's father) and Qulittalik traded wives at some point. At first, Maliki was with Natsiq and Qulittalik was with Ujaralaaq (Toota's mother). (See the next family tree diagram.) According to Tuinnaq Kanayuk Bruce, in those days the people of this region, the Aivilingmiut, tried to partner within their group, mostly to avoid Nattilingmiut, from the Arctic coast to the northwest, whom they feared. In keeping with this practice, Tuinnaq (Kanayuk) was betrothed to Mikitok Bruce. The two actually share an ancestor, Ujaralaaq, as demonstrated in Family Tree 2.

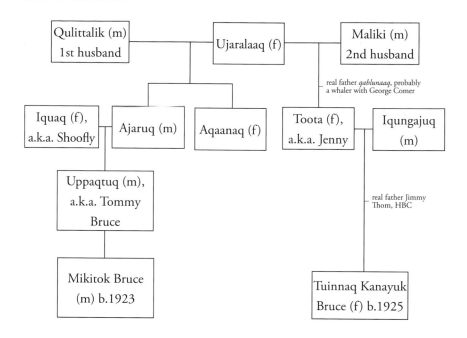

Iquaq, shown in Family Tree 2 as Mikitok's paternal grandmother, is the much celebrated and documented Inuit woman from George Comer's days as a whaling captain in Hudson Bay. Comer called her "Shoofly." Comer is generally considered the most famous American whaling captain in Hudson Bay active in the early twentieth century. In the whaling records, Shoofly's Inuktitut name is given as Nivisinaaq.

Iquaq had two sons with her first husband, Ajaruq. The second of those, Uppaqtuq, was given the name Tommy Bruce by the whalers. When he was just two years old, his father, Ajaruq, committed suicide, tortured by his own past, which included witnessing a horrible multiple murder and being required by his stepmother to execute his father.

Iquaq, the renowned "Shoofly," had four sons by two different husbands. The details of some of her descendants, and thus Mikitok Bruce's (and his siblings') ancestry are provided in Family Tree 3.

FAMILY TREE 3

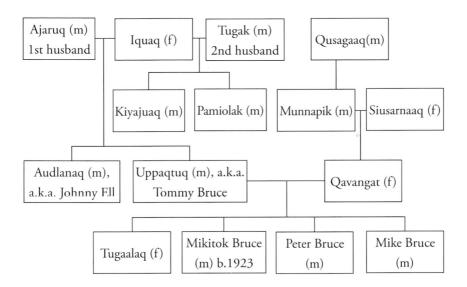

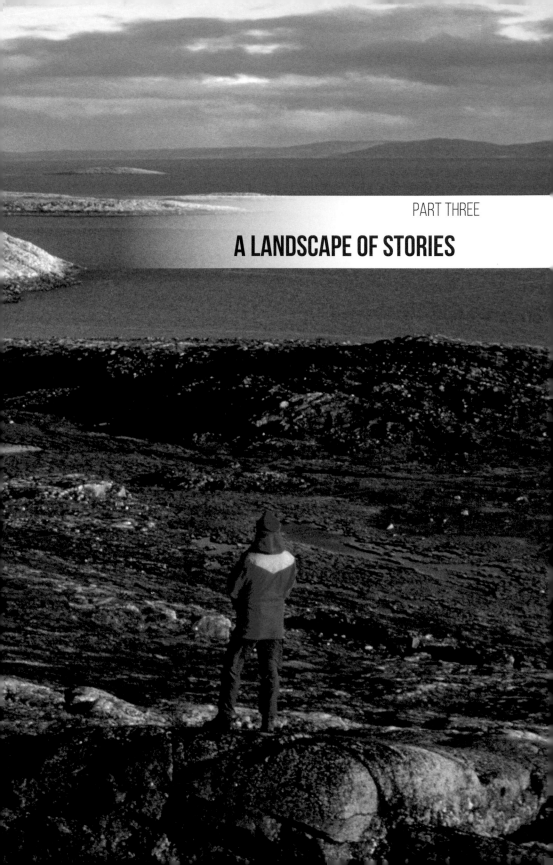

PART THREE

A LANDSCAPE OF STORIES

Previous page:
Hiking in the hills overlooking the Paliak Islands along the south shore of Wager Inlet.

Nunavut Gov/Donna Barnett

INTRODUCTION

These stories have their genesis in the oral-history accounts provided by the informants of the previous section. Where necessary, additional historical and archival research was used to supplement the stories arising from the land and its people. Quotes from the informants — there are many — are not individually footnoted; they all come from the interviews of the 1990s.

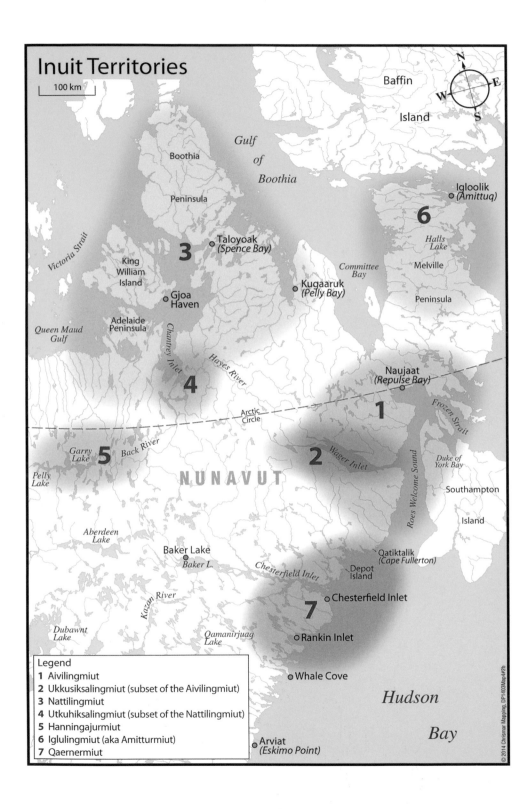

Inuit Territories

100 km

N · E · S · W

Baffin

Island

Gulf

of

Boothia

Boothia

Peninsula

Igloolik
(Amittuq)

6

*Halls
Lake*

Melville

Peninsula

Victoria Strait

*King
William
Island*

3

Taloyoak
(Spence Bay)

Committee
Bay

Kugaaruk
(Pelly Bay)

Gjoa
Haven

*Adelaide
Peninsula*

*Queen Maud
Gulf*

Chantrey Inlet

Hayes River

4

Naujaat
(Repulse Bay)

Frozen Strait

1

Arctic
Circle

Back River

5

*Garry
Lake*

2

Wager Inlet

Roes Welcome Sound

*Duke of
York Bay*

Southampton

Island

*Pelly
Lake*

N U N A V U T

*Aberdeen
Lake*

Baker Lake

Baker L.

Chesterfield Inlet

Depot
Island

Qatiktalik
(Cape Fullerton)

Kazan River

Qamanirjuaq
Lake

7

Chesterfield Inlet

*Dubawnt
Lake*

Rankin Inlet

Whale Cove

Hudson

Bay

Arviat
(Eskimo Point)

Legend
1 Aivilingmiut
2 Ukkusiksalingmiut (subset of the Aivilingmiut)
3 Nattilingmiut
4 Utkuhiksalingmiut (subset of the Nattilingmiut)
5 Hanningajurmiut
6 Iglulingmiut (aka Amitturmiut)
7 Qaernermiut

© 2014 Chrismar Mapping, DP1403Map4r2b

TWENTY-FOUR

CONNECTIONS INLAND

W hile sailing into Wager Inlet may not have led the eighteenth century *qablunaat* explorers to the Northwest Passage, what the long, fjord-like arm of the sea did offer, unbeknownst to them at the time, was a way to penetrate the unknown interior of continental North America's most remote northern reaches. As time would reveal, these travel routes were well known to Aivilingmiut around Ukkusiksalik, who had long headed inland from the end of the inlet to hunt for caribou and muskoxen. Across the tundra plains to the west were friendly people, the Hanningajurmiut, living in the valley of the Back River around the two biggest lakes, Pelly and Garry Lakes. To the northwest, closer to the Arctic Ocean, there were strangers, known to the Aivilingmiut but feared. "They were known to be murderers," said Tuinnaq Kanayuk Bruce, speaking of the Nattilingmiut, reflecting the sentiments of her people from a time long before the arrival of *qablunaat*. These strangers lived on the coast to the north, around the mouths of the Back River (and upriver to Franklin Lake) and Hayes River in Chantrey Inlet. By coincidence, they too called their home territory *Utkuhiksalik* (same word, same meaning, but slightly different dialect[1]).

The connections among different groups of people provide some insights into the tapestry of travel routes that covered the land in the time before the *qablunaat* arrived. The people living directly around Ukkusiksalik were part of the larger group known as the Aivilingmiut, who occupied the entire northwest corner of Hudson Bay. Historically, they were most closely related, culturally speaking, to the Iglulingmiut to the north. They were not closely related — which some, even today, often hasten to point out — to the Nattilingmiut, the coastal people to the northwest around King William Island and the Boothia Peninsula, nor to the people who lived on the tundra inland from Ukkusiksalik to the west, chiefly the Hanningajurmiut.

As the stories unfold, and the fear of strangers wanes, the travel route between Ukkusiksalik (Wager Inlet) and Utkuhiksalik (Back River) becomes more and more well-trodden. In 1879 a search party looking for clues to the fate of Sir John Franklin was guided across this route by Inuit.* In 1926 the Hudson's Bay Company traders were led by Iqungajuq over this route to make first contact with the Nattilingmiut, hoping to encourage their trade.** From their posts on the shores of Hudson Bay, both the RCMP and the Roman Catholic missionaries followed suit.***

While some Inuit from Utkuhiksalik, looking to trade their fox skins in the mid-1920s and later, went northwest to the Perry River on the Arctic coast, and some went south to Baker Lake, others went southeast to Tasiujaq in Ukkusiksalik. The post journals there record occasional arrivals of Inuit travelling across this inland passage.

> **March 16, 1926:** "Keemallinckgo arrived in p.m. Keemallinckgo is the first of the natives from Hayes River."

> **May 15, 1926:** "Kaam-o-kauk [Qamukkaaq] and Kec-malliaukz with families arrived in from Backs River. Took thirteen days."

The oral testimony collected from the people associated with this area also relates travel along this route during the first half of the twentieth century.

Qamukkaaq and his wife, Arnalluk, both Nattilingmiut, had three daughters: Madeleine Naalungiaq Makiggaq in 1926, Monica Ugjuk in 1931, and Mary Qablu Anawak in 1932.[2] All three were adopted out. All three were baptized by the Roman Catholic missionary Father Buliard during one of his

---

* See chapter 28, "The Search for Franklin."
** See chapter 33, "The Hudson's Bay Company Arrives."
*** See chapter 30, "Policemen and Priests."

long trips by dog team from the Repulse Bay mission to visit Inuit families on the land. According to church records, this was in December of 1942, the time of Father Buliard's first attempt to reach the Back River by travelling inland from the head of Wager Inlet, all part of the church's ongoing efforts to recruit Inuit followers in the far-flung camps.

Madeleine was born at Ta'yaitquq, northwest of Tasiujaq. As the eldest, she remembered best the visit by Father Buliard. "We loved that man. My husband knew that Father Buliard wanted to travel, so he went to Tasiujaq to pick him up. Before they travelled farther, he baptized all of us in camp, so now we had first names. He named us after his family and relatives. He named my mother-in-law after his mother, Cecilia; my father-in-law after his father, Joseph; my husband after his brother Juani; me after his sister Magdelina; and my younger sister after his other sister, Monica."

Monica Ugjuk was raised in the interior along the Back River. She recalled travelling as a child all over the vast territory from the mouth of the Back River, up that river inland to the area known as Hanningajuq [the Pelly Lake and Garry Lake region], south to Baker Lake, and east to Hudson Bay. "My adoptive parents never lingered in one spot all the time," she reminisced much later, in her seventies. "I was with parents who travelled all the time. They travelled in the winter and summer, walking or going by dog team, always travelling." As part of this itinerant life, she recalled visiting the old HBC post established at Tasiujaq in Ukkusiksalik.

After baptizing the families in this area just west of Tasiujaq, Father Buliard wanted to travel north to the coast over the trail to the Back River. "Anawak and my husband took him to Utkuhiksalik by dog team," recalled Madeleine Makiggaq. "When they reached Amuyat, Father Buliard wanted to be left with the families there. They told him, 'Inuit do a lot of travelling, so you might happen to be left alone.' But he just said, 'That's all right.' So Anawak and my husband left him there." Much later, in the spring, as the weather started to warm, Madeleine remembered the day a bedraggled Father Buliard staggered into their camp: "The dogs were so skinny. And he had bad sore eyes from the sun. We caught him at just the right time. I had compassion for him." They nursed the priest back to health. "He was overjoyed when he knew that he was going to eat and drink tea." Then they delivered him back to the HBC post at Tasiujaq.

This inland territory surrounding the Back River became Father Buliard's mission in life. It was as if he looked beyond the hills at the head of Wager Inlet and dreamed of what he might accomplish for his church. Contemplating this, he wrote in a letter to another priest: "I am very happy. If only, I had an Oblate Brother to help me, a little house, a few fishing nets! Not a sick person would die without having seen the priest; I could visit all the Eskimos without fear of hunger!"[3]

He continued his travels through the region, always with this dream in mind. On more than one occasion, he travelled by dog team right through to Baker Lake, becoming more familiar with this interior country than any *qablunaaq* before him. Father Buliard established his mission post on an island in Garry Lake, Back River, in 1949, built his "little house," and engaged a young Inuk named Anthony Manernaluk to serve, in effect, as the Oblate Brother the priest had wished for. Manernaluk acted as his guide for several years as Father Buliard visited Inuit camps for hundreds of miles around his tiny mission at Hanningajuq. Then in 1956, while Manernaluk was down south in Manitoba to be treated for tuberculoisis, Father Buliard mysteriously disappeared in a blizzard at Garry Lake.[*] No one replaced him there, and within two years all the Inuit of Hanningajuq had either died of starvation or been evacuated to Baker Lake.

Monica Ugjuk remembered the starvation time. "We didn't have enough meat during the fall, while we were camped near Umingmaktuuq. The three of us were left in the camp [Monica, her adopted father, Tiinaaq, and adopted mother, Tinuuriq]. At that time food was hard to find, although my father tried fishing. My mother, at times, could not walk; she used to crawl on the ground, trying to gather lichens and moss for fire. Without my knowledge, my mother was saying to my father that she wanted to be left behind, because she could not walk, and she was an old woman, too. When we were just about to leave her behind, I remember crying so hard, going out of the iglu. My father and I started walking toward Hudson Bay. After we left her, she got picked up while she was still alive, by a man named Qabluittuq, who saved my mother's life. I haven't forgotten that; I will always be grateful, for the rest of my life." Eventually, they were all reunited in Chesterfield Inlet.

---

* For more on Father Buliard, see chapter 38, "The Mysterious Disappearance of Father Buliard."

All of these stories serve to weave together the places and the people that make up the larger view of the land lying inland from the head of Wager Inlet. Ukkusiksalik was not an area in isolation from its surroundings; it played a central role in the history of this remote corner of the Arctic as a result of its connections to the people and places lying inland to the west.

FURTHER READING

John Bennett and Susan Rowley, eds., *Uqalurait: An Oral History of Nunavut* (Montreal: McGill-Queen's University Press, 2004).
Charles Choque, *Joseph Buliard, Fisher of Men* (Churchill, Manitoba: Roman Catholic Episcopal Corporation, 1987).

TWENTY-FIVE

HUNTING TO SURVIVE

For the early hunters, mobility was the key to survival, to take advantage of the changing patterns of animal behaviour. Anthonese Mablik in Repulse Bay described this practice as "something that has been going on in the past and will probably be going on in the future, too. The unwritten policy was get enough to last you a whole year, no more. This was respected by the younger people, too; the older people made sure that they were going by this policy — that you don't waste the meat at all. If the oldest people figure that there is enough to last them a whole year, they will tell the other people that's enough, no more, and that's when they will stop hunting."

Notwithstanding all the uncertainty of life on the land, the Inuit who lived around Ukkusiksalik maintained a centuries-old pattern of mobility. Recent elders, who were in effect only one generation removed from a pre-contact lifestyle in Ukkusiksalik, shed some light on the patterns followed by their forefathers.

In the winter months, the Ukkusiksalingmiut gathered into two loosely associated groups. Each group reflects a somewhat distinct lifestyle. One was located not far from the mouth of the inlet, near Nuvuk&it, where an open-water polynya nearby facilitated the seal hunt. The practicality of that arrangement endured right up to the 1960s, as explained by Elizabeth Aglukka of Repulse Bay: "Nuvuk&it is where we had our winter camp, to be close to the floe edge, to hunt seals." Even after Aglukka's family had access to a trading post in Repulse Bay and some imported foods, they still depended on seals for much of their food, and on seal oil for their heat and light. In earlier times, the seals' meat, skin, and oil were all absolutely essential for the Ukkusiksalingmiut wintering at Nuvuk&it.

A second group was located farther inland, to the west, around Qamanaaluk, where caribou and muskoxen sustained them through the winter. Some years ago, Guy Amarok of Chesterfield Inlet pointed on the map to an area a hundred kilometres northwest of Qamanaaluk, an area he called Kuugarjuk and, referring to a time in the late 1930s, he said: "In the wintertime we moved up to where other people were living. I remember that we were eating muskoxen for food. There were muskoxen in that area. We travelled by dog team from the post at Tasiujaq up to where the other Inuit were. We slept one night and then reached the other Inuit the next day." Others told stories of men going caribou hunting in that direction.

This is not to suggest that the two groups — one centred around Qamanaaluk and the other at Nuvuk&it respectively — did not intermingle. They did, probably often. People from the more inland group sometimes moved down to the fruitful seal-hunting location during the winter. The more seal-dependent people from closer to the coast occasionally came inland in search of caribou, most often in summer. There are many accounts that suggest this pattern of mobility was in place before the Hudson's Bay Company established a trading post at Tasiujaq (see, for example, "Ilumigarjuk's Story" below, which illustrates much more than the necessity of mobility for survival by hunting, though certainly makes the point that families travelled far and wide in pursuit of food). Notwithstanding all this evidence, nothing about the hunting patterns can be described as rigid.

ILUMIGARJUK'S STORY

As told by Tuinnaq Kanayuk Bruce in 1996

Three young Aivilingmiut men went caribou hunting in August with their wives, far inland from Ukkusiksalik. They happened to meet two Nattilingmiut men from the Pelly Bay area who said, "There's caribou behind that hill." So all the men together made a plan to catch the caribou. Each of the Nattilingmiut men took one or two of the Aivilingmiut men and headed opposite ways around the mountain, leaving the

Aivilingmiut wives behind in camp. In a short while, the wives saw two men coming back. They recognized by their walk that the two men were the Nattilingmiut, people who were generally feared by Aivilingmiut — or, as Tuinnaq Kanayuk Bruce put it, "They were known to be murderers." They probably killed our husbands, thought the women. One of the young women had special powers of the sort that allowed her to become very small, so she went behind a small rock. The men came into camp and took the other two wives, but they didn't see the one hiding behind the rock. Later, she became normal again and returned to the older people back in her own camp, which explains how the story came to be passed down among Aivilingmiut. One of the two captured was Iqungajuq's father's sister, Arnaqtauyuq. [Iqungajuq was Tuinnaq Kanayuk Bruce's adopted father, so Arnaqtauyuq was her great-aunt.] Arnaqtauyuq had a daughter, who married Niqqi, and together they had a son named Ilumigarjuk (Iqungajuk's first cousin), who some years later stayed with the RC missionary Father Buliard in Garry Lake.

Later, when travelling up to the Arctic coast once, Iqungajuq met a young woman who told him she was the child of the other captured woman, with one of the captors, so "I'm related to you!"

During the time that Iqungajuq managed the HBC post at Tasiujaq, Ilumigarjuk and his brother Putuaq came there to trade. Tuinnaq Kanayk Bruce remembered their visit. She described Putuaq's wife as "outrageous and aggressive."

Before the ice broke up in early July, Ukkusiksalingmiut dispersed to various summer camps, often at the mouths of rivers where the char fishing was reliable. Later in the summer, hunters made long treks inland, especially to the north, in search of caribou, another mainstay of the diet and a principal source of skins for clothing, in prime condition at that time of year.

As summer ended and winter approached, Inuit waited for the sea ice to form so that they could travel easily, to return to their chosen winter camp, and the cycle began over again. Throughout the cycle, as inexact as it may have been, the principle of maintaining mobility for the sake of survival underlay life itself for the Ukkusiksalingmiut, as for others, from earliest times to the recent memories of these elders.

TWENTY-SIX

INUGARULIGAQJUIT

W alking across the land in Ukkusiksalik one day in 1996, Felix Kopak and Octave Sivaniqtoq reminisced about *Inugaruligaqjuit*.

Inugaruligaqjuit are little people, less than thirty centimetres (one foot) high. *Inugaruligaqjuit* children are no bigger than mice, the two elders explained. One time, an Inuit dog ate one of them. Even the adult men are so tiny that, as you approach, they look at your feet first and then raise their eyes, and grow as they look up at you, until they are the same size. Then they fight. If you lose, you'll die. If you manage to win, by putting them down on the ground, they'll stay there until you escape. If you go down, they kill you by putting their knee on you. But they are not always so aggressive. According to Octave Sivaniqtoq, some of the *inugaruligaqjuit* wanted to help and were very thankful to Inuit for sharing food with them. Others would fight.

Years ago, those little men helped Siutinuaq* put a very big rock up on top of some smaller rocks. He was looking for caribou, and when he heard something to one side, he looked and saw an *inugaruligaqjuk* (little man) pushing a big rock with his shoulder, to put little rocks under it, just to let

---

* Siutinuaq is something of a legendary figure now. He was the father of two of the informants, Mariano Aupilarjuq and Jackie Nanordluk, and the grandfather of another, Andreasi Siutinuar, who bore this highly regarded name.

Siutinuaq know how strong he was. Then he picked up a rock as heavy as Siutinuaq and told Siutiniuaq to do it, too, and he could because the small man had made it really light for him.

Felix Kopak once saw footprints of *inugaruligaqjuit*, about ten centimetres long. He recalled one time when another hunter caught a caribou, and as he was cutting it up an *inugaruligaqjuk* came and asked if he could have some meat. The Inuk said take it all and then walked back to the *inugaruligaqjuit* camp with the *inugaruligaqjuk*. He stopped just short of the camp and watched. When the *inugaruligaqjuk* arrived in camp, the meat was shared, everyone got some meat. In return, that Inuk had no problem hunting all through that summer and the next winter.

TWENTY-SEVEN

AK&UNGIRTARVIK

According to Tuinnaq Kanayuk Bruce of Coral Harbour, Aivilingmiut tried to make sure their daughters married within their own group, avoiding, in particular, Nattilingmiut men. One of the ways Inuit facilitated such liaisons was for culturally related people from far and wide to gather on occasion. Parents could then negotiate arranged marriages for their children, sometimes shortly after birth.

In the spring, often, there was a large such gathering of Aivilingmiut from afar at Ak&ungirtarvik,* on the north side of Ukkusiksalik. In 1996, Octave Sivaniqtoq, seventy-two at the time, recalled gatherings there during his youth and remembered hearing stories of people coming together there for many years before his time: "Not all one clan — some were from Ukkusiksalik and other parts of Aivilik, and even some from Nattilik. A lot of people used to come here because there is an abundance of young seal in the spring, so they would hunt them here. People from far away, from Pelly Bay and Gjoa Haven, from that area, and some of the original Aivilik people, told me about this. This area was mainly used in the spring for camping. If

---

* The ampersand symbol "&" is used to mark the so-called voiceless lateral fricative in writing Inuktitut. Designated ɬ in the International Phonetic Alphabet (IPA), the ampersand, combined with Inuktitut vowels, results in the approximate sounds: &u = "-shlu-"; &i = "-shli-"; &a = "-shla-".

they had enough hunters, they would catch more seals. For that reason they would have these celebrations in springtime, when they had more people in camp. The main idea was hunting for food. That's how they got to meet each other most times."

It was principally for the seal hunt that they gathered at Ak&ungirtarvik, but they took advantage of the assembly to hold games and dances. Sivaniqtoq recalled what he heard happened at this site in generations before his. "Somewhere here they used to hold drum dances in a big tent, a *qaggiq*. Inuit knew when to get together in one place by word of mouth, others telling others where to gather. I guess they planned to meet in one area for games and competitions. That's the only way they knew when to get here, and other areas of good hunting used as gathering places for Inuit, for food and survival."

The dominant feature at Ak&ungirtarvik consists of two rock pillars, the largest pieces of which are presumably glacial erratics deposited here as the ice retreated seven thousand years ago. Many of the other boulders, it appears, were rolled into position by humans. As Sivaniqtoq explained, "Many of them from different clans, they first started making this by rolling rocks together. I'm telling what I have heard. Then they started challenging each other. It was our ancestors that were using it for a contest among themselves. They were from different camps and each had competition on their

Demonstrating how the *ak&ungirtarvik* is used.

minds to find out who was best at these games." In order to hold a contest among the men, a rope made from bearded-seal skin was stretched across the top of the rock pillars to create a sort of "high bar," to spin around as used in modern gymnastics, called an *ak&ungirtarvik*.[1]

According to Sivaniqtoq, "They had different games on the rope back then. Sometimes they would sharpen a snow knife and tie it to the rope. Then a man would get on the rope and go around it, and if his arms loosened he could kill himself. When different people from other communities would get together, they would compete that way."

Another elder, Felix Kopak, recalled witnessing the game when he was young. "I once watched a man named Aarulaaq. The rope was very tight. He was asked to demonstrate the game once when he was passing through our camp. He said he might not be able to do it now, but he tried, anyway. He put on Uqtuqsi's wife's *amautiq* [woman's parka] and got up onto the rope. When he got ready to play the game, he straightened right up and started twirling around. The hood and the back end of the *amautiq* were just straight out because he was going so fast. He said he was going to *qariqtaq* (spin around, like on a high bar), so he straightened his legs and arms and did gymnastics. He repeated this a few times back and forth. It was so amazing. He was even funny with the *amautiq* he was wearing."

Later, Kopak added, "When I was younger, we tried this, not tied to rocks, but inside an iglu. My step-parents and the Puujuutit and Anaqtuunik families used to live in one big iglu with a high ceiling. We put a rope across the ceiling and made a hole on each side of the iglu when it iced up in the winter, and put each end of the rope through the holes and put pieces of wood to hold the rope from the outside. We tightened it and put a reinforced rope again in between and tightened that equally on both sides by shortening the ropes. That's what I remember."

All around Ak&ungirtarvik are scattered nearly a hundred tent rings, which housed the assembled families. Some of them have walls a metre high, built of very substantial boulders, which Inuit today suggest are the oldest. There are at least sixty old caches, where the hunters once stored the meat they caught. Plus there are a few graves. This was clearly a large and active community at times. There is one very large ring of stones, which marks the location of the *qaggiq*, the large skin tent used for communal gatherings: feasts, games, and dances. This was, after all, a time of celebration and plenty.

Kopak explaining where women went to give birth, at Ak&ungirtarvik, 1996.

There is one curious little tent ring which is little understood today. It is so small it looks like it might have been a grave, but that is not the case, as Kopak explained. It was the place where a woman went to give birth, a small compartment on the south side of the tent ring. She gave birth alone in there, then stayed in there with the baby for five days, being handed food and water by the midwife through the small opening on the east side. After that, she could return to the family tent with her husband.

Ak&ungirtarvik is certainly the most unusual archaeological site yet discovered in Ukkusiksalik, evoking memories of the way people lived many decades, possibly centuries, ago.

FURTHER READING

Karlis Karklins, *The Wager Bay Archaeological Survey, 1991–92* (Ottawa: Parks Canada, 1998).

TWENTY-EIGHT

THE SEARCH FOR FRANKLIN

After first Middleton and then Moor failed to find the Northwest Passage via Wager Inlet, the British turned their attention largely to the possibility of a more northern route, eventually determining that the most likely access to a passage lay to the north of Baffin Island through Lancaster Sound. Many expeditions sailed these waters, ultimately leading to what most people at the time fully expected to be the final, successful assault, led by veteran Arctic explorer Sir John Franklin.

As remarkable as it may seem, after John Franklin and his entire expedition of 128 officers and men disappeared with barely a trace in 1845, the search — which covered so much of Canada's Arctic — touched even Ukkusiksalik. This is an account from the oral history provided by Tuinnaq Kanayuk Bruce, recounted in 1996, when she was seventy-one years old, while camped at Tasiujaq near the western extremity of Ukkusiksalik.

There were two men, Tasiuq and Maliki, who used to be Inuit helpers on a ship. Tasiuq was Iqungajuq's father.* Maliki was Tasiuq's nephew. There were

---

* Iqungajuq was Tuinnaq Kanayuk Bruce's adopted father. He helped to build the HBC post at Tasiujaq in 1925 and later served as manager. See chapter 33, "The Hudson's Bay Company Arrives."

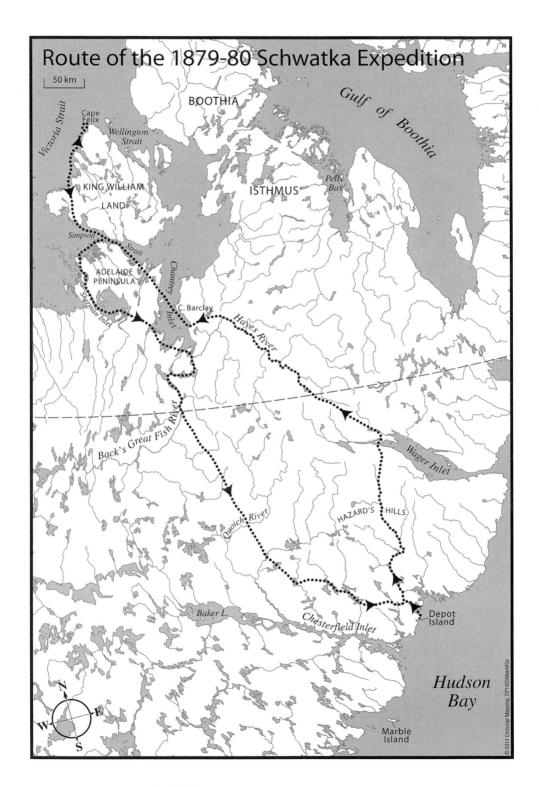

Route of the 1879-80 Schwatka Expedition

50 km

Victoria Strait

Cape Felix

BOOTHIA

Gulf of Boothia

Wellington Strait

KING WILLIAM LAND

ISTHMUS

Pelly Bay

Simpson Strait

ADELAIDE PENINSULA

Chantrey Inlet

Sherman Inlet

C. Barclay

Hayes River

Back's Great Fish River

Wager Inlet

Quoich River

HAZARD'S HILLS

Baker L.

Chesterfield Inlet

Depot Island

Hudson Bay

Marble Island

N
W   E
S

© 2014 Chrismar Mapping, DP1403Map#2a

these people on the ship, one named Henry, who was the cook. Henry* wore caribou clothing all the time and didn't want to get rid of them. I'm not sure who the other guy was, but he was the leader. Maliki and his wife, Ujaralaaq, had two *qablunaat* with them, and their guide was from Nattilik — I think his name was Ikusik. I think they started from near Qatiktalik [Cape Fullerton] and went by dog team up north. Ships used to get lost up north and they wanted to go look for them. I'm not really familiar with the story about people they were searching for on the lost ship and what route they took and so on. [This is her reference to the Franklin expedition, a name with which Tuinnaq Kanayuk Bruce was unfamiliar.]

There was one dog team or two, I'm not sure. They passed close to Ukkusiksalik, but the rest didn't know, only the Nattilik guy from near the mouth of the Back River. Apparently, their dogs got hungry along the way, but their guide knew where there were caches of fish, so they got some food. They said that the fish were cleaned very neatly; even the cheeks of the fish were skewered. That's also where they got their dog food from.

After they got the food from the caches, there was a camp close by. They were scared of getting murdered at a Nattilik camp, so they brought along guns — even the woman was given a gun. But apparently, the Back River people [those near the river mouth, called Utkuhiksalingmiut] were a lot friendlier than other Nattilingmiut. After staying there for a while, they gave the Nattilingmiut other items that they had, in a trade for food, then they left from this area to go farther north.

Along the way, they encountered another camp. The people in the camp were expecting their relatives to come in from hunting. There was a child with two dogs on a leash who came to meet them. When the child came closer to the sled, the dogs in the sled got nervous because they did not recognize the other dogs, and the child let go of the dogs and the dogs took off back to the camp. Even though the child was surrounded by the dog team, he just stood there when he realized that he was not

---

* Presumably this is Heinrich Klutschak, who acompanied Lieutenant Frederick Schwatka on a search in 1878–80 for clues to the fate of John Franklin's expedition. Klutschak was already a seasoned Arctic traveller, who advocated the merits of adopting Inuit ways of travel, which might explain his enthusiasm for caribou clothing. See more detail of their expedition later in this chapter.

supposed to meet these strange people. Tasiuq or Maliki put him on the sled to keep him safe.

When the two dogs came back to the camp, the people became nervous because they knew these people arriving were strangers. Right away, the men prepared themselves. At that time, people didn't approach a new camp right away. You stopped not too close to a strange camp, to have lots of room to move in either direction if something strange happened. There were two men getting prepared; apparently they were readying their weapons for killing. The Nattilik guide [with Schwatka's party] knew right away the two men wanted to kill. He was given a pistol by the *qablunaaq* leader, which was already loaded. He was to fight with the men approaching. As the two men approached the sled, the Nattilik man, with the pistol, started to stoop down right away. Back then, whenever they were challenging each other, they used to stoop down to fight. The people who just arrived by dog team stood by the sleds and the *qablunaat* stood still as well, watching those two men coming toward them.

One of the men who came from the camp stooped down, coming toward the Nattilik man, as soon as he stepped aside to challenge the man who wanted to fight. The rest of the men with the dog teams had guns as well. When the man from the camp stooped down to fight, the Nattilik man also stooped down.

The other man from the camp was standing farther away. The Nattilik man said, "Go ahead and kill me." As soon as the man from the camp harmed him, he knew the shooting would begin. Whenever the man from the camp would strike the Nattilik guide, caribou hair from the fur parkas would fly off because it was being cut by the knife. That's the way they fought. This went on for a while. They would back away and charge again.

Then the Nattilik man looked at the dog teams and when he saw the child on the sled, he stood up very quickly. I guess he thought the child was dead. When he stood up, the travellers beckoned the child to go back to the camp. He got home without anything else happening. The dog teams went on their way without camping there.

They overnighted somewhere and later they met some more people at another camp. They went not too close to the camp and spent the night there, because those people were not as vicious as [at] the first camp. In that camp there were children playing around the iglu, going in and out. The strangers didn't seem to bother them although they spent the day there. One of the *qablunaaq* men (the leader) lost his knife; he couldn't find it anywhere. He thought someone had taken it, and he said that if he didn't find his knife, he would kill someone. My grandmother, Ujaralaaq, who was travelling with the dog team, got very scared. She figured that if the leader killed someone, they would all start fighting. My grandmother told the people in the camp about the lost knife and someone returned the knife right away.

They took off on their journey. It was spring and much warmer than when they began their trip in the winter. The person named Henry walked all over the place looking for something. He went off a distance and he found something. Somewhere along the coast near Gjoa Haven, he found a grave. Apparently, someone made a cairn, an inuksuk, beside the grave and put papers in among the rocks. Henry found them. When he found the papers, they said that the doctor of the ship had died from sickness.

Henry and the others walked around to search all the time. Henry found some coins that were stashed away. He was always talking very loudly. When he found the grave with the letters and the money, the others could hear him shouting from quite far away because he was so happy. I think the letters and the money were contained in the same bag. The other *qablunaaq*, the leader, seemed to be embarrassed about Henry's actions and his loudness.

They also found a human shoulder bone in a pot. They couldn't figure out whether it was the skeletal remains of a person that died from hunger or whether the guy was murdered, and they didn't find any other letter saying how he died.

My grandfather [Maliki] walked and searched around with them. He found something buried in the earth but he didn't tell the others, knowing that he would have to dig it out. So he didn't tell the *qablunaat* about it. He was sorry later on for not telling the others because he figured there might have been valuable stuff in there.

They didn't find a lost ship, but they found a grave with letters and money. The *qablunaat* probably kept those things and took them back to their homeland [United States].

From the location of the find, they left for lower ground. I don't know what happened to them on their way back to their boat [at Hudson Bay]. But I've heard stories told about the time they arrived back to the ship. Henry was talking very loudly as usual, and was very excited, and still wore his caribou clothing all this time.

Apparently, my mother was born after they had returned to the ship. I guess her [natural] father was the *qablunaaq* leader.*

My grandmother used to tell stories about this to my mother after my grandfather passed away. I think my grandmother was very good at telling stories. My mother was like my grandmother, that's why she used to tell me these stories.**

⸻⟡⸻

That is the oral-history account provided by Tuinnaq Kanayuk Bruce. It is interesting to compare it with the historical record. There are three separate historical accounts of a search expedition led by Lieutenant Frederick Schwatka, U.S. Third Cavalry, in 1878–80. Each of the officers left an account: Schwatka himself kept a diary, which was published posthumously; his second-in-command, Heinrich Klutschak, published a popular account in German immediately after the expedition; and a journalist who accompanied the expedition, W.H. Gilder, wrote articles for the *New York Herald* and published a book. Taken together, these sources provide great detail about the expedition, much of which corroborates Tuinnaq Kanayuk Bruce's oral-history account.

———

In the early 1870s, one of the whalers wintering over in Hudson Bay heard accounts from Inuit of "a stranger in uniform who had visited them some years before, and who was accompanied by many other white men"[1] and, further, had left both papers and spoons in a cairn somewhere to the north. The introduction to the published version of Schwatka's diary puts it plainly.

---

* I believe Tuinnaq Kanayuk Bruce has (quite reasonably) conflated two events here. There is little doubt that Tasiuq and Maliki accompanied Schwatka's expedition. However, it is more likely that her grandmother, Ujaralaaq, became pregnant by a whaler on George Comer's ship some years later. See chapter 29, "The Whaling Era" and chapter 31, "A Multiple Murder."

** For *qablunaat* accounts of this expedition, see the suggestions in "Further Reading" at the end of this chapter.

For several years reports were received through American whalers wintering at, or visiting, the northern part of Hudson Bay, that books and other memorials of Franklin were known to exist in certain districts, to which the Eskimos would be willing to conduct the white man.[2]

The 1878 plan was straightforward enough. Schwatka's team would hitch a ride north to Hudson Bay with the whaling ships, establish a base camp on the mainland opposite Depot Island, just south of Cape Fullerton, engage some of the Inuit who had spoken of what were assumed to be Franklin's papers and spoons, and then travel overland to the Arctic coast and beyond to search for more clues to the fate of the 1845 expedition. Their thinking was that only during summer could they properly search the land for evidence left behind by Franklin's party, so a spring trip northward would put them on the coast in time to search during the summer of 1879, with the intent to return to the base at Hudson Bay the next winter. Klutschak put the key to their success into words: "We had to become Inuit," by which he meant the expedition's intent to adopt Inuit ways of survival and travel. Indeed, it is telling that Klutschak entitled his book, in German, *Als Eskimo unter den Eskimos* [*As an Inuk Among the Inuit*].[3]

Klutschak described the intended route as "a relatively short overland march to reach the Back River, whose lower course again promises to provide a good sledging route to the northeast and north." In fact, their northbound trip would take them across the inland end of Wager Inlet, through the heart of Ukkusiksalik.

In August 1878 the Schwatka party was dropped off by a whaler to establish its base camp. The men set about their tasks, essentially settling into a routine of survival over the winter and preparation for the next spring's travel. Heinrich Klutschak described his own role vividly. "By unanimous vote the provisions were turned over to me with the duty of satisfying five stomachs to the best of my abilities. Such a multifaceted job as mine, that is, artist, geometer, meteorologist, and cook certainly has its idyllic side, but it seemed best to me in the morning and evening when I was bustling about with pots and pans in my stone-built, roofless kitchen. After my work was finished I could enjoy watching the superb appetites of my boarders."*[4]

---

* Tuinnaq Kanayuk Bruce referred to Klutschak as "Henry, who was the cook."

Several Inuit families, mostly Aivilingmiut, attached themselves to Schwatka's camp and helped with the hunting required to ensure a steady supply of meat. The aim was to leave for the north on April 1, 1879. According to Klutschak, when the time came for this departure, they set out with three sledges, loaded with nearly five thousand pounds of gear and supplies, pulled by forty-two dogs, accompanied by the five *qablunaat* in Schwatka's party plus twelve Inuit. The Inuit leader was a man named Tulugak, who had his wife and his eight-year-old son with him. Klutschak also lists others: a young man called Mitkulik; another referred to as Eskimo Joe* and his wife; an older couple he does not name and their fourteen-year-old son, Kumana; an Inuit hunter named Ikusik and his family, his wife, Susy, their daughter (age five), and their thirteen-year-old son, Arunak. Both Ikusik and Mitkulik, he says, were actually of Nattilik origin, which Schwatka expected would prove advantageous as they approached the Arctic coast.**

The first part of the journey unfolded smoothly. They hunted as they travelled, of course; the inland region south of Wager Inlet provided ample caribou and, on one occasion somewhere just northwest of Ukkusiksalik, they took four muskoxen. Once over the divide and descending toward the Arctic Ocean, anticipation of the first encounter with a Nattilik camp took hold. "The Inuit were in a particularly high state of excitement, which betrayed both great curiosity and fear; our interpreter [Eskimo Joe], who for a long time had been dreaming of the ceremonies associated with meeting a strange Inuit tribe, was extremely anxious.... The first mutual encounter between different Inuit tribes always has a stamp of mistrust and

---

* "Eskimo Joe" was Ipiirvik, from the Baffin Island region of Cumberland Sound, nicknamed Joe Ebierbing by the whalers. He and his wife Tookoolito, known as Hannah, met Charles Francis Hall on his first expedition in 1861–62 and accompanied him on his two subsequent Arctic voyages, and then travelled to Conneticut with Hall. The wife referred to here is a new wife; Tookoolito died in the U.S. in 1876.

** The names of Inuit accompanying the Schwatka party as provided by Tuinnaq Kanayuk Bruce were as follows: Tasiuq, with his nephew Maliki and Maliki's wife, Ujaralaaq, and Ikusik, a Nattilingmiut man, as guide. According to Klutschak, the entire party was divided up into three teams and each team assigned to a sledge. Klutschak's sledge was guided by Ikusik, who Tuinnaq Kanayuk Bruce tells us was accompanied by Maliki and Ujaralaaq.

caution, and no matter how poor their weapons they stay in their hands until the parties involved have reached an understanding.""⁵

These people were Utkuhiksalingmiut, the splinter group from Nattilik who lived around Chantrey Inlet, the mouths of the Back and Hayes Rivers. "Among them we encountered the first relics of objects which once were either parts of the two ships *Erebus* and *Terror* or otherwise belonged to the Franklin expedition. Arrow tips, lances, snow shovels, in brief everything made of wood, copper, and iron, originated from the site of the Franklin catastrophe and had either come into the hands of these people via intermediaries, that is, via other Inuit, or had been found by them directly."⁶

One of the men in this camp, named Ikinilik, told the visitors that he had visited one of the ships where it was stuck in ice a few miles to the west of the Adelaide Peninsula. "When no sign of the whites or of any other sign of life could be seen, and since they did not know how to get inside the ship, they made a large hole in the ship's side near the ice surface. As a result the ship sank once the ice had melted. According to Ikinilik they had found a corpse in one of the bunks and they found meat in cans in the cabin."⁷ The Inuit helped themselves to items they thought useful, including some forks, knives, and spoons.

Another Inuk, whose name Schwatka recorded as Puhtoorak, later told the party of searchers about multiple visits to this same ship. He said he was sure there had been *qablunaat* living on board, who must have abanadoned the ship before it sank. He said he saw a corpse "in a bunk inside the ship" at Ootgoolik and confirmed the account of a hole being cut in the ship's side while it was frozen in ice. The name Ootgoolik corresponds to the area where HMS *Erebus* was found in the summer of 2014. Gilder, in his record of the encounter, said he learned that the ship was near an island called Keeweewoo, a small island near O'Reilly Island, which, as far as we know, corresponds very closely with the location of the shipwreck found in 2014. Gilder even records that "they [Inuit] had to walk out about three miles on smooth ice to reach the ship" by way of pinpointing the position. It is evident that this long-standing Inuit oral testimony pointed quite accurately to the ultimate modern "discovery" of the *Erebus* shipwreck.

---

* Tuinnaq Kanayuk Bruce: "They were scared of getting murdered at a Nattilik camp, so they brought along guns — even the woman was given a gun. But apparently, the Back River people were a lot friendlier than other Nattilingmiut."

During the summer of 1879 the Schwatka party examined the western and southern coasts of King William Island and much of the coast of the Adelaide Peninsula. Thanks, no doubt, to their Inuit guides and interpreters, the party uncovered some new evidence from the Franklin party, revisited some of the graves and cairns previously discovered by earlier search parties, and found some new sites. Schwatka is generally credited with confirming that both *Erebus* and *Terror* had been beset in ice in Erebus Bay, on the west coast of King William Island, in the winter of 1849–50. Inuit informed him that most of the ships' men were still alive then.

In mid-November the party loaded up the sledges, hitched up the dogs, and set off inland from the Arctic coast to begin the arduous winter journey across the tundra back to Hudson Bay. On March 23, 1880, they arrived at Marble Island, where they found a whaling ship passing the winter and, as usual during the whaling years, significant numbers of Aivilingmiut gathered nearby. The party's survival and safe return to the U.S. was now assured; it remained only to wait for the summer's ice-free sailing season.

Back from their long trek, resting in camp on the shores of Hudson Bay, Klutschak strongly, though roguishly, suggests they enjoyed themselves. "After being greeted by the female population of this relatively large [Aivilingmiut] settlement we crawled into various snow houses and were very well received." One can understand why Tuinnaq Kanayuk Bruce suggested above: "Apparently, my mother was born after they had returned to the ship. I guess her [natural] father was the *qablunaaq* leader." One might ponder who in the communities surrounding Ukkusiksalik today are descendants of the men in the Schwatka party. Tuinnaq Kanayuk Bruce suggested she could be among them.

FURTHER READING

William Barr, ed., *Heinrich Klutschak, Overland to Starvation Cove, with the Inuit in Search of Franklin, 1878–80* (Toronto: University of Toronto Press, 1987).

W.H. Gilder, *Schwatka's Search: Sledging in the Arctic in Quest of the Franklin Records* (New York: Charles Scribner's Sons, 1881).

E.A. Stackpole, ed., *The Long Arctic Search: The Narrative of Lieutenant Frederick Schwatka, U.S.A., 1878–80, Seeking the Records of the Lost Franklin Expedition* (Mystic, Connecticut: Marine Historical Association Inc., 1965).

TWENTY-NINE

THE WHALING ERA

Octave Sivaniqtoq offered an account unique among the former residents of Ukkusiksalik.

> As the story goes, there were [whaling] ships around the Cape Fullerton area. The captain of one ship was told about the whirlpool [at the mouth of Wager Bay], so he went to investigate. They made sure the ship was watertight, so that it wouldn't let in any water. They checked the hull in all places. The captain got all the crew inside the ship, all of them, and watertight, and he himself was just at the mast. When they went to the whirlpool, the ship was pulled down, right down to the bed of the sea. It wasn't very deep, so it went down to a certain point where it just stopped, and the ship was inside the water at the whirlpool and the captain was on top of the mast. They were there until the whirlpool started turning the other way around, as it switched between high tide and low tide. When the whirlpool started turning around they went back afloat. Then the captain knocked on the mast and the crew was happy to get out of there.

This is one of very few direct accounts in the oral history from Ukkusiksalingmiut describing the activity of the whalers. We do not know who the whaling captain in the story was. Perhaps it was George Comer, master of the *Era*, who sailed these waters more than any other, and showed great interest in interactions with local Inuit, to the extent that another whaler called Comer "native crazy," a moniker often repeated in the historical literature, true or not. He undoubtedly heard tales of the big whirlpool from his Inuit helpers, so perhaps he decided to investigate.

The first whalers arrived on the west side of Hudson Bay in 1860. British explorers had reported many whale sightings in northwestern Hudson Bay, "as is no where else to be met with in the known world."[1] With these reports in mind, the American whaling captain Christopher Chapel, in the *Syren Queen*, accompanied by his brother Edward in the *Northern Light*, pushed farther west into Hudson Bay than had any previous whaling ships. Said Chapel: "I expect to find whales and get a good cutt this fall & find a good winter quarters ..."[2] They over-wintered near Depot Island, south of Wager Inlet, and the next summer enjoyed a very successful hunt.

There is an oral-history account of these two whaling ships, the first *qablunaat* ever seen by some Inuit living in the area of Depot Island at the time. George Comer recorded that an Inuk named She-u-shor-en-nuck, when he first saw the ships, "could only think and compare the masts to sleds having been stood up but in telling this to the other natives they all went up on a hill and looked and concluded it must be the white man's ships which they had heard of."[3]

The *Northern Light* took home twenty-one thousand pounds of baleen that year alone, more than any previous American ship had ever achieved in the eastern Arctic. These Arctic whalers came in pursuit of both the oil and the baleen and, gradually over the years, expanded their commercial activity to include trade with the Inuit they met and often engaged to help with the whaling. Initially, the whale oil was used in lamps, both in Europe and in the U.S. This purpose was eventually served by petroleum products, but whale oil continued to be used in the manufacture of paint and perfume, among other applications. Whale oil greased a lot of the machinery of the Industrial Revolution. The baleen, on the other hand, became the most important product of the hunt. The curtain (called "bone" by the whalers at the time), which hangs in the bowhead whale's mouth to filter the edible morsels out of the sea water, became flexible enough when heated to bend and twist, so that springs, umbrella staves, corset stays, and fishing rods could be fashioned from it.

Following the success of Chapel's season, roughly fifty more ships sailed into the area between Chesterfield Inlet and Repulse Bay over the next ten years, firmly establishing this as a prime hunting ground. Activity ebbed and flowed over the next few decades, increasingly involving local Inuit, most particularly the Aivilingmiut. In 1903, the population of Aivilingmiut was estimated at 138 along this coast, many of whom had contact and often employment with the visiting whalers. It is reasonable to surmise that this also involved the Aivilingmiut living in and around Ukkusiksalik. We know that by the early 1900s — by which time the Scottish whalers had arrived in their steam-driven ships to join the Americans, who were still using sailing vessels — at least fifty Inuit men were working for just two of the American ships, as hunters during the winter and as whale-boat crews in summer. Inuit labour was essential to the success, indeed even the survival, of the foreign whalers.

Over the winter of 1909 to 1910, the *Ernest William* anchored just inside the mouth of Wager Inlet, and others occasionally followed suit in subsequent years, but this was unusual. Depot Island, near Cape Fullerton, at the southern limit of the Aivilingmiut territory, was the most popular location

Inuit on Captain George Comer's whaling ship the *Era*.

for the ships to over-winter. Breakup came earlier at the offshore islands than in the bays along the mainland coast, freeing the ships to get to work on the summer's whaling.

The whalers sailed up and down in Roes Welcome Sound, mostly concentrated in the stretch from Cape Fullerton to Wager Inlet. When the lookout in the crow's nest sighted a bowhead or right whale, several whaling boats were launched to pursue the chase. These boats, twenty-six to thirty feet in length, were each manned by six men, including the harpooner. They rowed after the whale until the harpooner could launch his weapon, thereby attaching the boat to the whale by means of a long rope which was allowed to run out from the boat as the whale thrashed and dove. When it surfaced again, the boats' crews were ready with lances to complete the kill and then tow the carcass back to the ship. It was a highly dangerous procedure. Many Inuit served in these whaling boats.

An American trader, George W. Cleveland, was landed from the whaling ship *Francis Allyn* in July 1900 on the north side of the entrance to Wager Inlet. He was to establish a new shore station there on behalf of the Thomas Luce whaling company, based in Massachusetts. The trade for sealskins, walrus ivory, polar bear, and muskoxen hides had been added to the whalers' role. Cleveland, with help from local Inuit, built a twelve-by-twenty-four-foot warehouse. By his own account, it "was a case of getting among the Eskimos or starve.... I was taken among them as one of their own brethren."[4] Sivaniqtoq recalled that his mother, Navaq, lived with these early traders before he was born, originally as their cleaning lady and later as a companion for Igalik ("person with glasses"), one of Cleveland's assistants. Inuit knew George Cleveland as Sakuaqtiruniq ("the harpooner"). He operated at Wager for four years and eventually moved everything farther north along the Hudson Bay coast to build a post for one of the Scottish whaling companies at Repulse Bay. Later he established a station at Cape Fullerton for a New York furrier, then worked variously as a free trader and for the Hudson's Bay Company. He continued living in the region until the 1920s and died in 1925. He sired many children during his time among the Aivilingmiut, so there are undoubtedly many in the region who can boast the bloodline.

Between 1860 and 1915, there were a total of 145 whaling voyages into Hudson Bay, about 105 of which over-wintered at least one year. The last of the whalers to visit this region was George Comer in the *A. T. Gifford*, shipwrecked in 1915. That marked the end of the era that had ushered in a new way of life for the people of Ukkusiksalik.

FURTHER READING

Dorothy H. Eber, *When the Whalers Were Up North* (Montreal: McGill-Queen's University Press, 1989).

W. Gillies Ross, *Whaling and Eskimos: Hudson Bay 1860–1915* (Ottawa: National Museum of Man, 1975).

THIRTY

POLICEMEN AND PRIESTS

Explorers, whalers, and traders were not the only *qablunaat* to visit the Ukkusiksalingmiut. The first police patrol to Wager Inlet occurred in the summer of 1904, by boat from the newly established Royal North West Mounted Police post at Cape Fullerton. The police were guided by Inuit special constable Scottie on this trip, the first of many to check on the Ukkusiksalingmiut and the condition of local game. About this time, the government decided to restrict the hunting of muskoxen, so the police advised Inuit that they were not to shoot muskoxen except in circumstances of dire hunger. Inuit, on the other hand, wanted to trade the muskox skins to the whalers. And some of the whalers, including George Comer, encouraged the hunt notwithstanding the anti-hunting regulation.

Similar patrols became a part of the routine for the Mounties stationed at Cape Fullerton. One such patrol, by Sergeant D. McArthur, set out from Cape Fullerton on December 4, 1907. As McArthur reported later, "from information received from Natives around Fullerton that some of the Ivilicks natives [Aivilingmiut] were sent muskox hunting in the vicinity of Wager bay or inlet I thought it advisable to make a patrol and investigate."[1] On arrival at Wager he found no one, so continued on toward Repulse Bay. "I found on arriving there that three men and their families intended to go on a muskox hunt. I gave them all to understand that they must not kill muskox unless they were starving, and in that case they had to hand over the skins to the Government (or police). They said they would not go and kill muskox as they did not want to get into trouble."

McArthur then pushed his dogs on to the Frozen Strait, where he found George Cleveland in the whaler *Ernest William*, who "informed me that he had orders from his firm in Dundee not to take any muskox skins under any circumstances, and not to allow any of his natives to kill any.

"Mr. Cleveland informs me that the natives told him that Capt. Comer told some of the Ivilicks [Aivilingmiut] to go muskox hunting last fall when Capt. Comer was in Repulse bay with the schooner *A.T. Gifford*. He also informed me that two natives by the names of By & By and Cock-Eyed Jack were at present at the Wager killing muskox [for Comer]." With that, McArthur headed back to Wager and on January 10 found the two hunters, whom he instructed to stop. By & By explained that Captain Comer had indeed sent them, and that he "thought because a white man told him to go it must be all right." The skins of nine muskoxen were turned over to the police. The patrol completed its journey, arriving back in Fullerton on January 22, 1908, after an absence of fifty days.

Two years later, the regulations had changed. Inuit were now permitted to hunt muskox for skins during the winter season, until March 20. Corporal M. Joyce reported on his patrol from Fullerton to Wager Inlet in February and March of 1910 to ensure that the cessation date was respected, but he discovered that only one muskox had been killed all winter. Apparently, the Ukkusiksalingmiut felt the muskox population had been depleted because there were so many wolves in the region.[2]

In 1910 the police chartered the schooner *Jeanie*, under Captain Robert Bartlett, to deliver supplies needed at Cape Fullerton and to deliver material needed to establish small outposts along the west coast of Hudson Bay, including the most northerly at Wager Inlet, part of a plan to facilitate regular winter patrols of the Ukkusiksalik area. The *Jeanie* sailed into Wager Inlet on September 7 and anchored in a bay along the south shore of the inlet some fifty kilometres from the mouth. As Constable J.G. Jones reported, "This harbour is on the direct route taken by the dog teams in winter to Repulse bay."[3] The men began to build the new station, a small wooden building. On the ninth, a severe gale blew the schooner onto the shore. The ship was wrecked and the men stranded. They eventually made their way back to the Fullerton post in a whale boat. The *Jeanie* never left, and nearly a hundred years later, older Inuit spoke of seeing remnants of its hull when they were younger.

Guy Amarok of Chesterfield Inlet recalled at least part of the story. "One story I heard, from before I was born, there was a wooden ship with sails that came in, and it was shipwrecked. The place where it was wrecked, there used to be a little shack that was probably used by the whalers. That's where that wreck happened. After that ship got wrecked, people used the ship for firewood."

A police report dated January 31, 1911, indicates that the total population of Aivilingmiut then was fifty-five men, sixty-five women, forty-five boys, and thirty-one girls. There is, of course, no way to assess the completeness of their census taking.

The RCMP never established a permanently manned post in Ukkusiksalik. "There was no RCMP there," confirmed Guy Amarok. "The only time that they ever came was if somebody did something wrong. That's when they would come up. But there was no post, no permanent RCMP, there. They just went in for patrols, or to work on a case." One of those occasions was the death of Amarok's grandfather, Siksaaq, in the mid-1930s.*

"The RCMP came by dog team in winter," recalled Tuinnaq Kanayuk Bruce from her childhood at the Tasiujaq post. "I am not sure for what reason they came, but I think they were investigating the deaths of two men, Siksaaq and Sutuqsi." Like Siksaaq, Sutuqsi had disappeared while out hunting and was found some time later, lying on the ground.

———

The first missionaries arrived in Ukkusiksalik in 1915, but in the years that followed, like the RCMP, the Roman Catholic missionaries passed through with some regularity. Mary Nuvak of Chesterfield Inlet remembered both. "There were police patrols going up there. They went up by boat and they went up by dog team. They would go up to Repulse Bay, but I don't know if they went in to Ukkusiksalik on a lot of those trips. I remember the first bishop for this diocese; he was here [in Chesterfield Inlet] and there were

---

* For more details of this mystery, see the accounts of Francis Kaput (page 57) and Guy Amarok (page 85).

other priests here, and they travelled up to Ukkusiksalik, to conduct baptisms, stuff like that. The priests travelled a lot up to Ukkusiksalik."

As a young man, Octave Sivaniqtoq actually worked for the RCMP, although not in Ukkusiksalik. "When I was in my late twenties, I was working for the RCMP, stationed out of Chesterfield Inlet. Then I was told that my wages were too small and they didn't have enough money to give me at that time. So what they did was they asked the headquarters in Winnipeg, or some place, if they had heard about this building that had belonged to the Hudson's Bay Company. They asked the Hudson's Bay Company if I could have that building, and they said yes. So I was told to get that building. When I was going to get it, Father Didier found out and he told me that I was not to use that building, that he was going to take it himself. I gave this building to the priest. We took it apart and even helped him bring it down to Nuvuk&it."

From that time on, through the 1940s and 1950s, the priest from Repulse Bay made occasional trips down to Nuvuk&it in order to visit the people there, using the small building that remains today. Elizabeth Aglukka, who spent the winters there from 1951 onward, remembers his annual visit. He stayed approximately two weeks. "They used to come by dog team. When the priest came, we would have services, and he would teach us when he was there." Elizabeth Aglukka was baptized in that little mission building.

During Theresie Tungilik's early childhood in Ukkusiksalik in the 1950s, the priests' visits were a highlight. "I remember Father Didier, who was the one who arranged for my parents to be married to each other. He would come in by his own dog team. He had his own team of husky dogs. The priests knew how to provide for themselves. They were well taught and they knew how to make their own iglu, hunt their own food. They didn't need a guide. He would travel and come and visit us, and I remember rejoicing then because he would bring me some candy. And butter. Those two things I remember the most. I remember one time, one of the priests brought me a windup toy mouse and we had it running around on the floor in the iglu."

Today, although the need for visits to the outpost mission has vanished, a small cross still hangs just inside the door of the building at Nuvuk&it — a reminder of its history.

THIRTY-ONE

A MULTIPLE MURDER

This story originated with Tuinnaq Kanayuk Bruce, who recounted it while camped at Tasiujaq in 1996. She called it "Qulittalik's Story." Qulittalik was Tuinnaq Kanayuk Bruce's grandmother's first husband. Qulittalik was also the great-grandfather of Tuinnaq Kanayuk Bruce's husband, Mikitok.

——✳——

Qulittalik was a man whose name means "person with a coat." His wife was Ujaralaaq. Qulittalik and Ujaralaaq had two children: a son, Ajaruq, and a daughter, Aqanaaq.

There was another couple, a man called Maliki and a woman named Natsiq. The two men traded wives, so now we have Qulittalik with Natsiq, and Maliki with Ujaralaaq. Ajaruq stayed with his father, Qulittalik.

While Qulittalik and his younger brother were hunting, they encountered a Nattilingmiut man also with his younger brother, and the four of them started crawling toward a bearded seal. The older Nattilingmiut man was crawling behind the other three. Somehow he crept up behind Qulittalik and sneakily pulled the trigger on Qulittalik's rifle. The shot killed the younger Nattilingmiut brother and wounded Qulittalik's brother. The older Nattilingmiut man blamed Qulittalik for this and attacked him, trying to kill him, but failed. So instead, he used his shamanistic powers to make Qulittalik lose his mind. Qulittalik got crazy and even tried to kill his other brothers.

Later Qulittalik, his new wife, Natsiq, and his son, Ajaruq, left from Iriptaqtuuq in Ukkusiksalik to head inland toward Tasiujaq. Ajaruq remained very attached to his father. Along with them travelled two of Qulittalik's brothers, their wives, and one small child, a girl about four years old. They saw some caribou beside Tasiujaq, just west of where the HBC post was later built. Qulittalik went hunting but came back with no caribou and no explanation. At that point, the others started to think he was becoming strange, because they knew he was actually a very capable hunter.

After this unsuccessful hunt, they made camp, built two iglus. Natsiq had a miscarriage that night so Qulittalik built a little annex on one side of their iglu for her to be alone in there, in accordance with the custom. Later that night he started to fix his rifle. They were relaxing in the iglu; the younger brother was lying down with his head on his wife's lap. Qulittalik fired his rifle, hitting his brother and just nicking the young wife. The brother did not die, however. Then Qulittalik grabbed his snow knife and went toward them. The young wife took her ulu and tried to defend them. She could have been successful if she had managed to cut him over the eyes, but she missed. Qulittalik stabbed them both with the snow knife.

Natsiq, confined in the annex, heard all this but did not know what to do. We know about this today because Ajaruq was there and he survived. Qulittalik began to butcher the two bodies, his brother and his sister-in-law, and he said to his son, Ajaruq: "I've just killed two wolves; you go tell my younger brother." But Ajaruq was too anxious to use this opportunity to get out, so his father suspected something and stopped him.

Qulittalik went to the other iglu the next morning. His brother was icing his sled runners. Qulittalik stabbed his younger brother. The little four-year-old girl, who was watching, ran to the iglu. Qulittalik followed and stabbed both the little girl and the mother with his snow knife. He started eating them like animals. He saw them as animals, because he had lost his mind.

Then Qulittalik went back to his iglu and asked his wife to come out. After that, he never slept. Later, when Qulittalik went out of the iglu, Natsiq said to Ajaruq, "I'm going to make your father sleep, and you're going to kill him." She had that special power — there are two kinds of powers that some people had back then. [One, the] ability to hide behind even a very small rock and [two, the] ability to put people to sleep.

After several days, Qulittalik became tired, lay down, and went into a deep sleep. Natsiq gave the sign to Ajaruq to take the snow knife out from under Qulittalik's bed and to stab Qulittalik in the chest. The boy started crying. Remember, he was so attached to his father. Natsiq whispered, "We must, or we will be killed and eaten like the others, and no one will know what happened to the others." The boy continued to cry, but nonetheless he did it. He stabbed his father.

Qulittalik felt the knife going into him and grabbed it with both hands. Natsiq said, "Pull the knife!" Ajaruq did and cut both his father's hands. All this was very difficult for Ajaruq, because he was so attached to his father.

Afterward, Ajaruq made a little sled out of a caribou skin. Natsiq was very skinny, having spent several days starving in the iglu annex. Natsiq kept saying, "Just leave me here to die. Go on yourself to tell everyone what happened." But Ajaruq did not listen to her; he just kept dragging her, sitting on the caribou skin, for miles and miles. Later, when he stopped for a rest, she insisted he must go on alone. They cried together. Then he left, but she said as he left that her wish for him was that he would find a seal on top of the ice, one that had lost its hole, far enough away that it would be too late for him to turn back to her, but soon enough to save [himself].

He found a seal, killed it, and the sight of the blood made the faces of all those his father had killed appear before him. Nevertheless, he ate some seal and continued on toward Iriptaqtuuq. As he approached, he was afraid to face the people and thought of killing himself; he actually tried but failed.

When he arrived in camp at Iriptaqtuuq, Ajaruq found his real mother, Ujaralaaq, and her husband, Maliki. They believed his story, but others camped there thought maybe he did all the killing, since he was the only one to survive. But he was telling the truth, his mother could tell. She said, "This child was brought up with love all around him, and could not have done that."*

---

* After finishing this story, Tuinnaq Kanayuk Bruce looked up and said, "I am saying the same words to you that Ajaruq said to his mother when he told this story. It is not a legend. It is a true story."

The precise story, as recorded above, was passed from Ajaruq to his mother, Ujaralaaq, who passed it to her daughter Toota, who in turn passed it to her own daughter Tuinnaq, who recorded it in 1996 with translation by her daughter Manitok.

Ajaruq later married a woman named Iquaq, also known by the nickname "Shoofly," and they had a son named Uppaqtuq, later known widely as Tommy Bruce, the name given to him by the whalers. Tommy Bruce was the father of Mikitok Bruce, Tuinnaq Kanayuk Bruce's husband. When Uppaqtuq was only two years old, Ajaruq committed suicide because he was still so upset at having killed his father years before. The shaman in camp tried to save him, but his mother did not properly understand the shaman's instructions, so he died. After Ajaruq died, Iquaq got a new husband, and her first-born she named after Ajaruq: John Ayaruaq.[*] Tommy Bruce always called that boy, actually his younger half-brother, by the Inuktitut name Ataatakuluga, "my little father."

Meanwhile, Maliki and Ujaralaaq had a baby, called Toota, who later would be Tuinnaq Kanayuk Bruce's mother. Her real father was *qablunaaq*, probably one of the whalers on George Comer's ship.

It is noteworthy that Tommy Bruce's son Mikitok would ultimately marry Toota's daughter Tuinnaq. Both of them were descendants of the same Ujaralaaq, although one from each of Ujaralaaq's different husbands. Aivilingmiut tried to marry within their group like this, according to Tuinnaq Kanayuk Bruce, in order to avoid Nattilingmiut, their immediate neighbours. They were afraid their daughters would be mistreated among the Nattilingmiut, especially if there were times of famine. The Aivilingmiut wives would surely be the first ones left to starve. Also, they felt that keeping their daughters within the Aivilingmiut group helped avoid the infanticide of little girls.

———

There was an eerie postscript to the story as told in 1996 on the shores of Tasiujaq. A few days afterward, Tuinnaq Kanayuk Bruce proposed that we walk up toward Qamanaaluk to the site of the murders. It was August 9 — I will never forget the day — a special time for her whole family, including three daughters and several other members of her extended family.

———

* See John Ayaruaq's story in chapter 32, "A Fatal Accident."

Tuinnaq Kanayuk Bruce at Qamanikuluk in 1996, showing some relatives the old snow knife found at the scene of the murders.

We walked alongside the Brown River, upstream past the first big bend in the river, to Qamanikuluk. She remembered the spot —— her father, Iqungajuq, liked to camp there with his family, to fish in the river with *kakivak*. Though she had not been there for fifty years, she walked straight to the spot without hesitation.

We arrived at Qamanikuluk, the scene of some of the murders described in Qulittalik's story. One iglu had been on the south side of the river where we walked, close to the rapids where we stopped. The second iglu had been downstream somewhat, on the other side of river. We felt surrounded by the presence of the haunting story, although there was no apparent evidence that anything had ever happened there.

But while we lingered to enjoy the land, one of her daughters found something lying hidden in the grass: part of a very old snow knife. At that moment, the spiritual and the physical came together for us in a very powerful way.

THIRTY-TWO

A FATAL ACCIDENT

Life on the land was fraught with danger. That was the reality for Inuit, a way of life recalled clearly by the elders who inform this work, who knew life as it was before and will never be again.

About 1920, when John Ayaruaq was five or six years old, his family travelled south by boat along the coast from the Repulse Bay area toward Chesterfield Inlet. It was July, so there was still ice, although breakup had begun. There were three boats in total. Ovinik, Ayaruaq's father, had twelve people in his boat. All three boats were blocked by ice while trying to cross the mouth of Wager Bay. One pushed on south; the other two turned back and ended up trapped in some ice floes near a small island on the north side of the entrance. They pulled the boats up onto the ice in order to survey the situation. Ayaruaq remembers, as a child, sitting in the boat looking down into the water at the rocks and seaweed on the bottom, when suddenly the ice shifted and a big ice floe overran and crushed the two boats, submerging them and throwing everyone into the water, some of them beneath the ice. Some died, including both of Ovinik's wives, and several were injured, including a man named Siksaaq, who spent a considerable length of time trapped beneath the ice until others were able to chop him free. It was a gruesome event, dramatically demonstrating the power of the ice and the currents at the mouth of this inlet, the same forces that had played havoc with Captain Middleton's expedition in the *Furnace* and the *Discovery*, and the same swirling currents that struck fear into the hearts of the whalers. Inuit to this day travel through that area with extra caution and particular respect for the power of the tidal currents that operate there.

This is John Ayaruaq's account of what happened when he was a boy, as he recorded it in 1968.

—⸱ᐧᐧⰀ—

I would like to tell a story of what I remember. Inuit and *qablunaat* both remember incidents that have occurred. This incident is something that I experienced. I will not say anything I do not remember, as I know if I am writing something that is not true, it is not right. I will make my story as accurate as possible. These stories can be used by anybody, either Inuit or *qablunaat*. This can be used as a reference. If I am asked to tell a story, I am willing to tell anybody about my experience. If there are any questions arising, I am willing to answer them.

The stories I will be writing will start from the time I can remember. These incidents have not been written about before this. I am the first person to write about these incidents. The incidents I am writing about are the ones which I was involved in as a child.

However, I would like to start with my parents. My father's name was Ovinik and my mother's name was Eekoark [Iquaq]. My older brother's name was Okpaktook [Uppaqtuq]. However, Okpaktook had a different father. We had the same mother. My father had two wives. His wives' names were Eekoark and Sakooluk. My sisters' names were Kanguk and Tugak. We had the same father and mother. I am the youngest of the three children of Ovinik and Eekoark. I was the only son of my parents. I know that my parents loved me. I remember that two of them loved me. My father and Sakooluk really loved me. My real mother did not love me as much. Sakooluk also had a son that she had adopted, and he was the younger brother of Kubluitok.

During the year 1914 to 1915, it seems I had just woken up. We had an iglu made of snow because it was winter. My father and a man called Maree were being turned into shamans. Two people went to get seal blubber, Maree and Seekooyuk. Since Maree was to become a shaman, he was forbidden to ride on the *qamutik*. He walked. But Seekooyuk was riding on the *qamutik*. So Maree did not arrive at the same time.

People in camp knew Maree was going to arrive. They arranged everything on the floor before he arrived. When he arrived, it became very scary. He was in a drunken-like shaman's state and they started to fight with him. When I heard about this, I became so scared that I do not remember what happened.

A few years later, I remember when we left for Cape Fullerton. I think it was around the middle of July or the end of July. We were leaving from Tayaniq, which is near Repulse Bay. I remember very clearly when we were at the Ukkusiksalik entrance, near the Chesterfield Inlet side of the entrance.

We had stopped because there was too much ice in the entrance. In each boat, there was somebody who was in charge. My father was in charge of our boat. Angotinmagik was in charge of the second boat. Mikuiseenilik was in charge of the third boat. There were three boats that were trying to get to Cape Fullerton.

All the men who had wives brought their wives on this trip. In my father's boat were Kanguk, Siksaaq, Eekeetinuar, and his wife, Salookteetak, and their son, Eegoonatsiak, and their daughter, Puyatak, and Sammurtok. This man, Victor Sammurtok, is still alive. My father, my mother, and my sister were in the boat. I called my real mother, Eekoark, as my sister.* I called Sakooluk my mother, but she was not my real mother. The reason why I called her my mother was I liked her. Also in our boat were my sister, Kungulik, and my stepsister, Tugak, and my stepbrother, who was adopted by my parents but I do not know his name, even though I remember him. There were twelve people in our boat.

In Mikuiseenilik's boat there was Mikuiseenilik and his wife Taqaugaq and his wife Nagmalik. There were five people in his boat.

In Angotinmagik's boat there was Angotinmagik and his wife and the adopted son, Kayakyuaq, plus Mannie and his wife Nanaouk, Peeluayuk and his wife Niaqukittuq. Peeluayuk and Niaqukittuq are still alive but they are not husband and wife now. And Akeaguk and his wife Nungak, and Mannie's mother, who was an older woman. There were ten in Angotinmagik's boat.

We were stuck at the Ukkusiksalik entrance because there was too much ice. We pitched our tent on a small island and pulled up our boats. We were

---

* This is the Inuit tradition. Children are often given the names of deceased relatives. Thus, if you are named after your maternal grandparent, you will call your mother "daughter."

on the island for a few days. Because we were there for a few days, people had to walk across the ice to get moss and berry vines for firewood. Then the ice started to float away. I remember one woman crying very hard. Somebody had to go get her by boat. This happened while we were still on the island.

While we were still there, there was a seal basking on the ice. My father went on the ice and shot the seal. He did not bother to retrieve the seal. He just came back to the camp and said to his wife that it looks like his mother. His mother was already dead. I remember my father's mother, who was blind. Her name was Ikpikark. After my father caught the seal, he told my mother that the seal looks like his mother. He did not even go to the seal he shot. He just left the seal on the ice. Since we did not have a lot of food, Kanguk, Siksaaq, and Eekeetinuar went down on the ice to get the dead seal. They ate the seal, since there was very little food.

Since my father was a shaman, he knew there was no navigable water to get to Cape Fullerton. We decided to go back to Repulse Bay. Two of the boats decided they would go back to the Repulse Bay area. My family and Mikuiseenilik's family decided they were going back. Angotinmagik decided he would try to go on to Cape Fullerton. He informed the others that if he could not get through he would turn around and follow the others back to Repulse Bay.

We went back across to the other side of Ukkusiksalik. When we reached the other side, there was too much ice. We could not get through that way, either. We came across some ice that was stuck in shallow water near a small island. There was an ice floe which was jammed in between the two big ice floes. We landed our boats on the ice floe that was jammed in between two other pieces of ice. The men were trying to find a way to get through the ice, looking for open water on the big pieces of ice. One of the women was on one side of the boat, relieving herself, on the ice where we had pulled up our boats.

I remember there were four of us waiting, sitting in our boat. I was in the middle of the boat, facing toward the water, looking at the bottom of the ocean. I was watching the seaweed in the water being carried away by the currents. The big ice floe broke apart and dragged our boat underwater. The only part of the boat that was above water was the mast. The other boat was also dragged under, but we could see the stern. The two boats were wrecked by the ice at the same time, dragged under the ice floe. Two people were killed instantly, Eekeetinuar and his son Eegoonatsiak. Sakooluk was holding her adopted child in the water among the chunks of ice. People attempted to take her out of the water. My father, Taqaugaq, Kanguk, and Sammurtok were trying to pull her out of the water.

They could not reach her because she kept getting dragged under by the ice floe. Finally, they were able to pull her on top of an ice floe. I came up where my stepsister was, right beside a large ice floe. When I saw her, I succeeded in pulling myself out of the water. I climbed onto a piece of ice to take a look back at the water where the accident occurred. I could only stand on one foot on this piece of ice. I will never forget this piece of ice I was standing on with one foot — it helped me get out of the water. I think that I might have been about five years old. After I climbed onto the ice floe, I saw people together on top of the ice floe, because my mother Sakooluk was dying. There were cuts and broken bones all over her body. Someone took her adopted child, who is still alive.

Where is my sister who is my real mother, Eekoark? She's not here, and I do not see her. I heard from these people that when we got caught in the broken ice, my sister — my real mother, Eekoark — could not see me. She jumped into the water, and her body has not been seen since. Her intestines were seen when the ice floe flipped over. Then I started to search. I saw the mast for our boat.

We heard a voice from under the ice. We heard just a voice, we did not see anyone. It was right where we were, but we could not do anything. There was nothing. We were just people. We lost all our equipment, everything. The ice could not be moved. We could hear a voice although we could not see the person. My heart went out to the person.

After this happened and the ice slowed down, Angotinmagik's boat, which tried to continue on to Cape Fullerton, could be seen. They were returning because they could not get through heavy ice. As soon as they saw us, they tried to get us as fast as possible. They had no engine and it took a long time to reach us. They used paddles and oars. The tidal current was not flowing anymore. The current had caught us. When they finally arrived, they did not even come to us. They went by us because land was close to us. The island was close by, so they brought other people and women first. Then they returned to me.

I do not remember how scared I was. We kept on hearing the voice under the ice. They used an axe and an ice chisel to pull out the person under the ice. When they pulled Siksaaq out, he had broken his pelvic bone. Two people died after they were on land. They were afraid to get one body that was on the ice. They left it on the ice for a number of days.

know it was there because they went out to check Sakooluk's body on the ice. There were five people who had injuries. My father, Kanguk, Taqaugaq, Sammurtok, and myself had eye injuries. I heard from other people that our eyes were very red.

We spent about five days on the island. After waiting these days, they decided they were going back to Tayaniq, near Repulse Bay. The people who could walk were going to go overland. The others who could not walk were taken by boat. The people who were walking overland had to be brought across the river by boat.

The river flow was too strong to cross by foot. They would get across the river with the boat. After we had reached the people in Tayaniq, I experienced something that was very scary. My father started to do bad things while we were in the boat. Maybe it was because he had lost two wives and he also had a broken leg. He was missing his two wives that were killed in the accident. The injury and the death of his two wives had a bad effect on his mind. He started to fight while he was in the boat and everyone was crying. I remember this because it was very scary. People prevented him from killing himself.

I remember the accident but I have never before told the whole story.

FURTHER READING

John Ayaruaq, *The Autobiography of John Ayaruaq* (Ottawa: Department of Indian Affairs and Northern Development, 1968).

THIRTY-THREE

THE HUDSON'S BAY COMPANY ARRIVES

"We went to Ukkusiksalik, Toota and Jimmy Thom, Iqungajuq and Niaqukittuq, and Iqungajuq's brothers. They started building the Hudson's Bay post. Iqungajuq's mother went along, too. My mother was Toota. My real father was Jimmy Thom. I have heard that my real father left when I was a year old. My Inuit [adopted] father was Iqungajuq." These reminiscent words come from the youngest member of the group that arrived in Wager Bay in 1925, Tuinnaq Kanayuk Bruce. She was less than a year old at the time. She looked back fondly and often on her days at Ukkusiksalik, during her long life in Coral Harbour with her husband, Mikitok Bruce. Much of what we know of the history of the HBC post at Ukkusiksalik has been recorded for us by Tuinnaq Kanayuk Bruce.

The Hudson's Bay Company's schooner *Fort Chesterfield* sailed into Wager Bay in September 1925, looking for a suitable site to establish a new trading post. Jimmy Thom, the HBC manager assigned to the new post, travelled with the group of Inuit from Repulse Bay to Wager Bay by smaller boat, where they met the *Fort Chesterfield*. They built the future trading post on the shore of Tasiujaq (named Ford Lake by the HBC), above the reversing falls at the head of the inlet, near the western extremity of Ukkusiksalik.

It was a time of expansion for the HBC. Posts were already operating at Baker Lake, to the south, and at both Chesterfield Inlet and Repulse Bay along the Hudson Bay coast. The people who lived around

Fort Chesterfield arriving and unloading at Tasiujaq, September 1925.

Ukkusiksalik were certainly well aware of this access to trade goods. However, the new post at Tasiujaq was not principally for them. The HBC had in mind to attract the people from farther inland, the country near the Back River extending down to the river mouth in Chantrey Inlet. By coincidence, the area around the Back River's mouth was also known by Inuit as Ukkusiksalik (actually, as *Utkuhiksalik* in their own dialect). And the connection between the two Ukkusiksaliks was already well established as a traditional hunting route.

The HBC's real motive behind the new post was revealed in a letter from the district manager of the area north of Churchill to the fur trade commissioner, his superior in the HBC management structure, dated February 5, 1925.

> I am forwarding you requisitions and plans of a new Post to be erected at the extreme west end of Wager Inlet. The object in establishing a Post in this quarter is not so much for the purpose of developing the country, but to prevent the majority of the Eskimos hunting between Wager Inlet, Backs River and northward to the Arctic coast, from trading at [Revillon Frères'] Baker Lake Post.
>
> From the strategic position in which Revillon's Post is situated at Baker Lake, there is a great possibility in the future of their managing to gain a good footing in this particular sphere, unless we endeavour to cut off the Backs River and Arctic coast trade from them.[1]
>
> — W.R. Mitchell

When the schooner sailed a week later, leaving Jimmy Thom in charge of the new post with the assistance of Sam Voisey as clerk, along with Iqungajuq and his brothers, the post journal records that the house walls were up, finished except for the roof, and the store was floored. With the incentive offered by the arrival of winter's first snowfall that week, construction moved along quickly. As hospitable as Tasiujaq may seem today, in the autumn of 1925 it must have felt the most desolate place on Earth to the early traders.

Their story is recorded in detail in the daily entries to the post journal; the mundane routine, the good humour, the pain, and the joy are all there. The five-room, uninsulated house in which the two traders, Jimmy Thom and

Sam Voisey, lived was thirty feet by eighteen feet, the nearby store slightly smaller. Around them were the tents or iglus, depending on the season, of the few Inuit families who attached themselves to the post.

Even as the traders settled into routine over that first winter of 1925–26, mindful of their ultimate purpose in establishing the new post, they were not long in laying plans for a trip toward the Back River country. With Iqungajuq (called Native Dick or Wager Dick by the *qablunaat* traders) lead-ing the way, the small party loaded up two sleds and set out overland in early February 1926. They were gone just over a month but eventually found some camps near the mouth of the Hayes River, just to the east of the Back River. Here, with Iqungajuq's assistance, they announced to the Utkuhiksalingmiut the establishment of a new trading post just five days away.

Back at Tasiujaq, on March 16, 1926, the trader Jimmy Thom wrote in the post journal: "Keemallinckgo arrived in p.m. Keemallinckgo is the first of the natives from Hayes River," adjacent to the mouth of the Back River, on the Arctic coast, 250 kilometres to the northwest of Tasiujaq. This is the first recorded instance of Inuit from that distant heartland of undeveloped territory — as seen from the HBC perspective — travelling the long estab-lished route down to Ukkusiksalik in order to trade their fox skins.

Tuinnaq Kanayuk Bruce does not remember that first winter, the time when Jimmy Thom was manager, though she does remember some of the later managers and clerks.[*] Her mother worked for many of them as cook and housekeeper. As a little girl nicknamed Tuinnaq, a derivative of "looks like a doll," she had free run of the house and store, although initially her family lived in a tent on a slight rise behind the buildings. "I used to come through here for a bath — the white man would give me a bath," she recalled, standing in the kitchen door of the traders' house. Much of the contents of that house were familiar to her, although she found [that] many things had been displaced when she visited it seventy years later, in 1996.

Standing outside her childhood home, Tuinnaq pointed across the water to the east, to a giant boulder overlooking the bay where a young man, Amitnaq, had laid the dead body of one of his dogs, a measure of respect for his late father and the dogs that had carried him and his mother to safety

---

[*] For a list of the HBC managers and clerks at the Tasiujaq post, see the end of this chapter.

The old HBC post at Tasiujaq, as it appeared in 1996.

at Tasiujaq after his father's death. Just south of that, along the hillside, is another grave, where Samson Ipkarnaq buried his young wife within a year of the post's establishment, before the couple had been together long enough to produce any children. When Tuinnaq turned to look toward the north end of a ridge lying alongside the post, where a pile of large stones stood out against the horizon, her eyes fell upon her grandmother Arnnagruluk's grave [Arnnagruluk was sometimes known as Tulugak]. Iqungajuq and his brothers entombed their mother there, where she was protected from marauding animals by the huge stones. The grave is still evident today.

She has a lot of happy memories, too. Tuinnaq described visitors, Inuit from far away, walking into the post during the summer. She recalled people coming overland to trade fox skins. "I remember people came from Back River, those people with those wooden sunglasses that they made. I was wondering what kind of people they were, because that was the first time I saw people like that. They seemed different people. Their dialect was different from ours. How they dressed was different from us."

One of the visitors she remembered was Siksaaq, a Nattilik man who some years earlier was lucky to escape with his life from the boat accident at the mouth of Ukkusiksalik. Siksaaq's death during the early years of the HBC post's operation provides one of the many spiritual stories of the Ukkusiksalingmiut. His son, Francis Kaput, who lived later in Rankin Inlet, described his father as originally from Nattilik, and said the family moved gradually south to the Chesterfield Inlet region. In that process, they spent several years around Ukkusiksalik. In the late 1930s, they were living near Qamanaaluk when, in need of food for his family, Siksaaq set out for the post at Tasiujaq. Tuinnaq Kanayuk Bruce, by then a teenager helping with the work at the trading post, remembered his visit.

"Siksaaq's family owed too much to the store in Naujaat [Repulse Bay], so they couldn't buy from the store in Tasiujaq. So our family, Iqungajuk's family, had to supply some food for Siksaaq. We were doing it out of love. It was all from our own supplies. So we gave a little bit of food to them. And he was going back to his family. He was walking at that time. He got to Kapik [one of his sons] in Qamanaaluk, and after Kapik's, he walked to Kreelak, his oldest son.* He never got there. He was not found until the snow melted the following spring, and we figure that he had built an iglu. Some say he was attacked by a polar bear."

Kreelak's son Guy Amarok, who was six or seven years old at the time, remembers his grandfather's death. "The story behind that was he was taken by evil spirits. People looked for him for a long, long time. What had happened was, he had built an iglu. But he was pulled off the bed. His feet were on the high part [sleeping platform] and his body was on the floor, but he was pulled down and killed by spirits. There was nobody else in that area. My grandfather was an *angakkuq* [a shaman]. It looks like he was killed by another *angakkuq*, another spirit."

Siksaaq's youngest son, Francis Kaput, confirmed the involvement of shamanism in his father's death. "He did not die of starvation. He did not die because of illness. Nobody attacked him or anything. I can recall in those days, there were medicines and shamans. I remember, when we walked from Chesterfield Inlet, the first night when we got to where my brother Kreelak was staying [near Qamanaaluk], early in the morning, I heard him [my father] say when he was getting ready to go out hunting again, 'I'm tired of being

---

* There is conflicting information as to whether Kreelak or Kapik was the eldest son. They were probably close in age and almost certainly the two eldest of Siksaaq's five sons: Kreelak, Kapik, Okpik, Taparti, and Kaput.

around Ukkusiksalik and I'm tired of these demons, the shamans trying to get at me. Next time I see this person again, I'm just going to give up and not even fight back.' It was Udlut's wife's brother that was always after him; I guess he was a shaman. That's what my father was telling my older brother. I guess that's what got him, a demon or a shaman. I guess he never fought back, like he told my brother. That following winter, that's when he never came back.

"I can only assume that, after what I heard from him, saying that he was tired of these demons and shamans trying to get at him, and if they tried him again, he was just not going to fight back, I can only assume that that's what got him. My mother knew, too, that some day this would happen. I assume that this is what happened." There was no doubt in either Kaput's or Amarok's mind about what happened.

The next winter, after the body had been found, young Guy Amarok remembers travelling past that place. He fell off the sled, and when he looked up a giant raven-like bird was coming toward him. No one else saw the bird, but he remains convinced to this day that "it was associated with that particular incident" — the death of his grandfather Siksaaq.

In some ways, incidents like this one were simply taken in stride by people in the area, and life at the post went on as usual. Growing up at Tasiujaq was a happy experience for Tuinnaq. "When we were children, we would fish for those small, ugly fish that come out from under the rocks. We used to look for siksiks [ground squirrels] and pick berries. We never used to be bored, even though there weren't that many people living in the area." And some special events stick in her mind. "I remember when they used to have square dances. Tommy Taqaugaq was really good at the accordion. Even though he had an injured arm, he was really good at playing accordion." She recalls one Christmas when, for some reason, her family was not at the post but was camped at Tinittuqtuq, the peninsula out in the main body of the inlet. But the post manager did not forget her. "I remember when it was Christmas, the Bay manager sent me a little doll and candies with the doll." Nevertheless, she often wishes she knew more of what happened during those years at Tasiujaq. It was all recorded, she remembers, in a diary kept by her father, Iqungajuq, but that diary has been lost.

On Sunday, November 6, 1927, a notable entry from the post journal records the arrival of another child who would become a central player in the story of Ukkusiksalik.

The HBC ship *Fort Severn* serving the HBC post at Tasiujaq, early 1930s.

The *Fort Severn* fighting its way through the ice of Hudson Bay en route to the HBC post at Tasiujaq, early 1930s.

Inuit men working at the Tasiujaq post to help unload the *Fort Severn* during its annual visit, early 1930s.

-10 Clear with decrease in wind. The wind blew so strong last night that driven snow was forced thru the window frames of both bedrooms and kitchen. Also a pile of lumber flooring was scattered about like matches. During the early hours of the morning native Dick's wife Tootah gave birth to a boy.

The boy was called Robert Tatty. His natural father was W.E. "Buster" Brown, post manager at Ukkusiksalik for the outfit year* 1926–27, but he left before his son was born. Tatty's mother, Toota, was one of Iqungajuq's wives, so naturally Tatty became Iqungajuq's adopted son. For both Tuinnaq and Tatty, Tasiujaq was home, in the deepest sense possible, and they retained that attachment for the rest of their lives.

Life at the post beside Tasiujaq consisted mainly of the fox trade for the next few years. A new manager and clerk arrived almost every summer on the annual supply ship, and the expanding family of Iqungajuq became an ever more permanent fixture. By the early 1930s, that family consisted of Iqungajuq, his two wives Niaqukittuq and Toota, and all the children: two girls, Avaqsaq and Tuinnaq, and three boys, Napayok, Tatty, and Tattuinee.

The post journals** are a telling mix of comments on engines, the first airplanes, and the introduction of shortwave radios, with observations on fish, caribou and seals caught, the weather, and the local people. The journal keepers left behind a vivid picture of their life and a record of historic detail whose impact increases with the passing of time. It seems unlikely that any of them would have anticipated the far-reaching significance of their words.

December 3, 1928: Slightly overcast — no wind. Samson off to traps in a.m. Sicsak in with some fish. Men hauling water and feeding dogs. At office work.

November 4, 1929: Visibility very poor today — cold north west wind changing to north towards evening. J. Spence [clerk]

---

* In HBC parlance, the outfit year — similar to today's use of "fiscal year" — commenced on the first day of June each year and concluded on the last day of May the next year.

** For an in-depth excerpt of the post journals, see the appendix, "The Traders' Journals."

with natives Dick & Sutoni [Sutoqsi] left this morning to set some traps up by Kauminalook [Qamanaaluk]. Self employed compiling records from Outfit 256 and making out last months forms. Lamps have to be lighted at four o'clock. The last few days are really the first winter days we have had, frost showing on windows and doors and generally feeling wintry, especially when one wakes up in the morning.

December 25, 1929: Dull and overcast, calm, snowing a little. Had all the natives in tonight, gave them a feed and presents, after which they enjoyed themselves dancing for the rest of the evening. The music was supplied by native Tommy on a five dollar accordion. Everyone enjoyed themselves. Ipooyauak and Enukshuk, being Back's River natives and as Dick would say "First time see 'em Christmas" were greatly amused and no doubt it made an effect upon them.

January 13, 1931: Keeluk [Kreelak] has now had a young wife bestowed upon him, she is Samson's wife's eldest girl and needless to say, Keeluk is all tickled up the back and elsewhere, I suppose.

As 1932 passes, the journal notes that the local Inuit have been without food much of the time, and that only one, Samson Ipkarnaq, has come into the post to trade. Foxes are scarce. Spirits are low.

January 4, 1933: Natives Deaf Johnny, Angatinuak [Angutinguaq], Sutoxi [Sutoqsi] and Nowya arrived at post this evening and they all were in a sorry plight with frost bite, hunger and tiredness. The majority of their dogs had died on them through lack of food and they had but seven dogs amongst them when they arrived here. None of these natives had any [fox] fur [to trade].

January 5, 1933: Gave the natives a dance tonight to cheer them up, as they all seem very downhearted and miserable owing to the scarcity of fur.

March 27, 1933: Still no signs of any natives arriving, so I guess they are getting very little fur.

April 4, 1933: It is time some natives were showing up to trade. They must be getting very little fur, if such is the case the longer they stay away the better.

April 9, 1933: Native Tommy and wife arrived in a.m. He had one fox. Wager Inlet this year is beyond the pale — it is enough to make any self-respecting trader feel like a rest cure patient at the Health Spa.

May 10, 1933: Natives Arngnawa and Nowya with wives and family arrived at post tonight 12 p.m. They bring in the same story which we have been hearing all winter — absolutely no fur in the country.

May 31, 1933: This brings to a close Outfit 263, one of the poorest fur years since this post was established, and it is with absolutely no regrets from either member of the staff that we write "finis" to this most disastrous outfit.[2]

This "disastrous outfit" produced only $1,216.22 profit, barely half of the previous year's profit. It is not surprising then, that the decision was made by HBC superiors to withdraw the staff from Wager Inlet. What is surprising is that no record of that decision has survived in the journal. The last complete entry is on Saturday, August 26, 1933. The next day's entry seems to have been interrupted in midstream, after only the usual opening line about the weather. Did the summer supply ship come into view just as the manager, W.A. Heslop, was catching up his journal? Did he run out to meet it, only to learn that he was being transferred? The ship's log of the *Fort Severn* notes her arrival in Tasiujaq at the Wager Bay Post at 11:56 a.m. on the twenty-eighth, whereupon she "commenced loading Wager supplies," which process finished on the thirtieth, in time for the ship to sail at 12:45 p.m., with the manager and his journal embarked.

Tuinnaq Kanayuk Bruce recalls the day clearly. "When my family and I were at Qamanaaluk fishing, some people came to us and asked Iqungajuq if he could take over. That ship came to Tasiujaq and those people came to us in their little boat. He really didn't want to take over, but they told him as long as you write down everything that is sold — they persuaded him. Iqungajuq didn't want to take over because he didn't know what to do."

Iqungajuq did take charge, with remarkable success. The story of the HBC post at Tasiujaq, after the withdrawal of the *qablunaat* traders, continued for several more years.[*]

HBC MANAGERS AND CLERKS AT THE TASIUJAQ POST

Outfit	Years	Manager	Clerk
256	1925–26	J.A. (Jimmy) Thom	Sam Voisey
257	1926–27	W.E. (Buster) Brown	H. McHardy
258	1927–28	H. Leith	H. McHardy
259	1928–29	Archie Hunter	J. Spence
260	1929–30	J.L. Ford	J. Spence
261	1930–31	J.L. Ford	N. Irvin
262	1931–32	J.F.G. Wynne	N. Irvin
263	1932–33	W.A. Heslop	A. Paterson
264	1933	W.A. Heslop	A. Paterson
	1933–45	Iqungajuq (a.k.a. Wager Dick)	

1. The outfit (similar to today's use of "fiscal year") commenced on the first day of June each year and concluded on the last day of May the next year.
2. The term of the manager/clerk did not exactly coincide with the outfit, in reality. Usually, the new manager and/or clerk arrived on the

---

* See chapter 35, "An Inuk Manager for the HBC."

supply ship (*Fort Chesterfield* or *Fort Severn*) in late August, and the departing manager and/or clerk left on the same vessel, so the period of overlap for purposes of a "turnover" was no more than a few days.

3. W.E. "Buster" Brown also returned to Tasiujaq as manager of a tractor transport project over the winter of 1928–29, a failed attempt to open up trade with the Arctic coast to the northwest, and in the 1930s served as the district manager.

4. The final pair, Heslop and Paterson, left on the *Fort Severn* on August 30, 1933 — the end of a *qablunaat* presence at the trading post in Tasiujaq. Iqungajuq took over upon their departure.

THIRTY-FOUR

THE FOX TRADE

The presence of a trading post nearby changed the way of life for most of the Ukkusiksalingmiut. Mary Nuvak of Chesterfield Inlet explained why the post was established: "The reason why they opened the post up in Ukkusiksalik was for fox skins, fox fur. They wanted to be accessible to trappers. That's what they were going after. They had competition, so they wanted more people to trade with them. That was the reason they opened that post there. They wanted to make sure they got the business." For people in the area, the post was a source of trading goods, of supplies to supplement the hunt. It provided access to market for highly valued white fox skins, as well as the pelts of a few other animals. "When I was in Ukkusiksalik," recalled Octave Sivaniqtoq, "we never traded with sealskins at all. It was only foxes and wolves." It was also a source of help in times of need. For the most part, it was a straightforward exchange — furs for goods.

The trapper laid his furs out for the trader's appraisal and received so many HBC tokens, which he then immediately spent by selecting trading goods from the shelves. "What the traders used as money was a piece of wood about half an inch thick and four inches long [1.25 centimetres by 10 centimetres], sometimes cut in half," described Felix Kopak. "That is what we used as currency. This is how they used to trade, with a block of wood. My parents used to trade them, first of all for bullets, and then for powder and the other stuff you need for the rifle, and they used to trade tea and

An Inuk brings his fox pelts into the HBC for trade.

biscuits, and sometimes sugar. The fox price used to vary from year to year. On a good year, you could buy a hundred pounds of flour with one fox. In a bad year, you would buy it with two."

"Tea, tobacco, sugar, biscuits, flour, porridge oats, those are the foods that I remember," said Guy Amarok, who traded at Tasiujaq with his family in the 1930s. "They weren't using food that we have today, which is perishable when it's frozen. It was basic food that was being traded."

Invariably, the trader was called upon to do more than barter for furs. In the absence of greater expertise, he became doctor, dentist, nurse, and priest when necessary. Felix Kopak was once so sick that he "could not see — I became blind." The HBC manager at Tasiujaq fixed him up. "Ikumalirijialuk [Buster Brown] got a tablespoon and he mixed an equal part of that — a white liquid, one that is really stinky; rubbing on the skin, it feels hot — with molasses, and he made me swallow it. I thought I was going to die. Fortunately, shortly after that, I started feeling better."

For the Ukkusiksalingmiut, life came to focus more and more on the trading post. "The people from Ukkusiksalik did their trading mostly at Tasiujaq," said Sivaniqtoq. "We used to go up to Repulse Bay if we needed something that was not at Tasiujaq, but we did our trading with Iqungajuq most of the time."

Tuinnaq Kanayuk Bruce, Iqungajuq's daughter, remembered people coming in to trade from different directions, by different means of travel — by foot, by dog team, by boat — and at different times of the year.

In 1933, the HBC withdrew its *qablunaat* staff and left the operation of the post in Iqungajuq's hands. "I have heard, I might be wrong, but I have heard, there weren't enough foxes and not enough people were going there. And there wasn't enough trappers to get foxes for the post," offered Tuinnaq Kanayuk Bruce by way of explanation.

THIRTY-FIVE

AN INUK MANAGER FOR THE HBC, 1933–45

In later life, Robert Tatty said that he remembered growing up to manhood in Ukkusiksalik. He recalled the active post, the manager they called Qauluniqsaq, meaning "the one with lighter hair," the comings and goings of hunters from the camps with their foxes to trade, the abundance of wildlife all around. "They were good times" he said. For him, that territory was always home. He returned many times, often for long periods.

Robert Tatty's natural father was W.E. "Buster" Brown (Ikumalirijialuk), post manager for the outfit year 1926–27. When the last of the *qablunaat* managers left in the summer of 1933, Tatty was not quite yet six years old. He recalled the arrival of the *Fort Severn* when it came on August 28, 1933, to withdraw the staff of the Wager Inlet post. "I was not old enough to work yet. I remember when the manager left. He asked my father, Iqungajuq, to take over the post. We moved into the small HBC house [actually the warehouse, originally] then. I remember the little open putt-putt boat the manager came to get us in from our camp down the lake."

His older sister, Tuinnaq Kanayuk Bruce, also recalled the day. "Iqungajuq didn't want to take over because he didn't know what to do. When my family and I were at Qamanaaluk fishing, some people came to us and asked Iqungajuq if he could take over. He really didn't want to take over, but they told him as long as you write down everything that is sold — they persuaded him." Iqungajuq was familiar with the post operation, having been there

Iqungajuq, manager of the trading post at Tasiujaq, 1933–45.

since its construction in 1925, but to be the manager was an unexpected challenge. The more so because, with the withdrawal of *qablunaat* managers, the HBC also ceased the annual visit of a supply ship, and left it to Iqungajuq to fetch his own trade goods from Chesterfield Inlet or Repulse Bay, the two closest HBC trading posts.

"When that [supply] ship stopped going to Ukkusiksalik," continued Tuinnaq Kanayuk Bruce, "Iqungajuq used to go to Chesterfield by

Peterhead boat to get supplies for the store. One time he went to Repulse Bay by dog team to get more supplies for the store. I don't remember how many times he went to Repulse Bay or Chesterfield Inlet to get more supplies." On these occasions, it was left largely to Tuinnaq to operate the trading post, to conduct the trade.

Even though she was no more than a young teenager, Tuinnaq became increasingly involved in the post's operation, often helping out in the store. "When winter was almost over and it wasn't that cold, then my father would go to Repulse Bay by dog team to get more supplies for the store. In summer he would go by boat. Then I would do the trading for him. We used small pieces of wood as money [HBC tokens]. I would write down in Inuktitut things that were traded. I didn't like trading because some people weren't happy. Some people would bundle up the fox fur and I wouldn't realize that they had rips or holes in them if they were all bundled up like that. People traded for bullets, flour, tobacco, lard, ingredients for making bannock, tea, things like that. They weren't expensive at that time. I had to write it all down in Inuktitut. I learned to write and read by myself. When I was a little girl, I memorized a song, and someone gave me words to that song

An aerial view of the post at Tasiujaq taken during the time that Iqungajuq was the manager.

Tuinnaq Kanayuk Bruce during a 1996 visit to the old trading post where she grew up.

written out in syllabics, so I started reading it by what I had memorized. I learned to read by myself."

Iqungajuq served in this position as ad hoc manager of the Tasiujaq post most ably, with the help of his whole family. He managed the store more profitably than his *qablunaat* predecessors. All his inventory and trading records were meticulously written down in Inuktitut syllabics. The Company provided him with trading supplies and (later) some coal to heat his house in return for his service. He managed to turn a profit with very little support from his remote supervisors, who were duly impressed. A small commission on his trading profits was left to accumulate for him at the Repulse Bay post. Once or twice a year he would make the trek out to this closest HBC post to deliver the fox skins he had collected from other hunters and to restock his outfit. Tatty, a young boy quickly learning to be a man, frequently made these trips with his father. "When my father and I went out — hunting, or trapping, or to Repulse — we left my two older sisters in charge of the trading."

Hunters came to the post in summer, by foot from inland or by sail from down the inlet, to get bullets, tea, and tobacco on credit, which they would pay back in skins during the coming winter. All winter long, occasional hunters came by dog team to turn in their fox skins. "It was a happy time, when lots of people came," recalled Tatty.

In the early 1940s, HBC trader Bill Robinson made a spring trip from the Repulse Bay post to visit Iqungajuq at Tasiujaq. His observations offer another perspective on life at the post with an Inuk as manager.

> The warehouse consisted of one huge room with a back porch. It resembled an immense iglu with a snow tunnel entrance. At one end of the room two double beds were placed end to end. Dick [Iqungajuq] and his family seated themselves on one bed while his brother and family sat on the other. Individual caribou-hide sleeping bags were placed on the bare mattresses, marking each member's allotted spot on this giant substitute snow bench. An overturned packing box and a wooden bench along one wall completed the furnishings in the room. A Primus stove and seal-oil lamp shared the surface of the packing box. Other than the seal-oil lamp, no heating arrangements

existed. This was Dick's summer quarters. During the cold days of winter the families lived in a couple of cozy iglus.

Since the departure of a Company manager in 1933, Iqungajuq had turned the Ukkusiksalik post at Tasiujaq into a small but consistently profitable operation. He was a man who could find his way simultaneously in two different worlds. He took his responsibilities to the Company seriously, kept his records straight, and never provided a problem for his distant supervisors in Repulse Bay. Yet he maintained the values and traditions of his own heritage within his family structure. He was admired by all who came to know him.

In his annual report dated May 31, 1944, at the close of Outfit 274, Repulse Bay manager D. Drysdale summed up the state of the Wager Bay trade and the valuable contribution made by Iqungajuq.

Dick will not be here with his results till August or early part of September. Last year it was September 22nd before he got here, so he is liable to be just as late this year, since his boat engine is in very bad repair, and he has to sail most of the time.

Dick brought me an Inventory of his stock taken sometime in February. He thought he would get another fifty foxes at the most from Back River natives in the later part of April or early in May. I sincerely hope he managed to get them, but I am doubtful as fur seems to be pretty scarce this year. I always stress the point about debts, and no doubt he has often been told about this. He is a pretty careful old fellow and I am sure doing best he can. And no doubt when fur is scarce he has a hard time saying NO to anyone who comes to ask for a few pounds of tobacco or tea.

Last fall he had a very narrow escape somewhere in Wager Bay, got caught in a very bad gale which wrecked his old motor boat and he had a very hard time keeping the Peterhead off the rocks. But he says the Peterhead is still in sailing condition — but says the bottom is getting pretty soft and won't stand a rough sea.

These proved to be prophetic words.

In the meanwhile, it was time for Tatty, nearly eighteen, to have a wife. Accordingly, in March of 1945, on one of their resupply trips by dog team to Repulse Bay, Iqungajuq and Tatty picked up his betrothed from Anaruaq's camp. "I was pretty young," recalled an elderly Annie Tatty, who was fifteen, just a month shy of her sixteenth birthday, at that time. "It would be pretty young for *qablunaat*, but Inuit used to get married young. Inuit used to make plans who is who that will marry." Annie's adopted parents (her mother died in childbirth), Joseph Kakak and Paula Angnaujuq, had not shared their plan with her. She grew up in Ukkusiksalik, near Piqsimaniq, and had visited the post at Tasiujaq on a number of occasions. She remembered seeing Iqungajuq and Tuinnaq and even Tatty. But "I did not know he was my future husband." So, in the spring of 1945, as best she could, she settled into her new life with Tatty's family at Tasiujaq. "I was uncomfortable, because I never have been without my parents before and I was homesick for quite a while. They treated me very well, but I did not want to leave my father and mother."

That summer, the whole family set out by boat from Tasiujaq for Repulse Bay, to get the year's supplies. The HBC had promised that a new boat for Iqungajuq would come in on the annual supply ship from down south — reason enough, it seems, for the whole family to make the trip. The ship was late. They waited patiently in Repulse Bay. That trading post, too, was nearly out of supplies. Finally the ship arrived, with supplies but no new boat for Iqungajuq. The family had no choice but to head home in the old, rotting boat. As Annie Tatty recalls it, "our boat was not hard wood. The side of the boat was peeling off and it started cracking. Also we did not have a motor." Travel conditions were less than ideal. It was already September; sea ice was forming.

"We tried to go back to Wager in the old boat, loaded with our supplies, but it was already freezing and the ice severely damaged the boat," recalled Robert Tatty forty years later. "We tried to axe a way through the ice. But eventually it was frozen in and we had to abandon it." They were about halfway down Roes Welcome Sound toward the inlet, at a place Inuit call Umiijarvik.

His older sister, Tuinnaq Kanayuk Bruce, was also there. "The ice was scraping on the sides of the boat. My parents got scared so we landed on

Mikitok Bruce telling stories during a 1996 visit to the old post where his wife grew up.

shore. Our boat wasn't wrecked. We came to the beach before it really got wrecked. We got our supplies on land. We had to put up our tents in that area where we beached, and we spent the winter there. It was already icing up. The ice was getting thick. It was really cold. When we got to shore, Iqungajuq built a house with ice blocks. It was really nice to live in that ice house for a while because we could see through [the walls]. But when winter came, we built an iglu and moved into it." The ice house became the trading post, with walls the height of a man, the boat's sail spread overtop as a roof, and the supplies neatly piled inside. That incident changed the course of history. The family had planned to stay at Tasiujaq, thinking that Tatty would take over as manager of the store. But Iqungajuq simply resumed his trading from a new location.

"We had more business there than before, at Tasiujaq," recalled Tatty. "There was a lot of fox that year. But that was the end of the HBC in Ukkusiksalik. During that winter I went back to the old post to do an inventory and to pick up the remaining supplies."

"We had left our dog team in Ukkusiksalik," recalled his sister, Tuinnaq. "Agulaq was going to look after them. But he was too old to look after them properly. Siulluk left for Chesterfield Inlet at the same time when we were going to Repulse Bay. If Siulluk had looked after the dogs instead of Agulaq, they would have survived. Tatty went back to Tasiujaq [from Umiijarvik] that winter. He was quite young then. He was riding with Angutinguaq on one dog team. He was planning to get [our] dogs and come back [to Umiijarvik] and get the family and then go back to Tasiujaq. But the dogs weren't being fed, so they starved. We didn't have a dog team any more because they starved. I think they brought a few things but not that many, because it was winter and it was quite far from where we were camping [at Umiijarvik]." For lack of a dog team, the family never returned to Tasiujaq. And so the colourful history of the HBC post at Tasiujaq, a uniquely remote post with an Inuk as manager for twelve years, came to an end. Fortunately, the stories of the lives which unfolded in those buildings are preserved.

———

What happened to Iqungajuq and his family? With the winter's accumulation of fox skins, they made their way north to Repulse Bay, to cash

Tuinnaq and Mikitok's great-grandchildren during a 1996 family visit to the old post where their great-grandmother grew up.

in the results of Iqungajuq's final year as a trader. The next year, in the spring of 1947, his daughter Tuinnaq's betrothed, Mikitok, (this was still the era of arranged marriages) arrived in Repulse Bay to pick her up. The young couple returned to his family in Duke of York Bay, on Southampton Island. Iqungajuq and Toota followed in the summer. Not long after, Toota died at Duke of York Bay, probably of tuberculosis. The combined families lived there for about six years and then moved to live on the south coast of the island, on the outskirts of what is now Coral Harbour, where Tuinnaq and Mikitok lived until their deaths in 2012 and 2013 respectively.

THIRTY-SIX

QARMAQ

After visiting the *qarmaq* (sod house) where his family lived in Piqsimaniq in the 1950s, Jackie Nanordluk described the construction of a *qarmaq* as he recalled it.

━━◆━━

I have seen Inuit making a *qarmaq*, a sod house. I will explain to you what I know. First of all, before they started making sod houses, the weather and the ground had to be colder. Most of the people had a similar way of building sod houses. Some made it just on the land and some dug into the sand first and made a ditch for the sod house. When it is on the sand, they try and make it simple as possible. The walls of the sod house usually were sod, but some made it also with rocks; these are the differences in the building of these sod houses. If they are going to make a *qarmaq* just out of sod it had to be a little bit frozen in the fall.

The *qarmaq* couldn't be done in one day. Some took a few days, being careful not to make the sod too thin; they had to make it quite thick in order for it to hold. They could not use the sod for the roofing. They needed to make the walls higher using the sod, to the height they wanted it — which varied from builder to builder. As soon as they finished the bottom part of the walls, then they would put the canvas tent over the top for the roof and set it up like a tent with poles. Some were made slanted; this varied as well

Jackie Nanordluk standing beside the entrance stones to his family's old *qarmaq* at Piqsimaniq in 1996.

from builder to builder. I guess each person had their own custom in building a *qarmaq*. Some had a steeply slanted roof, because they will be just using it to sleep in. The bed was at the end in the lower part. Some built their roof higher, even though it was slanted.

Once they put the canvas tent over it, then they would also put poles to make it more even. If they had enough wood around, this would make a good frame for the *qarmaq* with canvas on it. This is the way I saw a *qarmaq* being built. In the past they did not have measuring tapes, so they did it by sight, and for that reason they had different heights. They would decide if it was the right size by looking at the height they've created. They would use different kinds of wood in the frame of the *qarmaq*. The canvas tent was put inside it, put in last. Finally, they would collect bushes to put in as insulation between the tent and the sod, and on the top of the *qarmaq* they would put more bushes to finish it up.

The door would be quite narrow so that it let in less wind through it. It was not done in such a way that it would just face any direction. They would make the door to face the south wind, where there would not be a snow buildup. They would make the *qarmaq* by looking at the landscape. If the land is facing down then they would make the doorway facing down instead of making the doorway on a higher level.

They used rocks that would fit best in the *qarmaq* and make them fit accordingly to each rock beside it. They would try and collect rocks that were more square and level, even if larger. Flat rocks were best to use, as that would make it much easier to build, and get it done faster as well. The height would be done faster, too. But they used any size of rocks, as long as they are not too heavy to carry. It's very hard work to build up the walls. They tried making the inside of the *qarmaq* more carefully than the outside. They used a lot more sod than rocks, because the rocks are so heavy to use and hard to work with. If there is enough sod around, they could figure it out more, how high they want to build the walls. They were not that high. They were more or less built like tents, with enough room to stand in it, but lower on the side. When you see them from outside they looked quite low. Even if it is low, once you go inside it is higher, because they have dug in to the sand to make more space in height and make it more comfortable to live in. They made the *qarmaq* larger according to the size of family.

I have heard, but have not seen it with my own eyes, that they used to use bowhead whale bones, especially the ribs, for beams. They had to use things that were long enough for beams.

The window of the *qarmaq* was made out of a bearded seal's throat skin.* The way they used the skin of the bearded seal's throat was by carefully peeling it off the layer of the throat while it is still damp or soft. It's hard to peel it off. Peeling off the throat skin is like the way you prepare the intestines of the animals. It's thin, so that it could be used for the window, to let the light come in to the *qarmaq*. In those days, they did not have anything else to use for a window. The bearded seal is much larger than a ringed seal and much tougher, so it tears less. They would put them all together from more than one throat skin to make it large enough for a window and sew it together.

---

* In some places, Inuit also used bearded seal intestines, sewn together, as a window.

THIRTY-SEVEN

MASIVAK

"This was our trail; we walked along here," recalled Octave Sivaniqtoq during a visit to Masivak on the south shore of Ukkusiksalik in 1996, when he was seventy-two years old. Together with Felix Kopak, he walked upstream along a path beside the river, from the landing beach up to his family's old *qarmaq*. Over the next two days, he offered many more insights into life at Masivak.

⁓◦⁓

My grandfather used to tell me stories and things that happened. When he was asked a question like "Why is that area called Masivak?" he apparently knew exactly how it got its name. When the fish go upriver, just before winter sets in, Inuit used to bury their cache of fish when the weather was so they can no longer dry fish. At Masivak they buried their fish, many of them, all over the area, to be used for food during winter. Apparently, when the wind was right, in a certain direction, you can smell their gills from afar because there were many caches. It was the gills that got really smelly. "Masik" means a fish gill, so that's why this is called Masivak, because of the smell. There used to be a lot of fish in this area long ago, and the river was wider.

They called him Piyausuituq, although he had another name. His real name was Arnar'naaq, but when other kids pestered him in the Nattilingmiut dialect, he was trying to say, "I don't want to be pestered" — *piyausuitunga*. That's why his nickname is like that, but his real name is Arnar'naaq.

Piyausuituq Arnar'naaq used to tell us that the stone weirs at the far end, at Masivak, used to be used for fishing in the spring. Before ice breakup, apparently, people used to fish there. But he wasn't around then, when they fished at an old weir that was used in the spring, where the fish could reach during high tide. He used to fish in the old stone weirs in the main river, used in August, but even some of them have dried out over time. I think there are three stone fish weirs around Masivak. They used to be in the water, but with the water drying out they are quite far from water now. There is another weir farther upriver for use when fish are coming downriver in spring.

This area was used for camps before guns were brought to Inuit. People used them if they did not have bow and arrows and *qajaq*, or had trouble walking, and they couldn't hunt caribou. So they fished at the stone weirs, mostly for the winter's food.

Some people had difficulty walking because of old age. Some Inuit had disabilities, such as long-term illness, such as backaches, leg injury, or what have you. Some had difficulty seeing because of old age. There were people who didn't have older children to provide food for them. And some people were without a *qajaq* and other hunting implements, because of old age and poverty. This area was a fishing place for all those people. The other rivers were too strong, so they used this river. It was the easier.

They camped and lived mostly in Masivak because of the abundance of char and caribou. I know by experience, when I was still a child, that there were a lot of caribou around and fish going upriver. There were plenty of fish back then.

When you could not get them with a fishing hook, you could make a stone weir by putting rocks around the water, for fish to get trapped into while they're climbing upriver. Make it like [the base of] an iglu with an entrance facing downriver, so as they go up, they go through the entrance and they get trapped. You measure the entrance with your foot to make sure it's wide enough or narrow enough so fish don't escape back downriver. That's the way they used to do it.

Once they get inside the stone weir they get into the *qaggiq*,* which is

---

* This is the original meaning of the word *qaggiq*, the holding pen in a stone weir where the fish – lots of them – are gathered. The word was then applied to a large gathering place, as in a tent or iglu, where the people would come together for celebrations.

the main round swimming area where fish are trapped. Then you plug the entrance when there's enough fish trapped. That's the way they did it back then, and you can spear as much as you want.

If a fish is fully grown, the entrance is just right. You have to make sure there are no holes in the walls of the weir so fish don't get out. They can try to escape on either side, but as long as it's plugged, there's no way out for them. You make the trap with rocks and lay them out higher than the water. Around the open trapped area, called *qaggiq*, you have to make sure to put stones higher than the water flowing, so it's not moving and fish don't escape. It's okay to keep the bottom of the weir lower. That's why the top of the stone weir has to be higher than the water, because fish try to continue to climb.

They can go right to the tip of the weir as far as they can, but they can't escape as long as the stones are all there and any holes are plugged. We put a light, flat stone to plug the entrance of the weir after the fish are in.

I can't say for sure how many fish might be inside the trap. Sometimes the trap is filled right up and sometimes there's not very many. I can't estimate how many there would be. Sometimes fish are so many they are just stacked one on top of the other and they are so crowded they can hardly move. You can spear them with *kakivak* starting from anywhere in the weir. But I can't say what the number would be. I'm sure there were more than a hundred sometimes. Inuit spearing the fish bonk them and string them together as they keep spearing them. Some get so many on a line or string and when the string gets full of fish they go to the land and dump them and go back again and spear some more. I'm sure the numbers were over a hundred.

The *kakivak* was made out of caribou antler, oval shaped, with a prong in the middle and a string put in like a harpoon. Some made a *kakivak* out of the caribou front leg bone and some used polar bear foreleg bones. They were different.

Some had strings to thread the fish by the mouth. With the string, you can't ruin the fish or lose it, because you're stringing it as you spear it. There could be five people in the weir, spearing fish. That was their only source of food, so they started using string to keep tally of, or ownership of, the fish.

Nowadays, they don't fish at the stone weirs.

Felix Kopak joined Sivaniqtoq and they led the way farther uphill toward a large rock. Kopak remembered stopping here when he was a young adult on his way from Chesterfield Inlet north to Repulse Bay by dog team. He pointed up the valley that cut through the hills and said that was his route from Chesterfield Inlet. Sivaniqtoq recalled hunting caribou up in those same hills many years ago.

After several hundred metres, the path led to a large, prominent rock on an elevated area overlooking the river valley farther inland. Sivaniqtoq sat down beside the rock to explain its importance. Years ago, if you broke your *kakivak* in the river, you had to get away from the river to work on it, to fix it. This rock was where Sivaniqtoq did that work, away from the river. The work was always done on the side of the rock away from the river, so that you could not see any of the water in the river as you worked. Otherwise, the fish would move somewhere else and there would be no more fish going up this river. That was the creed understood by Inuit years ago. All rivers were treated in the same way, added Kopak. If someone broke the law, the fish would stay away for exactly a year and return on the anniversary of the infraction.

In those days, the shamans controlled such things. "Whatever a shaman said to do, or not to do, we would follow," said Sivaniqtoq. If someone did

Sivaniqtoq beside the big rock during a visit to Masivak in 1996.

not obey, the shaman would search for the person and make him confess. That way, the fish would return a year later. If the shaman did not find the person, perhaps the fish would never return. And if the shaman found the person but he refused to confess, that person would get ill and stay ill until he confessed.

Similarly, in traditional times, as Sivaniqtoq explained, Inuit always tried to put their tents behind rocks away from the river, out of respect for the fish. Children were told not to play in the river to make sure the maximum number of fish came upriver into the weir.

THIRTY-EIGHT

THE MYSTERIOUS DISAPPEARANCE OF FATHER BULIARD[1]

Late October on the barrenlands is a stormy time of year, the wind howling and the early snow of winter whipping across the frozen tundra and newly formed lake ice. It is a difficult time for travel — not enough snow on the land for easy sled travel, and lakes where the ice can be precariously thin.

On October 24, 1956, Father Joseph Buliard, a veteran of seventeen years in the Arctic who must surely have understood the difficulties and dangers of travel at this time of year, made the fateful decision to leave his tiny mission on an island in Garry Lake, on the Back River, some 450 kilometres west of Tasiujaq and 300 kilometres northwest of Baker Lake. Though it was not a particularly cold day, he dressed warmly in a caribou-skin inner coat under a heavy duffel parka, caribou-skin pants, and caribou-skin *kamiit*. As he left his cabin, he did not lock the door — it was his habit to lock up only when going on extended trips. He expected to be absent only a few hours. He hitched his six dogs to the sled, ready to depart.

Emerging from his tent a hundred metres away, John Adjuk noticed the missionary's preparations and approached to talk. (Father Buliard spoke fluent Inuktitut.) Adjuk expressed concern that the weather was deteriorating. As he recalled, there was already a white haze enveloping the landscape and a light snow was falling; that, combined with the warm air, offered a warning sign — a blizzard was coming, thought Adjuk. It was not a good

Father Buliard pulling fish from his net in 1955.

day for travel, even a short distance, implored the Inuk. There are fish in the net and the dogs are hungry, countered the priest. He was determined to go, despite the weather and the warning, and his own weaknesses.

Shortly after his arrival in the Arctic many years earlier in 1939, Father Buliard fell through the ice near the Repulse Bay mission and severely froze his hands. Though his fingers were all saved, they were never the same. He suffered terribly from cold hands and a loss of dexterity. That, on top of his extremely poor eyesight, made him ill-suited for travel alone in Arctic conditions. He had, in fact, become lost and disoriented on more than one occasion. For several years prior to 1956, while based at his mission in Garry Lake, Father Buliard had been more than a little dependent on his guide and companion, Anthony Manernaluk, to keep him safe and comfortable. Although they had travelled hundreds, if not thousands, of miles together by dog team, it was always Manernaluk's skill that kept them alive.

Manernaluk, living in Rankin Inlet years later, remembered his years with Father Buliard fondly; he spoke of him as he would a father, more so than a Father. "Before, he was always cold, hands and feet," recalled Manernaluk, who came to live with the priest as an orphan at age fifteen. "But when I travelled with him, he was never cold. I kept his mitts and *kamiit* clean, no snow, not frozen." Always, when they stopped for the night, Manernaluk built their iglu in great haste — the priest never managed to acquire this skill — so Father Buliard could take shelter inside while his young Inuit companion fed the dogs and organized the camp. By the time Manernaluk crawled into the iglu, "Father Buliard had tea and bannock ready," he added with a smile.

In the summer of 1956, Manernaluk became so seriously ill that he was flown out to Baker Lake, and then Churchill, where he was diagnosed with tuberculosis. "When I was in that hospital in Churchill, Manitoba, and when the doctor told me that I had to be sent down to Brandon, to hospital, I tried to tell the doctor that I didn't want to go. I knew that Father Buliard wouldn't make it on his own and I wanted to be with him, so I tried to force the doctor to send me back home." But to no avail, with the result that Father Buliard was left to fend largely for himself.

Adjuk and his wife — in need of religious education so she could be baptized — came to camp nearby the mission. Another young man (identified in RCMP reports alternately as Andy Semigia or Anthime Simigiak, who himself perished in a storm a year later while hunting, at age nineteen) stayed some of the time with the priest in the mission. But none of them were as devoted to helping and caring for Father Buliard as Manernaluk had been full-time. So it was that, on October 24, 1956, when he set off to check his nets for fish, Father Buliard travelled alone.

"I tried to tell him that a storm might be coming," said Adjuk, who survived to over ninety with the memory. "But Father Buliard said he needed food for the dogs, and he left anyway. Shortly after, a blizzard started. The

Father Buliard with local Inuit at his mission in Garry Lake.

winds were very strong, so that the snow was blowing. He didn't make it back home. He was never seen again. If he had listened to me, he would not have died."

There has been much speculation about what happened to Father Buliard. The first version of events — ultimately proved incompatible with the facts — came with the news of Father Buliard's disappearance, which reached the outside world only several months later. An Inuk reported the third-hand details to the mission in Gjoa Haven, whence Father Pierre Henry sent word south in January 1957, saying: "This is the story. Anthime Simigiak had been visiting Father Buliard's mission. Before nightfall, Fr. Buliard accompanied him home with the dogs of the mission. Anthime's father, Sabgut, had his tent set up on the opposite shore of Garry Lake. On returning, after having accomplished this kind deed, the missionary turned away on glare ice proceeding toward the mission. Unfortunately, the dogs went straight ahead, without taking the detour to avoid the undercurrent which freezes only very late in the season. That is how the catastrophe took place."

Adjuk, who was closest to the scene, by his own account actually saw Father Buliard *after* Simigiak had departed the mission. Apparently the last to see the priest alive, Adjuk told it this way to the RCMP, an account which he has repeated on many occasions over the last fifty years of his life. After the missionary left with his dog team, the wind picked up, and the snow started drifting. Visibility reduced such that the priest could not be seen, even though his nets were, on a clear day, within site of the mission, just a few miles away across the ice. The next morning, Father Buliard had still not returned, and the storm continued. Nevertheless, Adjuk walked out to where the nets were and found nothing: no sign that anyone had been there, the ice apparently undisturbed, the nets untouched. There were no tracks visible; the blowing snow had obliterated whatever clues the dogs and sled had left. Worried, he walked to Sabgut's camp on the mainland, where he told Sabgut that the missionary had not returned. Over the next few days, Sabgut and Adjuk made some effort to search on foot for Father Buliard, or at least for some clues to his disappearance. They found nothing and, quite naturally, accepted his loss as part of the delicate balance between life and death on the barrenlands. In one Inuk observer's words at the time, "We accept death from causes such as starvation, drowning, freezing to death, much easier than white men do, as we live with it all the time." As Sabgut later told the RCMP, the dogs probably smelled some caribou and chased after them. Then the father, with his poor vision, could not find his way back home. Perhaps, he suggested, the dogs had run away with the sled — it was known that Father Buliard was adequately but not highly skilled with the dogs. Nor could he build an iglu. Probably, he froze to death, lost on the tundra.

There are, however, other theories, which may reveal nothing more than the vivid imagination of some non-Inuit writers and RCMP investigators, but which must nonetheless be told. Adjuk dismissed them unequivocally. "A person who was not there to see wrote about someone drowning Father Buliard, wrote lies about the Inuit. This liar wrote that some Inuit men drowned Father Buliard. It was his imagination. He had never even been to Garry Lake." Adjuk was referring to a book, *The Howling Arctic*, written by Ray Price, published in 1970, several years after the events, which contains a chapter about Father Buliard's disappearance. By this account, which the RCMP tried in vain to confirm through repeated investigations, a self-declared shaman named Kukshout plotted to murder the priest. (Kukshout was undoubtedly a powerful figure in the Garry Lake area but, according to Adjuk, he did not perform any "wonderful" acts, as befitting a shaman.) Kukshout had had disagreements with Father Buliard, according to the priest's diary, even though he was baptized Roman Catholic and had previously served as a guide for the missionary. The police based their rationale for motive on Kukshout's desire to remove Father Buliard's influence, which, they argued, served to diminish Kukshout's power over "his" people. The RCMP claimed to know, absolutely, that "Fr. Buliard while at Garry Lake always slept with a loaded rifle next to him at all times," because he feared attack from someone in the area.

The police theory held that Kukshout intercepted Father Buliard on the ice, en route to his nets, shot him dead, and then — with the help of two other men, Sabgut and Simigiak, who both lived in the same camp as Kukshout — put his body through a hole in the ice, where it disappeared, never to be seen again. To a significant extent, this thinking is based on what happened to the priest's dogs. Sometime later (there is confusion about whether it was days, weeks, or months later), five of the dogs returned to the mission. No one ever said they were coated in ice. They were no longer attached to a sled. Someone, theorized the RCMP, had released them. And clearly, they had not plunged through thin ice, taking Father Buliard with them. One thing is clear in the RCMP reports — a year later, Kukshout was using these dogs as his own. That, it might be argued sensibly, was only practical.

The other curious circumstance that the police offered to support their theory was the untimely disappearance of Simigiak, one of the supposed witnesses, while out hunting a year later with Kukshout, who returned to camp with Simigiak's rifle in hand. Many years later, in 1978, Sabgut reportedly committed suicide, tortured, some said, by allegations that he had played a part in the disappearance of Father Buliard. At the very least, it all adds up suspiciously. Not until the winter of 1979–80, a few months after the passing of their principal suspect, Kukshout (who, ironically, died as a result of breaking through the early winter ice on a lake near his home in Whale Cove), did the RCMP close their file on this case.

There have been other, even wilder, rumours. An officer in the Canadian army, who was responsible for retrieving Father Buliard's diary from the mission in 1961 while engaged in a northern mapping survey, reported hearing that the priest's body — with a knife still stuck in its back – had been found three hundred kilometres downstream, where the Back River reaches the ocean.

Some people suggested that an Inuk who disliked or envied Father Buliard had placed a curse on him and, when he died, a sense of responsibility befell those around Garry Lake who knew of the curse. An RCMP document records this idea and adds: "When Buliard became lost and did not return, this particular [Inuk] spread the word that his wish had been obeyed by the spirits and that he had gotten rid of the Father." Still others suggested that it was an Anglican plot to undermine the competition.

On the other hand, one police officer wrote: "To my knowledge there is no support for the rumour that Fr. Buliard was murdered." He goes on to describe other times the priest was lost on the land. "It was almost an annual occurrence with this wandering Priest, to go missing. Emergency messages were dispatched over the CBC Northern Messenger programme to the effect that 'Anyone knowing the whereabouts of Fr. Buliard travelling somewhere on the Barren Lands please contact your nearest RC Mission as soon as possible.' There was hardly a spring passed when the aforementioned did not happen. The fact this Priest would disappear and succumb to the elements of the Arctic is no surprise to me. It was surprising to me indeed that he survived as long as he did."

There were several reports that Father Buliard had predicted his own death. "Sooner or later," he told his fellow missionaries, "I'll finish by going through the ice, the rivers up there are so tricky in so many spots." One of his closest friends and his biographer, Father Charles Choque, reflects that "his idea was that time was short and he had to really do the preaching as much as he could in his life. He knew that something would happen to him. Because of the way he was living, he knew that one day something would happen." Adjuk's wife recalls that Father Buliard told her, not long before he disappeared, that the "next time he became lost, he would never come back," and he asked her not to worry, only to pray for him.

Father Choque, who served in Baker Lake during the time that Father Buliard had his mission at Garry Lake, has clearly given much thought to what happened on that tragic day in October 1956. "We don't know," he said. "We don't know exactly what happened, because we didn't see anything." Then, in what was perhaps a moment of surprising candour, he added, "Personally, I think that he was killed."

Most Inuit, however, and in particular those who knew Father Buliard, say that simply could not be. Adjuk, who was living beside the mission in 1956, points out that the Inuit needed Father Buliard; he was a source of tea and ammunition, and "because of this, we were happy about him being up there."

"We loved that man," said Madeleine Makiggaq, who was named at her baptism after Father Buliard's sister. "When I think back and start remembering him, I still feel compassion for him." Everyone who lived around Garry Lake, who survives today, says he was well liked and respected; no one speaks the slightest ill of him, or believes his death was anything but accidental.

None more so than Anthony Manernaluk, who was perhaps closer to the missionary than anyone. "When I heard of Father Buliard being lost, I felt I lost a parent." Asked to explain why the RCMP entertained their suspicions for so long, Manernaluk was blunt. "I don't know, and it's not true."

FURTHER READING

Charles Choque, *Joseph Buliard, Fisher of Men* (Churchill, Manitoba: Roman Catholic Episcopal Corporation, 1987).

THIRTY-NINE

THE CYCLE CONTINUES

The HBC's departure did not herald the end of Inuit living in Ukkusiksalik. In fact, the cycle of life continued much as before. Some families moved into the area for just a short while, a year or two, and then moved on. Not long after the post at Tasiujaq ceased operation, Peter Katokra's family moved down to Ukkusiksalik from the Repulse Bay area. He was about sixteen at the time. "We moved to Ukkusiksalik to be near game. In those days, it used to be hard to stay alive. You had to go from day to day with whatever you catch. The main reason why we moved to Ukkusiksalik was to survive, to be able to hunt caribou. The immediate area of Repulse Bay didn't always have caribou; caribou was our main reason why we moved, because there is caribou in Ukkusiksalik year round. There's also seal there and Arctic char there. I know we moved to Ukkusiksalik so we can have a better living and so that we can be happy.

"I had my grandfather Akkiutaq; my grandmother Kinakuluk; my mother, Arnarqriaq; and my father, Ulikataq; my uncle Marc Tungilik; my sister, Qiluk; my brother, Aqiutaq; also my grandparents' adopted son, Iyakak. Also, there at that time were the families of Sivaniqtoq, Tavok, Sangnirqtaq — I think there were about five families. This occurred after most people left Ukkusiksalik. Before our time, there used to be a lot of families in Ukkusiksalik area. I am quite sure that when the trading post shut down, some people left there. Although there were not as many people there, there was always somebody in Ukkusiksalik."

Other families, like Tungilik and Tavok, stayed in Ukkusiksalik for the longer term. In the mid-1950s, Marc Tungilik moved his family back down to Ukkusiksalik, when his daughter Theresie Tungilik was just old enough to remember. "We had been travelling by dog team, and it was getting dark, so we stopped for the night. I saw my father building an iglu and he was getting all frosty on his moustache from hurrying. Finally he finished the top and we got in there and I remember being too small to climb on the bed.

"I just remember my mother telling me that we used to live mostly around Ukkusiksalik when the Hudson's Bay Company and the missionaries would allow only working people to live in the settlements. Every time I think of Ukkusiksalik, I see beautiful landscape — mountainous, hilly — and fast rivers flowing." At age seven, Theresie Tungilik went away to school in Chesterfield Inlet. "That was the first time I didn't sleep in caribou bedding — it was sheets, and it was too hot. I really had a hard time sleeping that first night." At that point, Tungilik moved his family back up to Repulse Bay. Several other families made a similar move about the same time, as the community living around the trading post and the RC mission at Repulse Bay began to grow. By 1960, there was only one family left living in Ukkusiksalik — Tavok.

Tavok's daughter Elizabeth Aglukka was born on the shores of Ukkusiksalik in 1950. She grew up there, to age eighteen, when her ailing father decided it was time to move the family to the growing settlement at Repulse Bay. That marked the end of an era of occupation in Ukkusiksalik. Tavok had lived there most of his life. "The main thing that my father did when we were in Ukkusiksalik was gathering food all the time, to make sure we had enough meat and enough fish. He was constantly hunting, for our food and clothing, and to make sure the dogs had enough to eat. The clothing we had was made totally out of caribou skin; be it summer or winter, we had nothing but caribou clothing. The other main thing that my father did was constantly trap foxes and hunt seals for the skins because there was a demand for those. He used to come about twice a year [to trade in Repulse Bay]. He would come in about December, because in November the ice is still too thin, and again in May, and those would be the only two trips."

To maintain this livelihood, Tavok followed a pattern similar to the long-standing cycle of life in Ukkusiksalik. Every winter he took his wife and children to Nuvuk&it, where he built an iglu for the winter, and he hunted at the *aukanaqjuq*, "the place that does not freeze" (polynya), for

Elizabeth Aglukka at Nuvuk&it in 1996, sitting with an old cooking pot she recalled being used by her mother there, now sunk into the ground with tiny flowers growing out of it.

seals to provide meat for his family and his dogs, and oil for the *qulliq*. When Elizabeth Aglukka returned to the site of her family's camp some thirty years later in 1996, she was filled with emotion. "I felt a lump in my throat and I felt like crying but I held it back. It was to do with the fact that I haven't been here for many years and I felt the overwhelming joy in me to see it again." No place in Ukkusiksalik offers a stronger attachment for her.

Walking around Nuvuk&it in 1996, Elizabeth Aglukka's emotions were triggered time and again by the tiniest of discoveries: a medicine bottle she remembered the priest providing for her sick sister, part of her father's sealing harpoon, the mouthpiece used with a bow drill, her father's smoking pipe, a beaded bracelet she had as a child, and an old tobacco tin filled with family treasures like bullets, coloured pencils, sewing needles, and other tiny reminders of a long-forgotten past. "I would like to leave these things here," she said, looking around at Nuvuk&it with tears in her eyes. "This is where it belongs.

"This is where we had our winter camp, to be close to the floe edge, to hunt seals. In those years, we had no Coleman stove. We used only a *qulliq*; that's why we had to be near the seals."

From about November to May they lived in an iglu on that island. Other families joined them there, notably Sannertanut and Inuksatuajuk, because it was more productive for the seal hunt to have more men working together. When the days began to get warmer in May, they moved a few hundred metres east on the island, to set up their canvas tent on a gravel beach. The seal hunting continued. When the ice started getting "bad," it was time to move onto the mainland, initially to the peninsula and, once the ice cleared, each family returned to its own summer camp. The Tavok family usually spent the summer around the mouth of the Piqsimaniq River.

"In the summer months we used to have to walk by foot to look for caribou out in the land, due to the caribou being scarce. The caribou were not in a particular area — they would be all over the place, but not near our camp." Hunting caribou inland, occasionally catching seals near the river mouth, and fishing for char kept the family well occupied during the summer. When the char started to run upriver in August, attention shifted to the fish weir a few kilometres upstream. For a week or two, there were lots of fish, and the family would work together every day to empty the trap, clean the fish, and put them away in a stone storage cache. "We went all together to check the weir. When we got close we could see lots of splashing in the water. That was the best time. We enjoyed arriving to see that."

Most years Tavok stayed in his summer tent until there was enough snow, usually in December, to build an iglu upriver beside the fish weir, for ease of access to the stored food. One year, 1962, because there was a new baby girl in the family, Tavok built a *qarmaq*, a sod house. "It seemed really warm when we moved in here from the tent," remembered Elizabeth, standing at the site of her one-time home. "When we got low on seal oil, it was time to move back to Nuvuk&it." And the cycle began once more.

Finally in 1968, Tavok decided the time had come to move on. "During the winter he got very ill, to a point where he almost died," recalled his daughter Elizabeth Aglukka many years later. They were at Piqsimaniq, then moved to Nuvuk&it when he was well enough to make the move. "After that, he feared that he might leave us behind, so he headed to Repulse Bay." Presumably, he went to make arrangements. Shortly after he returned, Pie Sannertanut and Elizabeth's future husband, Honore Aglukka, arrived at Nuvuk&it to help move the whole family up to Repulse Bay. Tavok was the last to abandon what was left of the traditional way of life, to leave behind the pattern that he and many generations of Inuit before him had lived so successfully in Ukkusiksalik.

FORTY

THE TATTY FAMILY RETURNS*

Annie Tatty was adopted at birth, in 1929, by Joseph Kakak and Paula Angnaujuq, who lived near present-day Repulse Bay. They later moved down to Ukkusiksalik, to Piqsimaniq, because the hunting for caribou and seals, and the fishing for Arctic char, provided such a reliable source of food.

"The animals that we eat were the only food that we had at that time, so we had to keep on moving in order to survive. We would travel inland to hunt caribou. We would cache the meat so that the men could go get them in winter. [In September] we would start hunting seals because we would have to use the *qulliq* to make water, boiled meat, and tea. We would travel where the seals were closer, to hunt, and we would have a camp there, at Tikiraarjuk. We had a huge iglu, [so big] we had to use four *qulliq*. The *qulliq* was the only thing that can make heat either in summer or winter. The ringed seals and the caribou were hunted most often. When it was spring and summer we used to catch many fish, with *kakivak*, and sometimes we would use nets — the ones that Inuit made."

Annie Tatty remembered her father leaving their camp at Piqsimaniq or Tikiraarjuk to take his fox skins to the trading post, either at Repulse Bay

---

* In 2010, Parks Canada arranged for Annie Tatty and some of her family to visit Tasiujaq for a few days, during which time I had the opportunity to interview her for this project.

Annie Tatty during a visit to Tasiujaq in 2010.

or at Tasiujaq, at the very western (inland) extremity of Ukkusiksalik. Sometimes she went along. She knew the people who lived there — Iqungajuq, who eventually became the post manager, his daughter Tuinnaq, and his son Tatty — but she never imagined then that she would one day marry into that family and live at the post. As she relates, "Inuit used to make plans who is who that will marry," meaning it was an arranged marriage, put into effect when she was not quite sixteen years old.

———

Robert Tatty's father was W.E. "Buster" Brown, post manager at Ukkusiksalik for the outfit year 1926–27. Tatty's mother, Toota, was one of Iqungajuq's wives, so naturally Tatty became Iqungajuq's adopted son when Brown departed. After the final *qablunaat* staff left the HBC post in 1933, when Tatty was nearly six years old, Iqungajuq took over. Soon young Tatty was helping out, in effect helping to run the family business.* As a result, although he left as a young adult, for the rest of his life Tatty thought of Tasiujaq as home.

---

* See chapter 35, "An Inuk Manager for the HBC."

Robert Tatty at Tasiujaq ca. 1979.

Fast forward many years, and it is no surprise that Robert and Annie Tatty decided in 1978 to move their family back to the old Tasiujaq post in Ukkusiksalik. Robert loaded some of his family and an array of supplies (including building material used to repair houses) onto his Peterhead boat in Rankin Inlet — where he and Annie had raised their family since 1959 — and they headed north to Ukkusiksalik. She remembered it well.

"Tatty wanted to come back here. We heard about polar bear hunters, those *qablunaat* from America. If they were to come here to hunt polar bears, he [Tatty] wanted to make money because the mine was closed at that time in Rankin Inlet. He needed a job. We have some pictures of the polar bear hunters that went hunting in this area. In the winter, when the spring was near, he guided them around the Nuvuk&it area. I think there were two hunters. There are pictures of them. You could tell it was a cold, cold winter — they all have their thick caribou parkas."

The family lived at the old HBC post from the summer of 1978 until the summer of 1980. Tatty and his wife stayed in the larger building at the back, known by the HBC as the "Native house." Others came with them. The Ukaliq family stayed in the old store, the smaller building on the west side of the site. "Kaluk's [Annie's son Paul Tatty] family came here with us at the same time." They stayed in the old manager's house, the building to the east. "When Kaluk's family went home to Rankin Inlet, Kakak's [Annie's son John Tatty] family came here to live with us." At this time, the generators were moved to the old manager's house, the porch of that building was shifted over to the old store, and John Tatty's family lived in that porch. Robert and Annie Tatty continued to live in the old "Native house," with their younger son Simeoni's family (wife, Minnie, and young daughter, Dorothy) living upstairs in the loft. Food from the land was abundant. Life, it seemed, was good. Tatty was back at his true home.

Robert Tatty (centre) and other family members at Tasiujaq ca. 1979.

"During the summer we would go buy food supplies, but people from Rankin Inlet would travel to where we were [and bring some store-bought food]. We got many fox skins. We have some pictures — the fox skins are hanging. They caught many foxes. The fox skins are easy to clean but the wolf skins are harder to clean because they are very thin. I did not have any help. People, mostly from Repulse Bay, used to visit, people who went hunting to this area. They knew they can fill up their gas from here, so they used to come here to hunt.

"If Tatty did not get ill — he was ill for quite a while — we would have stayed there longer. When he got ill, we went to Rankin Inlet and right after we went to Rankin Inlet, he went away for medical — he had to have surgery. He was ill and I also told him our children have to go to school as well. He started to think that I was homesick so we went home. After the two years we have stayed here, we never did come back here," said Annie, with a hint of sadness, sitting by the shore at Tasiujaq during a 2010 trip to Ukkusiksalik with her family, going home one last time. It was a long while since 1980, when Robert Tatty moved his family back to Rankin Inlet, never to return again.

With that, the long and legendary history of the HBC buildings at Tasiujaq came to an end, fifty-five years after their hasty construction started in the autumn of 1925. All the buildings soon began to decay. The three buildings remaining at Tasiujaq are now recognized Federal Heritage Buildings because of "their historical associations, and their architectural and environmental values."[1]

FORTY-ONE

A LEGACY

Ukkusiksalik remains a special place in the hearts of the families in the Kivalliq region, on the west side of Hudson Bay, whose ancestors lived there. Some still hunt there, though not nearly as much as their forefathers did. Some see it as a tourism opportunity, knowing the landscape's intrinsic appeal as they do. In the mid-1980s, three men with family connections to Ukkusiksalik opened Sila Lodge on the north shore of Wager Bay, to attract naturalists and provide employment, but the economics of the operation could not be sustained. Even at that time, there was already talk that one day, after the land claims were settled, the federal government would establish a national park there. Wager Bay had been selected in 1978 as a potential site for one of five proposed national parks north of sixty (north of the provincial boundary across the top of Manitoba, Saskatchewan, and Alberta).

The process accelerated in the 1990s, especially after the Nunavut land claim was settled in 1993 following many years of negotiations between the Inuit of Nunavut and the federal government. The settlement allowed developments of all sorts to move forward, from mines to national parks, and gave Inuit a measure of self-determination within the new territory. In 2003, Parks Canada signed the Inuit Impact and Benefit Agreement, which provided the green light to begin operation of Ukkusiksalik National Park, one of Canada's most remote. Nevertheless, it means that a few local Inuit now have jobs with Parks Canada and others may in the future find opportunities

Theresa Kopak (left) and Sarah Sivaniqtoq — each of their grandfathers was a valued informant — visiting the land of their ancestors around Ukkusiksalik in 1996.

in guiding and outfitting. Inuit retain their right to hunt for subsistence purposes within this and other national parks in Nunavut.

Francis Kaput, an elder in Rankin Inlet, said, "I would like to see Ukkusiksalik become a national park. Every bay, every point around Wager Bay has a name because this is where so much happened. It is important to preserve that knowledge. Ukkusiksalik is us. It's part of our culture."

Guy Amarok of Chesterfield Inlet added his support: "If it becomes a national park, then there will be no development that will destroy the land."

These are ringing endorsements which, while not universal, are widely shared among Inuit of the region. Such is the emotional attachment to Ukkusiksalik still today.

There is a reverence among Ukkusiksalingmiut toward their homeland. Yet, when asked, there was nowhere that any of its former residents thought should be off-limits to visitors, but always with the important proviso that visitors not harm the land or the old sites, and that they not interfere with Inuit use of their traditional hunting grounds.

During a return visit in 1996, her first in nearly thirty years, Elizabeth Aglukka sat on the ground at the site of her family's old spring camp in

Nuvuk&it, examining the artifacts they had left behind, and she said, "I would like these things left here, alone, untouched." It's acceptable in her eyes (though against the law that protects archaeological sites) for someone to pick up an item to look at it, she offered, so long as they "put it back where it belongs" afterward. "I would not like to see someone take something from here to put in a museum or to sell. I'd rather leave all the things here." Even Elizabeth left the site of her childhood home without taking a souvenir.

Today, Wager Bay is one of those spots, found frequently in the North, where a wild and rugged landscape opens the visitor's eyes to a new sort of beauty and appreciation of natural splendour, yet which somehow remains in complete harmony with its depth of historical occupation by other humans. The duality is a difficult one for the typical visitor from southern Canada or the United States or Europe, where the experience of human occupation has typically meant the destruction of the natural setting. Here in Ukkusiksalik history is everywhere, and yet it is apparent only upon close inspection. As with a wildflower, you can't see it from the air, but once standing on the shores of Ukkusiksalik, when you look down at the ground beneath your feet, the colour and detail and enduring nature of that tiny flower — and the history of that land — will enter your soul. Once discovered, it is captivating.

As Marc Tungilik said only weeks before he passed away in 1986, reflecting back on his life, "People are always happy to go to a plentiful land — that is how I felt about going to Ukkusiksalik."

ENVOI

The elders whose stories are the centrepiece of this tableau all understood — indeed, offered the very embodiment of — the importance of Inuit traditional knowledge, not only in the existential *Inuit Qaujimajatuqangit* sense — as a way of seeing the world — but equally in the value of the old stories as a reflection of where they had come from.

When Tuinnaq Kanayuk Bruce recounted the story of the tragedy at Qamanikuluk and then said: "I am saying the same words to you that Ajaruq said to his mother when he told this story. It is not a legend. It is a true story," we can believe her. For this is how stories from the land have been transmitted through the generations for centuries.

I hope we have all learned from this experience: learned that the land is more than empty tundra, beautiful though that is; learned that the landscape is a matrix of old trails and travel routes; learned that the spirits of people who travelled there remain a fundamental part of that landscape; and learned that their stories are woven into this complex tapestry's dimensions of time and place.

THE TRADERS' JOURNALS

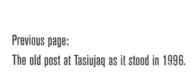

Previous page:
The old post at Tasiujaq as it stood in 1996.

THE TRADERS' JOURNALS

These excerpted passages from the *qablunaat* traders' HBC post journals reflect Inuit activity at and visits to the post, as seen through the eyes of the traders. The original post journals, preserved at the Hudson's Bay Company Archives (B492 a/1 to a/10) in Winnipeg, Manitoba, are hardcover books approximately ten by fourteen inches. They are organized by "outfit" in the manner used by the HBC from the beginning in 1670. An outfit commenced on the first day of June each year and concluded on the last day of May the next year. The spelling and syntax of the originals have been retained. In particular, the more careful reader will note that the *qablunaat* authors of these journal entries often had great difficulty with Inuit names and terminology. As much as possible, the text below adheres accurately to the varied spellings used by the traders.

September 7	MS *Fort Chesterfield* successfully made passage through falls and came to anchor here in harbour. Mssrs. Learmonth and Thom arranged site for buildings. Discharged about half of freight.
September 9	all hand on house building, schooner left for Repulse in A.M.
October 1	Very cold and snowing.
October 6	harbour frozen over almost to entrance.
October 8	Finished all outside work on store.
October 9	Brought food from tents to store.
October 10	Very raw weather, commenced work on outside of dwelling house.
October 14	Snow falling all day, finished ceiling inside house.
October 25	calm and cold, men have four seals.
October 26	Very cold, Samson's wife who has been failing steadily since spring died in the early hours of the morning. This necessitates the secession of work of the community for three days and five for the husband.
October 30	Cold and clear with a sharp wind from North. Hauled motor boat out on ice with dogs and arranged her for winter. Tessyooyuk [Tasiujaq] covered with ice.
October 31	extremely cold, hanging linoleum, five deer [caribou] passed within a mile of post, got all five.
November 1	Pupick in from camp killed five deer, also saw six wolves within one half mile of post.
November 2	Occupied house for first time last night. Owing to the unsuitability of snow — only one native occupies igloo so far.
November 9	Attuk in from camp on his way to pick up sled on land, brought some very fine salmon trout [Arctic char].
November 10	Atttuk and Keeluck [Kreelak] out in a.m. Tommy after seal on ice, but failed to get one. One set of shelves completed.
November 11	Sik-Sak [Siksaaq] got seal on ice. Wolves still in vicinity but very wary.

November 12   All natives now occupying igloos, last of them moved today from tents.

November 25   Pupick in and out, reports no sign of deer [caribou], and very little sign of foxes.

November 28   Men in from traps. Killed six deer and got one fox on way in — signs of foxes very scarce according to their reports.

December 6   Omitted to mention that men intend to cover as much trail as possible towards the Backs River or Ookeshikshellik [Utkuhiksalik] natives, mainly to assist the guide Sik-Sak [Siksaaq] who seems rather hazy on it as it must have been almost ten to fifteen years since he was across it.

December 10   Papak in from camp, first visit since freeze-up. No deer around. Although managing to kill seal from time to time at open water.

December 11   Papak left early morning for camp.

December 12   Attak in from camp.

December 25   Spent a very quick Christmas as all natives are away at present. Intend to hold New Year instead.

December 31   Drifting hard, cannot see shore from house. Men in from trapping grounds, saw only one deer [caribou], but it got away. Also saw tracks of several muskoxen on land, but did not go after them much as they would have liked to.

January 1   Held dance in evening, also gave supper to natives, enjoyable day spent by all.

January 22   Keeluck [Kreelak] and Kaffee [Kapik] in from camp on Kaminallo [Qamanaaluk], killed several deer a few days ago.

January 23   Keeluck and Kaffee left in early morning for camp.

January 29   Men in from traps; were delayed on account of drifting weather. Managed to kill eight deer [caribou] and got a few foxes. Samson got a wolf.

February 3   Left with two sleds, natives Samson and Dick for Backs River or native camps in that vicinity.

March 7	Arrived home 8 p.m. last night. Found natives after travelling all over the country (it seemed) living on the sea ice close to the mouth of Hayes River where they exist by fishing — not one of them has ever been in this direction, but now have hopes of seeing them in spring now that we have opened the route. The journey although taking us all this time, as we had no knowledge of the country, can easily be accomplished in the spring in five to six days average travelling. Dogs in very poor condition although plenty deer met with, but intensely cold the whole time. Came home in seven days.
March 16	Sik-Sak [Siksaaq] and Keemallinckgo arrived in p.m. Keemallinckgo is the first of the natives from Hayes River. They report no deer [caribou] near Sik-Sak's igloo but many wolves.
April 10	left for Backs River today taking Sik-Sak as a guide. Intend to try and catch up with them — have hopes of bringing any natives back who wish to trade.
April 23	Arrived in evening. Many deer inland.
May 15	Kaam-o-kauk [Qamukkaaq] and Kec-malliaukz with families arrived in from Backs River. Took thirteen days for Johnny, but mainly on account of deer [caribou] hunting, failed to find cache of meat that we left for him — killed nine deer on way in.
May 26	Thaw commenced in earnest it seems.

OUTFIT 257, 1926–27

June 3	Sik-Sak and family in, also Papak.
June 4	Papak, Kudlo, Kaffee and Keemalliark-jo out in a.m. to camp down inlet. Papak who has returned from Chesterfield reports the world is to cease in three years time citing one of the priests as his authority.
June 27	ice in harbour broke up.

August 14	Mr. Brown and natives Dick, Nugjuq and the latter's wife and their children, arrived at the post about 9 a.m. Worked around the post and unloaded motor boat. Natives Tommy and Deaf Johnnie arrived back from a seal hunt in early p.m. Brought in several deer. Rationed natives Dick, Tommy, Deaf Johnnie and Nugjuk with the intention of sending two of them to hunt dog feed.
September 9	Schooner arrived at post about 8 p.m.
September 10	all hands busy unloading cargo. By night nothing but coal remained to be taken off.
September 11	The remainder of cargo was unloaded, some of the schooner's crew off to the creek to draw water as the supply is finished aboard. The schooner is expected to pull out tomorrow. A dance was held for the natives tonight and turned out a great success.
September 12	The *Fort Chesterfield* pulled out for Chesterfield around 8 a.m. Deaf Johnnie and family and dogs went with her. The said native is expected to be employed at Chesterfield until such time as he can take Mr. J. Robertson back to Wager Inlet.
September 17	Gale from the east — snow — outside work impossible, staff busy at odd jobs inside.
September 27	Natives Sik-Sak and Kumallinjook with Dick as interpreter had their accounts explained to them as they are no longer needed at the post.
September 29	Staff busy erecting a water closet.
September 30	Dick off deer [caribou] hunting this morning. Mr Brown working on W.c. Mr McHardy started making drawing table for his room. Tommy, Kudluck, Kudlo and Sutoxi came in on motor boat around 10 p.m. bringing seals from cache. They sailed the whole trip as none of them understood motors.
October 8	22°F The well known superstition of the natives, forbidding the making of deer [caribou] skin clothes until it is possible to build an igloo had no effect on Dick's two wives when Mr Brown wished them to start right away making some clothes for him. It is interesting to note that the Chesterfield natives who are supposed to be Christians still hold to this belief.

October 18   21°F Mr Hardy discovered about fifty ptarmigan close to the post. Between them, Dick and Mr McHardy got thirty-five and these kept Dick's two wives busy for some time plucking.

October 29   5°F The front door was blocked for the winter. Tessyooyak [Tasiujaq] now all frozen over.

November 10   3° The lamps had to be lit around 4:30 p.m.

December 16   Two natives by the name of Sooeeruk and Tnookritwayjook, both strange to the post, arrived around 6:15 p.m. Their camp is about three days from here on this side of Wager Inlet.

December 17   -18° Staff with Dick as interpreter traded with Sooeeruk and Tnooksituayjook.

December 25   The natives all enjoyed a good feed followed by a dance held in the house at night.

December 27   All natives who came in for Xmas pulled out for their various camps.

January 24   -58°F, last night temperature was 40° below with a sharp northwest wind.

February 1   -25°F, Mr Brown, Dick and Samson busy getting ready to pull out tomorrow. Mr Brown means to find out why the Ookushikshillik [Utkuhiksalik] natives have not visited the post.

February 2   Mr Brown, Dick and Samson left. Around 10 p.m. Albert and his wife pulled in from Repulse Bay bringing mail from the Post.

Febraury 4   Albert and Mr Brown and the whole troop rushed back to the post around about 3 a.m. The supplies and stuff were cached in an igloo about a day away. As Albert agreed to go to Chesterfield, Mr Brown decided to take advantage of the fact and get Wager Inlet mail ready.

February 13   -46°, Around 4 p.m. Mr Learmonth, Sam Voisey and Nowyak pulled in from Chesterfield. They took fifteen days for the trip.

February 26   Mr Learmonth, Sam Voisey and Albert and his family pulled out for Baker Lake.

March 2	-17°F, Mr Brown, Dick and Samson pulled out this morning to Backs River.
March 6	-40°F, with the exception of Kumallarjook, all hunters trading at this post are now camped out at various places down the inlet.
April 21	Gale. The force of the wind is so great that the snow was driven into both bedrooms coming in from the sides of the storm windows and now the inside ones.

OUTFIT 258, 1927–28

June 9	20°F, water on top of ice in harbour.
June 10	saw ducks.
July 3	lots of fish in net.
July 4	33 fish.
July 5	61 fish.
July 6	81 fish.
July 7	92 fish.
July 8	37 fish + 1 pair of loons.
July 9	45 fish.
July 10	50 fish.
July 11	16 fish + 1 loon alive.
July 12	18 fish.
July 13	7 fish, working on jetty.
July 14	Staff busy typing out inventory. Only three fish caught today.
July 15	Staff making ready for leaving. Only three fish caught.
July 16	Rations were issued up to the 16th of August. Staff making ready to pull out tomorrow if all well.
July 17	Dull with north wind and raining after. Staff loaded up and pulled out around 4 p.m. Had to wait a couple of hours at the narrows to make the passage safely. Went ashore in little harbour about 14 miles further on to find suitable spot for landing cargo in case supply steamer decides to come up this summer.

July 20	Fair with northwest wind. Raining once or twice. Passed Fullerton around 10 a.m., then Depot Island around 5 p.m. Arrived Chesterfield about midnight. Had sail and engine most of day. Batteries almost finished. While bucking wind and tide the engine downed gasoline at the rate of two gallons per hour.
August 5	The supply ship *Nascopie* pulled in around 5 p.m. Mr Parsons and Mr Berthé who is representing Revillon Frères were aboard. Capt Mack and Capt Jackson, both of the *Harmony* acted as skippers. A cargo, numbers of whale boats and canoes were landed tonight.
August 10	The supply ship *Nascopie* pulled out for Southampton around 2 p.m. Going out on her on furlough from this sub-district are Mssrs Copland and Skinner. Mr Skinner was later dropped off at Southampton to take charge as it was necessary for Mr Sam Ford to go out for an operation. Mr Leith, who has been appointed post manager of Wager Inlet, came ashore for good this afternoon.
August 11	Mr Leith and Mr McHardy busy gathering some supplies to go up to Wager Inlet immediately as the dependents of the post servants will soon be out of rations.
August 12	Dull with northeast wind. Mr McHardy with Deaf Johnny and Billy set off around 6 a.m. on the launch and with a whaleboat in tow. Both boats carrying supplies. Heavy swell all day. Were delayed for some time just north of Depot Island on account of dense mist. Dropped anchor about half way between Depot and Fullerton.
August 13	Fair and clear overhead. Strong head wind and choppy sea. As both boats were shipping water it was decided to stop for a little in the hopes that the wind would abate. While just finishing lunch a bear was seen sunning itself on the rocks close by. Johnny shot it. Pulled out around 3 p.m. with the wind decreasing and anchored for the night at Whale Point.

August 15	Fine day with slight head wind. Went shore at mouth of Wager to get some water and got caught by tide falling. While waiting Billy shot a couple of deer [caribou]. Got off safely but had continual engine trouble and considerable time passed before she would run anyway decent. As a matter of fact the outfit only got some twelve miles up the Inlet when the tide turned and they were forced into a small harbour for the boat was making no progress against the current. To give an idea of how the water drops it may be mentioned that the boats were anchored some 25 yards from a steep shore and in about 3 fathoms (18 feet) of water. When the tide went out the boats were aground.
August 25	Outfit pulled out at 3 a.m. taking with them Johnny's whaleboat and rest of supplies and arrived at post around 9 a.m. Plenty of fish being caught in the nets now.
September 28	Sik-Sak [Siksaaq], Pupic, Inookortwayack, Swesuk, Nugjook all pulled in to trade. With the aid of the first three the Peterhead [just arrived the day before from Chesterfield] was unloaded.
September 30	Kuluck, Kaffee, Kudlo, Sooklooto came in to trade. The Peterhead boat was beached in the afternoon. Ice forming in harbour. The said ice strong enough to sear the timber of a boat.
October 30	Dick, Samson, Tommy, Mulluk and Sutoxi pulled out in afternoon to hunt.
November 6	-10°F, Clear with decrease in wind. The wind blew so strong last night that driven snow was forced thru the window frames of both bedrooms and kitchen. Also a pile of lumber flooring was scattered about like matches. During the early hours of the morning native Dick's wife Tootah gave birth to a boy.
November 8	-17°F, Hunters returned, 21 deer [caribou], one fox sign seen.
November 10	-14°F, Kuluck came in with some fish to trade. Reports no sign of foxes around Kauminallo lake where he and Nigjook are camped
November 11	Inookaitwajook in to trade at night. He is camped some ten miles past the narrows. No fox sign to speak of.
November 21	-30°F, Tommy set some traps at head of lake, saw no fox signs but plenty of rabbits [Arctic hare] and ptarmigan tracks.
November 28	-42°F, Nogjook, Keeluck and Sooeisuk pulled in to trade.

November 30 -28°F, Around 11 p.m. natives Eelanack, Kaumakauk [Qamukkaaq] and two boys pulled in. Eelanack reports poor deer [caribou] hunting last summer and fall at Backs River, not many fox signs.

December 13 -20°F, Sik-Sak [Siksaaq] and Kudlo came in to trade. No fox signs or any game around. They are camped inland south of the post.

December 25 -35°F, A dance was held at night which proved a great success.

December 28 -52°F, Inookoitwajook pulled in to trade in the early morning.

December 29 -45°F, Pupic pulled in to trade in afternoon.

December 30 -50°F, Tommy on foxes. Dick and Mulluk pulled in from their traps. No foxes and no signs of any.

January 4 -47°F, Tommy pulled in from traps. No luck.

January 8 -49°F, Anungwak and Pulooagjook arrived from Repulse Bay with the mail from outside. They took six days to make the trip.

January 13 -38°F, Attuk and Nuvuk pulled in to trade. They say there are no foxes around.

January 15 -42°F, Keemalliajook and Elanack's son arrived today. They are to take the mail across to Baker Lake, also Mr McHardy accompanying them.

January 19 -33°F, Mr McHardy, Mulluk and Keemalliajook made a start for Baker Lake but had to abandon the trip shortly afterwards as Keemalliajook was in such pain that he was unable to walk. The cause of the pain is a mystery. Tommy on foxes.

January 21 -42°F, Mr McHardy and natives pulled out this morning for Baker Lake. Dick back from traps but no luck.

February 19 -15°F, Keeluck came in last night with three foxes. He reports that there are no signs of any foxes down the inlet.

February 20 -11°F, Dick back from traps. He got one fox and two ermine.

February 24 -11°F, Tommy back from traps, no luck.

March 22	-7°F, Mr H. Conn, General Inspector of the Hudson's Bay Company, accompanied by Mr McKechni arrived here today from King Williams Island. They had with them Elanack who acted as guide for them. They will stay here for a few days and will then proceed to Chesterfield.
April 21	+29°F, first snowbird [snow bunting] seen today, this being signs of an early spring.
April 26	+15°F, Tommy and Samson came in 4 o'clock this morning from Chesterfield. Mr Ford expected tomorrow from Baker Lake with the mail. Opick and Nuvuk came in with dog feed to trade.
April 28	+6°F, Mr Ford and natives arrived this morning at 8 o'clock from Baker Lake having taken 17 days to cross. Lots of deer [caribou] seen.
April 29	+4°F, Samson and Deaf Johnnie left to bring up more supplies from down the river where the coast boat was lost.
May 17	+1°F, Mr Leith arrived here late last night.
May 29	zero °F, staff busy on inventory.

OUTFIT 259, 1928–29

June 4	+19°F, snow disappearing fast, both creeks behind the post opened today, signs of an early spring.
June 8	16°F, Mr Leith, Mr Ford, natives left to go down to coast boat to look over the supplies that are still there. Very bad going.
June 17	16°F, Mr Leith, Mr Ford, natives back. After looking over the coast boat I find that there is no chance of saving her at all. As soon as the ice begins to move out I think she will go with it.
June 18	+33°F, Staff busy bailing up furs.
June 20	+30°F, caulking Peterhead boat. Set three nets out close to creek and caught 23 fish in two and half hours, but there is very little water opened up yet.
June 21	32°F, 27 fish caught.

June 22	31°F, 58 fish.
June 23	35°F, 27 fish.
June 25	31°F, 59 fish.
June 26	33 fish.
June 27	33°F, foggy, 39 fish.
June 28	32°F, rain, 40 fish.
June 29	35°F, 15 fish.
June 30	33°F, 38 fish.
July 1	Plenty of mosquitoes around. 25 fish.
July 2	32°F, 51 fish.
July 3	32°F, 21 fish, rations issued.
July 4	42°F, mosquitoes very bad today, 17 fish.
July 7	35°F, the fish are getting very scarce, ten fish.
July 8	32°F, one fish. Everybody indoors today as it is too wet.
July 14	43°F, Staff busy getting ready to leave for Chesterfield. The Inlet is still frozen solid but will try to work along the shore.
July 16	34°F, Staff and natives loading up Peterhead boat and motorboat to be ready to leave tomorrow. Giving out rations at night. Tommy and Sutoxi staying behind to look after seal nets and also the post.
August 18	Arrived back at post by MS *Fort Chesterfield* from Chesterfield Inlet. Five days journey up, good weather all the way. Unloading deck load, part of hold load. Weather fine.
August 19	Finished unloading schooner today, also Peterhead boat which was towed up by schooner.
August 20	+41°F, Schooner pulled out 10:30 a.m.
August 21	caught 30 fish.
August 27	Mr Hunter working in store and office. Messrs Spence and Ogilvie working on wireless outfit.
September 4	St Paul, Winnipeg, Toronto tonight on the radio.
September 30	skin of ice over harbour.
October 7	No sign of schooner yet, afraid she is not coming.
October 8	MS *Fort Chesterfield* with Mr Learmonth aboard arrived in p.m.
October 9	Finished unloading schooner by dinnertime. Trading with schooner crew.

October 10	cold and drifting snow. Schooner pulled out at 8 a.m. today.
October 14	harbour frozen right over.
November 4	rest of staff skating in a.m. Listened to church service from Winnipeg and Yorkston in evening.
November 6	Listened to election results tonight from Winnipeg and various American stations and learned that Hoover had walked off with it.
November 11	Sunday observances as usual.
December 3	Heard the first hockey game of the season between teams of the CPR and CLK, broadcasted in p.m. Also that King George's condition was much about the same.
December 16	Writing letters for packet, which soon ought to be down from Repulse.
December 20	In office typing requisitions etc.
December 25	Xmas Day. Usual festivities for natives.
December 26	All hands recuperating from yesterday's party.
December 29	Dick laid up with cold. Learned that the MS *Fort Chesterfield* is wintering at Churchill. Also received greeting from Mr Parsons to the northern staff.
December 31	The *Nascopie* probably will visit Repulse and Wager next summer.
January 6	Repulse packet arrived tonight accompanied by Albert and Mad Eye.
January 7	Fixing up mail which will go to Baker Lake by way of Backs River.
January 8	Blowing and drifting.
March 11	Kaffee and Keiluck arrived in, report that their father Sic-Sac is sick.
April 6	Rations issued. Wonderful display of northern lights at night.
April 7	Kaffee and Keeluck arrived in — five foxes.
April 10	W.A. Harding and Deaf Johnny pulled out for Chesterfield with mail packet about eight this morning.
April 14	A snow bird [snow bunting] was seen today, being the first one of the season.

| April 21 | Angi-oo-kuk and Oak-koo-slook, brothers from Backs River, in with 11 foxes. |
| April 23 | Mun-u-lak and Keeluck came in, 1 fox, 8 seals. |

OUTFIT 260, 1929–30

September 5	Sky overcast drizzling practically all day. *Ungava* arrived at 11:30. General Inspector Hugh Conn, Mr Learmonth and Mr Ford the new post manager on board her. All hands busy unloading cargo in the afternoon. Everything ashore by evening. The carpenters on board the *Ungava* commenced on the foundation of the 20' x 15' warehouse being built at the harbour.
September 6	The *Ungava* pulled out about six this morning. Mr Brown, Mr Hunter and Mr _____ who are going out on furlough went on board.
September 22	Fine day, no wind. Harbour frozen over right out to point. Ice about ½" thick. Dick's two wives are both down with the flu today.
September 28	Dull day, wind as yesterday. Rations issued as usual. Staff skating on the harbour ice in the afternoon. Attukta's boy came in this evening wanting some medicine, as Mrs Attukta is sick. Wonderful radio reception tonight.
September 29	Tootah, Dick's wife, is still confined to bed yet with the flu.
October 3	Dull, snowing, wind SE. Samson's mother who has been failing steadily of late passed away about midnight last night. She was buried in the forenoon only a short distance to the north of the post.
October 7	Attukta arrived in this evening to report that his wife had died five days ago. According to native Dick the old lady strangled herself to death. Apparently she has been very ill for some time and had given up hopes of recovering and wanted to die so, while her husband was away from camp she ordered the children out of the tent and committed the deed.
November 4	Lamps have to be lighted at four o'clock.

November 6   Eelanak reports lots of fox tracks around Backs River. Very little deer [caribou] shot during summer by natives around Backs River; result, natives hungry.

November 8   Sutoxi is going away with the former [Eelanak] in accordance with the wish of his father [Dick] who thinks he will be able to get more furs at Backs River. Eelanak stated he gets more goods for his fur here than at KWI [King William Island] so I asked him to show the natives around his camp just what he got for a fox so that they too can see the reason he has of trading at the post. Eelanak also stated a native who was dying told his relatives how he came across a beacon a few years ago; he looked into the base of same and found some books which he tore apart and practically destroyed them all — his guilty conscience must have worried him, as this was absolutely the first time he ever mentioned anything to any natives about his find. I asked Eelanak to try and bring some pieces if he could get any into the post when he comes in, in the spring.

November 11   Dick banking up his igloo. Weighted one of the fish Eelanak brought in, 40 lbs as it was, frozen and ungutted.

November 12   Around 10 p.m. Keeluck arrived in, has 6 bear skins to trade. According to him fox tracks are fairly numerous all the way in and foxes have been around dog feed caches down the Inlet.

November 19   Arngnawa, Attaka and Nowyak (Johnny's boy) arrived in tonight with some foxes to trade. They report foxes fairly numerous but seal and deer [caribou] especially the latter very scarce. Two days ago Deaf Johnny nearly lost his life. It appears he was off sealing when the ice gave way on which he was walking — luckily for him he was close to the land and managed, Lord knows how, to get onto the shore ice and after crawling a mile or so on his hands and knees reached his igloo and the next day was none the worse for his dunking except the loss of his rifle.

November 29   First storm of winter and drifts have formed around the building up to five feet deep in about four hours.

December 5   Clearer, wind not so strong, signs of storm abating. Samson, Puttik and Dick went up to the river and got two cometic [*qamutik*] loads of ice. Staff taking inventory of store, which by the way is a very cold job. Radio poor.

December 9   Three natives (Aeeoguak, Punetuk, and Tunney) arrived from Backs River with about twenty foxes to trade. They have been fairly hard up owing to the scarcity of deer [caribou] and their dogs are in very bad shape. It has taken them ten sleeps to reach here from their camp.

December 18   The sun apparently does not want to shine on the post, during the last week it has never made its appearance above the hills.

December 20   Native Munuluk and Attukta's boy came in tonight, report lots of foxes down inlet.

December 21   J. Spence issued rations to the families of Post Servants.

December 22   Native Muneelak and Eepukna left around 8:30 a.m. so as to make their camp tonight. They intend moving their camps further down the Inlet as they have heard that the foxes are fairly plentiful there.

December 23   Clear bright day with fairly light wind coming from north. Staff busy typing our inventory. Natives Sutoxi, Eeluetuk and Eenookruk arrived from Backs River today with fur to trade. Most of the Backs River natives are sick and I am afraid, according to Sutoxi, a few will have passed away before spring, probably an epidemic of flu.

December 24   Weather and wind as yesterday. Traded a few foxes with Tommy and Angnaw, who bought some clothes for party tomorrow. Cooking up for tomorrow's feed to natives.

December 25   Dull and overcast, calm, snowing a little. Had all the natives in tonight, gave them a feed and presents, after which they enjoyed themselves dancing for the rest of the evening. The music was supplied by native Tommy on a five dollar accordion. Everyone enjoyed themselves. The following are the names of natives who enjoyed the celebrations

December 30	Blowing and drifting from south. Owing to weather none of the natives left. Dick's wife Neeako [Niaqukittuq] had a baby boy this morning at 10 but unfortunately it died about three hours after its birth. Cause unknown. Samson and Dick making snow porch at side entrance of house. Staff busy on books, i.e. closing of December accounts and putting finishing touches on inventory.
December 31	Dull and overcast, blowing hard from south, milder. Dick and Samson finished snow porch. Staff employed at office work. None of the natives left owing to bad weather. Neeako's baby was buried today. So endeth 1929. May 1930 be a prosperous one.
January 24	Samson and Staff working in store, rather a cold job! Sun disappears at 2:30 and rises around 9:55.
February 4	Bright; blowing and drifting hard from north.
February 20	According to Mr Ford the natives are all scared of native Attuka, whom they are afraid has gone a little off his napper through losing his wife.
March 25	Samson and boy returned this evening, Samson with three foxes to his credit. Magnificent display of northern lights tonight.
March 29	The women are at present employed skinning and cleaning the fox skins.
April 2	Blowing yesterday and slightly worse if anything. During the night the wind swung around to its old position NW blowing so fierce at times that it was impossible to see tractor building. The front windows and door of house are covered over with snow.
April 27	three Backs River hunters arrived in
May 5	two Backs River natives in this afternoon
May 20	natives Arngnawa, Tommy and Samson left with their families for their spring camps. Water is beginning to come up through the cracks in the ice in front of post.
May 21	the partridge [ptarmigan] are literally out in the thousands, shot thirty-four.
May 23	snow melting today — this is the first Saturday for a year or so that no rations have been issued — sun sets around 9:30 now.

| May 27 | Lots of flies have come to life and are having a gay time after their long sleep trying to break the windows in store. |
| May 31 | still, dull, strong wind from east. The sun didn't make its appearance today. Staff working on inventory, a few ground birds were noticed around the Post, the first to be seen this spring. So endeth Outfit 260, which considering all things has been a fair one, as regards fur and not too bad in other ways. Here's hoping the Post never goes beneath the past Outfit figures. |

OUTFIT 261, 1930–31

June 1	The new outfit opened with the usual spring weather for this time of year. Dull but fairly warm, moderate wind from southeast. The snow is disappearing fast and little streams of water are appearing on the hillsides. Staff J.L. Ford, manager and J. Spence, clerk, tidying up dwelling house and sundry jobs. Water coming up the cracks in great style tonight, when tide came up.
June 3	Blowing a gale from northeast, drifting a little just the snow that fell yesterday as the rest of it is too wet to drift. Real wintry looking, apparently old man winter is dying with his boots on. J. Spence writing up Expenditure, J.L. Ford closing off 260 books.
June 8	River at the end of the harbour starting to run today.
June 12	J. Spence confined to bed with acute pains in stomach, probably appendicitis.
June 15	J. Spence worse today. Most of the snow is gone now — found a hawk's nest with three eggs in it. On looking over last year's diary I consider we are a week ahead of a normal year.
June 19	Natives Dick, Samson, Puttik, Munleeak and Pupic came in tonight. Dick's wife has a pretty bad hand and I intend going down to harbour tomorrow to fix it up.
June 20	J. Ford traded with the natives who came in yesterday. Left for Depot at Morso Harbour to doctor up Toota's hand, around 4 p.m.

June 24	Raining most of day, moderate wind from southeast. J. Spence still in bed, I intend sending him down to Chesterfield with Dick.
August 24	The Nascopie arrived yesterday at Harbour, unloading supplies inside two hours.
December 25	Min -42°F, Max -14°F. Had all natives in for the usual dance which lasted until the wee small hours.
December 29	Min -42°F, Max -16°F. All natives left this morning for their respective camps.
December 31	Min -40°F, Max -43°F. So endeth another year and needless to say we celebrated in the usual manner although the "spirits" were rather scarce, and tasted morish, Cheers 1930.
January 13	Clear and bright with moderate wind from northwest. Sutoni and Kaffee got a load of ice. Staff sundry work. Natives Keeluk and Kudlo arrived around 6:30 p.m. stopping here for a day or so enroute to Sic-Sac's camp at Cominalow [Qamanaaluk]. The former has now had a young wife bestowed upon him, she is Samson's wife's eldest girl and needless to say, Keeluk is all tickled up the back and elsewhere, I suppose.
January 21	Min -55°F, Max -44°F. Eladnak's wife and two sons arrived in around 6:00 p.m. with the very sad news of Eladnak's death.
March 22	Min -40°F, Max -20°F. Natives Tommy and Pupic arrived in around 4:15 p.m., their families are pretty short of grub and they wanted to trade tonight, so as to get away tomorrow, finished trading around 12 p.m. These natives stated that the floe at the mouth of Inlet is pretty bad, owing to the rough ice and a cometic [qamutik] can only get within a couple of miles from the water, they also think that ice has formed across to Southampton Island from Nuvuk.
March 27	Min -20°F, Max -2°F. Puttik and Nickotee came in around 5 p.m. and traded nine foxes, they intend leaving tomorrow for their parents' camp.
April 8	Min -26°F, Max +6°F. Most of the Backs River natives have lost all their dogs, through sickness, making it impossible for them to make the trip in.

May 31	Min +28°F, Max +62°F. Lots of water appearing around the shores this evening. Pupic and family left this evening for camp in Wager Inlet. Cheers 261, the best outfit since the post has been established for fur — here's hoping the future outfits will live up to your standard — so long.

OUTFIT 262, 1931–32

July 22	Min 44°F, Max 82°F. Natives Samson, Tommy & Arngnawa with their respective families arrived at post in very early a.m. having travelled up the Inlet in two whale-boats, traded, and left again shortly after noon with Dick, Sutoxi, Keeluk and their families, a great exodus.
September 6	Min 34°F, Max 52°F. Dick, Sutoxi, Ameanak, Arnenawa, Albert, Sooeesuk, Teeomiak and their respective families arrived at post at noon, in two whale-boats, shortly after their arrival Pupic and Auktuk arrived from Cominalloq [Qamanaaluk] Lake.
September 15	Min 26°F, Max 36°F. Keemilleajook and Toolooak, two Backs River natives, who with their families have walked the intervening distance between Wager and Cockburn Bay.
September 29	Min 20°F, Max 32°F. The supply schooner MS *Fort Severn* arrived here late this evening and successfully discharged all cargo by 3 a.m.
January 15	Sic-Sak [Siksaaq], Auktuk & Kaffee arrived about noon. They have been frieghting some of their belongings down to the floe. Toolooak back to normal. Armitingwak was doctored up in a.m. as he had managed to give himself a very bad freeze. All natives from Cominalow [Qamanaaluk] Lake are now in vicinity of post, en route to the floe — between them all they have an immense number of goods and chattels, much time will be taken before all their belongings are taken down to the floe, it can only be accomplished in relays. This is by far the best policy for these natives, as naturally in Cominlow [Qamanaaluk] vicinity seal hunting is impossible.
February 20	enjoyed a game of football on the ice with natives.
March 16	Blizzard raging outside.

May 17	Sic-Sac & Keeluk arrived at post at 10:30 a.m. They stated that Constable MacCormack of the Royal Canadian Mounted Police, and native Noovia, passed the mouth of Wager Inlet en route for Repulse Bay. An RC Missionary and two natives were also accomplying the Police team.
May 24	The Police and Mission teams both arrived at Repulse Bay. The mail for Wager Inlet was cached at Nuvukley Isles [Nuvuk&it] and a pole erected to denote location. Native Albert was commissioned by Const. MacCormack to collect mail at Nuvukley and deliver same to Wager Post.

OUTFIT 263, 1932–33

June 7	River and creeks now running at full strength.
June 11	snowbirds [snow buntings] and larks everywhere.
June 20	Dick arrived in late p.m. Reports seal hunting very good down the Inlet and the natives down there are laying in supplies, also many eider ducks down the lake towards the narrows. The ice is now in very bad condition for travelling. Dick kept on the shore ice all the way from the narrows, the dogs are of course wearing their sealskin boots.
August 17	Beautiful day with a cloudless sky and light to moderate breeze. Native Dick, Sutoxi, Tommy, Arngnawa and Keemilliajook arrived about 6:30 p.m. with their families in the former's motor-boat. Some of them intend to proceed to Kuminalo [Qamanaaluk] Lake and district to look for deer. They report the Inlet free of ice but much of it moving about at the mouth of the Inlet. Staff attending to sundry jobs about the post and trading with some of the above natives in the evening. Four fish today. Radio reception not so good this evening, distorted by static and fading badly. Dick reports having shot a walrus on the ice in the Inlet last spring. Also has been successful in securing two or three white whales [beluga] which are reported to have been very numerous down the Inlet.

August 27	The MS *Fort Severn* arrived here at 6 a.m. today. Started discharging the *Severn* immediately and were all through by 12 a.m. as the outfit for this post was fairly small. The MS *Fort Severn* (DG Morris Captain) sailed at 4 p.m.
August 29	Staff busy in store today opening up new merchandise and restocking etc. Traded two foxes with Johnny. Looked the net today but no fish. Finished the last of our deer [caribou] meat today. Gave the natives the use of house for dancing tonight, which was well attended and highly successful. Nice bright day with southerly wind.
August 31	Trading in store this afternoon and did some office work also. The natives could not pull out today owing to strong east wind.
October 1	All the natives who had gone off deer hunting with the exception of Samson, Johnny and Tommy, returned to night and report no deer [caribou].
October 2	Another bitterly cold day with almost no wind. The arrivals of yesterday pulled out today with the afternoon tide for down the inlet where they intend to try their hand again at the sealing. They seem to be pretty hungry and are losing no time hanging around the post.
October 29	Sutoxi arrived this evening from down the inlet and reports that the natives are killing the odd seal now and then.
November 5	Kudlu in — many deer seen near Kaminola [Qamanaaluk] Lake.
November 13	Very stormy and the heaviest snowfall we have experienced so far this fall. Quite a few natives arrived at the post today and reported the signs of it being a good fur year are far from favourable.
November 24	Deaf Johnny arrived here this evening and did a spot of trading in store. Reports that fox signs are rather scarce and he intends going inland at an early date.
December 15	Keeluk, Kaffee and Okpeek arrived here this a.m. from Whale Point where they had spent the late summer and fall and report that deer [caribou] were fairly plentiful in that vicinity. Traded with these men this afternoon.

December 19   Kameeliajook arrived here today, but merely on a visit, as he had nothing to trade. Fox signs are very scarce and this man seems to have lost all his enthusiasm for trapping.

December 24   Christmas eve tonight but no celebrations were observed.

December 25   The storm lasted all night but gradually decreased during the course of the day and towards evening had almost blown itself out. Staff passed a very quiet and uneventful Christmas day. Went for a walk in afternoon as we were feeling in need of a little exercise and in evening had dinner of consommé, roast turkey, green peas and hors d'houvres, followed by Christmas pudding with white sauce, and washed the same down with a few glasses of old '62 Burgundy from the cellar. Baked bread after this glorious repast.

December 29   Nice clear day with slight variable breeze. Staff busy with sundry jobs and traded with native Samson who arrived at post this afternoon. This man reports that there are practically no foxes where he and quite a few other natives are encamped, about five days by komotick [qamutik] NW of the post. Deer [caribou] are also very scarce and the natives had absolutely nothing to eat for five days. This was hard on the children, who were crying almost continually, Samson reports.

January 4   Natives Deaf Johnny, Angatinuak, Sutoxi and Nowya arrived at post this evening and they were in a sorry plight with frost bite, hunger and tiredness, The majority of their dogs had died on them through lack of food and they had but seven amongst them when they arrived here. None of these natives had any fur.

January 5   Gave the natives a dance tonight to cheer them up, as they all seem very downhearted and miserable owing to the scarcity of fur. Everyone in town attended this brilliant social function which went down very well. The ladies had quite a bit of searching around to find clothes suitable for the occasion, but ultimately compromised with makeshift outfits.

January 21	Decided change in the weather today — clear and bright overhead and intensely cold. The death occurred today of a child of which Nowya was the father, and which had been left in the custody of Toota, who is staying here while her husband Dick is off on a deer hunt, as our meat is finished. I didn't even know that the child was here until set down for me by Toota, who realized that something was wrong with the child, but couldn't be sure what.
February 11	It is almost one month since any natives arrived here, and this would indicate that foxes are still very scarce.
March 13	W.A. Heslop administering dental treatment tonight to Deaf Johnny's wife. The proceedings were very painful to the patient, but very funny to the assembled audience, owing to the maneuvres of the patient to alleviate the pain of the actual extraction, by having other torture inflicted upon her while A. Heslop was manoeuvring around for a half-nelson or stranglehold upon the offending molar. The operation was completed successfully and then the plucky patient joined in the general merriment.
April 4	It is time some natives were showing up to trade. They must be getting very little fur. If such is the case, the longer they stay away the better.
April 9	Native Tommy and wife arrived in a.m. He had one fox. Wager Inlet this year is beyond the pale — it is enough to make any self-respecting trader feel like a rest cure patient at the Health Spa.
May 2	Sutoxi and wife arrived about 9 p.m. from Nuvukly [Nuvuk&it]. He reports the Huskies [Inuit] at the islands are getting more seals now but no fur.
May 4	Sutoxi cleaning foxes.
May 10	Natives Arngnawa and Nowya with wives and family arrived at post tonight 12 p.m. They bring in the same story which we have been hearing all winter — absolutely no fur in the country.

May 16	Nowya arrived today from Kaminalow [Qamanaaluk] and traded two fish. Natives Kamokake, Teenak, Angititak, Inukshuk and Amiko of Backs River with families arrived here around 11 p.m. The party totaled thirteen humans. They had three komatiks [qamutiit] and there seemed to be no shortage of dogs. They had been three weeks on the way from Backs River, and had succeeded in killing sufficient deer [caribou] for their immediate needs, but report that same were far from plentiful.
May 31	This brings to a close Outfit 263, one of the poorest fur years since this post was established, and it is with absolutely no regrets from either member of the staff that we write "finis" to this most disastrous outfit.

OUTFIT 264, 1933–34

June 4	Still overcast with wind now from NE. Rather warmer however and lots of birds and chics-chics [siksiks (ground squirrels)] to be seen and heard. Snow going down most noticeably today. The remainder of the natives who were on Kiminalo [Qamanaaluk], including the Backs River people, with the exception of Kamokak, arrived at post tonight on their way down the inlet to the sealing grounds. They did not camp here but stayed long enough to partake of a hasty mug-up.
July 6	Native Dick arrived from the camp close to Shemick Island and Pupic and Neriksoo from camp on Kaminalo [Qamanaaluk] River in/out — they are living on seals and fish, eight fish caught today.
July 15	Only four fish in net today. It would appear that the run is now at an end and that we missed the best part of the run through not being able to put our nets in the water, on account of the break up being considerably later than last year.

July 20	Natives Sutoxi and Keenak arrived here today 4 p.m. They intend going north of the post to look for deer [caribou], apparently being tired of the seal-meat diet. Five fish in net.
July 30	Natives Angotingwak and Albert with wives and families arrived at post 12 a.m. Report the inlet absolutely free of ice from Shemik Island west. These people are going from here to Repulse Bay and from that point to Southampton Is. where they intend to spend the winter.
August 1	Native Dick and Deaf Johnny arrived at post 7 p.m. They report deer [caribou] fairly numerous inland from harbour. Dick's wife Toota gave birth to a male child on 24th July, but unfortunately same was still born.
August 27	Fine day, moderate to strong NW wind in a.m. and early p.m.[*]

---

* The post journal for Outfit 264 ends abruptly with this entry. We know that the *Fort Severn* arrived the next morning and departed two days later with the staff and remaining supplies embarked.

GLOSSARY

ak&ungirtarvik	A stone structure, with a braided sealskin rope strung between two rock pillars, on which high-bar-style acrobatics are performed, as found in Ukkusiksalik at Ak&ungirtarvik.
amautiq	Woman's parka, designed with a sort of internal pouch, in which a young child can be carried against its mother's back.
aukaniq / aukanaqjuq	"The place that does not freeze." A polynya, an area of the Arctic Ocean where the water currents prevent the sea ice from forming even in mid-winter.
aurnaq / auriaq	A form of seal hunting (of stalking the seal), by crawling slowly toward the basking seal across the sea ice.
angakkuq	Shaman.
iglu	Igloo.
iluiyuk	Inland, on the mainland.

---

* The ampersand symbol "&" is used to mark the so-called voiceless lateral fricative in writing Inuktitut. Designated ɬ in the International Phonetic Alphabet (IPA), the ampersand, combined with Inuktitut vowels, results in the approximate sounds: &i = "-shli-"; &a = "-shla-"; &u = "-shlu-".

inugaruligaqjuk	Little person (pl. *inugaruligaqjuit*).
Inuit	The people.
Inuk	A person.
kakivak	Fish spear, leister.
kamik	Boot (pl. *kamiit*).
qaggiq	Large tent or iglu for communal gathering, usually for feasts or celebrations; also the pool above a weir in a river where large numbers of fish are trapped.
qajaq	Kayak.
qablunaaq	White man (pl. *qablunaat*).
qarmaq	House built of rock and sod, often incorporating whale bone (pl. *qarmat*).
qamutik	Sled (pl. *qamutiit*).
qiuqta	Arctic heather.
qulliq	Seal-oil lamp.
uangnaq	The direction from which the prevailing wind blows, usually northwest.
ukkusik	Pot.
ukkusiksaaq	Material to make a pot (i.e., soapstone).
umiaq	A large boat, usually made of sealskin, used for transporting families and sometimes for whale hunting.
uqalurait	Snowdrifts formed by the prevailing northwest wind, which create a predictably oriented pattern on the snow surface, sometimes used for navigation.

NOTES

CHAPTER 2: THE FIRST PEOPLE

1. Karlis Karklins, *The Wager Bay Archaeological Survey, 1991–92* (Ottawa: Parks Canada), 36. It should be noted that not all archaeologists agree with this assessment of Site 70X123. The contradictory view is that the earliest human presence was the Thule culture, direct ancestors of today's Inuit, about eight hundred years ago. The question will remain unresolved until further archaeological work is completed at the site.
2. Margaret Bertulli, *Ukkusiksalik National Park — Archaeological Assessment 2005* (Winnipeg, Manitoba: Parks Canada), 2.

CHAPTER 3: THE EARLY *QABLUNAAT*

1. Hudson's Bay Company Archives, A.1/34-35.
2. *Dictionary of Canadian Biography*, "Middleton, Christopher."
3. Ibid.

CHAPTER 24: CONNECTIONS INLAND

1. Peter Irniq, personal communication, confirmed in Bennett and Rowley, eds., *Uqalurait: An Oral History of Nunavut* (Montreal: McGill-Queen's University Press, 2004).
2. David F. Pelly, Hanningajuq Project (unpublished document), Hunters and Trappers Organization, Baker Lake, 2004.

3. Charles Choque, *Joseph Buliard, Fisher of Men* (Churchill, MB: Roman Catholic Episcopal Corporation), 81.

CHAPTER 27: AK&UNGIRTARVIK

1. Igloolik Oral History Project, interviews with Noah Piugaattuk (IE-052, March 23, 1989) and Noah Siakuluk (IE-385, August 24, 1996). Both refer to this acrobatic rope game. Piugaattuk refers to it, in his dialect, as *ak&ungisarvik*. Siakuluk describes it thus: "They would use this rope to swing back and forth, then they would go over it and make a circle while hanging on to the rope. When they start to swing around, their arms are stretched and the legs are also stretched as they go round. At first it was hard to go round, but with practice one was able to make a full revolution."

CHAPTER 28: THE SEARCH FOR FRANKLIN

1. William H. Gilder, *Schwatka's Search — Sledging in the Arctic in Quest of the Franklin Records* (New York: Charles Scribner's Sons, 1881).
2. E.A. Stackpole, ed., *The Long Arctic Search: The Narrative of Lt. Schwatka, U.S.A., 1878–1880, Seeking the Records of the Lost Franklin Expedition* (Mystic, CT: Marine Historical Association Inc., 1965).
3. William Barr, ed., *Overland to Starvation Cove with the Inuit in Search of Franklin 1878–1880* (Toronto: University of Toronto Press, 1987), 26. Translated from original *Als Eskimo unter den Eskimos* [*As an Inuk Among the Inuit*] by Heinrich Klutschak.
4. Barr, *Overland to Starvation Cove*, 20.
5. Ibid., 62.
6. Ibid., 64.
7. Ibid., 65.

CHAPTER 29: THE WHALING ERA

1. John Barrow, ed., *The Geography of Hudson's Bay; Being the Remarks of Captain W. Coats in Many Voyages to that Locality Between the Years 1727 and 1751* (London: Hakluyt Society, 1852).
2. Christopher B. Chapel, Letter to Captain William Jackson, May 16, 1860 (New Bedford Whaling Museum, Massachusetts: Archives of the Kendall Whaling Museum, 1860).

3. Dorothy H. Eber, *When the Whalers Were Up North* (Montreal: McGill-Queen's University Press), 24.
4. Ibid., 124.

CHAPTER 30: POLICEMEN AND PRIESTS
1. Report of the Royal Northwest Mounted Police, 1908. Ottawa, 265.
2. Report of the Royal Northwest Mounted Police, 1910. Ottawa, 275.
3. Report of the Royal Northwest Mounted Police, 1911. Ottawa, 260.

CHAPTER 33: THE HUDSON'S BAY COMPANY ARRIVES
1. Hudson's Bay Company Archives, A92/19/71.
2. All of the excerpts from the post journals on pages 194–96 are from the Hudson's Bay Company Archives, B492 a/1 to a/10.

CHAPTER 38: THE MYSTERIOUS DISAPPEARANCE OF FATHER BULIARD
1. A previous version of this chapter appeared in *Above & Beyond* 17, no. 4 (2005). All of the Inuit quoted in the article were interviewed at that time, and the RCMP records were reviewed at the National Archives.

CHAPTER 40: THE TATTY FAMILY RETURNS
1. Parks Canada, Federal Heritage Buildings Review Office Heritage Character Statement, 2013.

BIBLIOGRAPHY

The principal source for this work was the collection of Ukkusiksalik reports and documents prepared for, and held by, Parks Canada, mostly by the author, David F. Pelly, over a span of twenty years, 1992–2012.

Ayaruaq, John. *The Autobiography of John Ayaruaq*. Ottawa: Department of Indian Affairs and Northern Development, 1968.

Barr, William, ed. *Heinrich Klutschak, Overland to Starvation Cove, with the Inuit in search of Franklin, 1878–80*. Toronto: University of Toronto Press, 1987.

Barr, William, and Glyndwr Williams, eds. *Voyages in Search of a Northwest Passage 1741–1747*. London: Hakluyt Society, 1994.

Bennett, John, and Susan Rowley, eds. *Uqalurait: An Oral History of Nunavut*. Montreal: McGill-Queen's University Press, 2004.

Boas, Franz. *The Central Eskimo*. Washington: Smithsonian Institute, 1888.

Choque, Charles. *Joseph Buliard, Fisher of Men*. Churchill, Manitoba: Roman Catholic Episcopal Corporation, 1987.

Eber, Dorothy H. *When the Whalers Were Up North*. Montreal: McGill-Queen's University Press, 1989.

Fossett, Renée. *In Order to Live Untroubled: Inuit of the Central Arctic, 1550 to 1940*. Winnipeg: University of Manitoba Press, 2001.

Gilder, W.H. *Schwatka's Search: Sledging in the Arctic in Quest of the Franklin Records*. New York: Charles Scribner's Sons, 1881.

Hall, Charles F. *Narrative of the Second Arctic Expedition Made by Charles F. Hall: His Voyage to Repulse Bay, Sledge Journeys to the Straits of Fury and Hecla and to King William's Land, and Residence Among the Eskimos During the Years 1864–69*. Edited by J.E. Nourse. Washington: U.S. Government Printing Office, 1879.

Karklins, Karlis. *The Wager Bay Archaeological Survey, 1991–92*. Ottawa: Parks Canada, Ottawa, 1998.

MacDonald, John. *The Arctic Sky: Inuit Astronomy, Star Lore, and Legend*. Toronto: Royal Ontario Museum and Nunavut Research Institute, 1998.

Pelly, David F. *Sacred Hunt: A Portrait of the Relationship between Seals and Inuit*. Vancouver: Greystone Books, 2001.

_____. "The Mysterious Disappearance of Father Buliard, o.m.i." *Above & Beyond* 17, no. 4 (2005).

Richards, R.L., *Dr John Rae*. Whitby: Caedmon of Whitby, 1985.

Ross, W. Gillies. *Whaling and Eskimos: Hudson Bay 1860–1915*. Ottawa: National Museum of Man, 1975.

Stackpole, E.A., ed. *The Long Arctic Search: The Narrative of Lieutenant Frederick Schwatka, U.S.A., 1878–80, Seeking the Records of the Lost Franklin Expedition*. Mystic, Connecticut: Marine Historical Association Inc.,1965.

Williams, Glyndwr. *Arctic Labyrinth: The Quest for the Northwest Passage*. London: Allen Lane, 2009.

_____. *The British Search for the Northwest Passage in the Eighteenth Century*. London: Longmans, 1962.

Wilson, Bryce et al., eds. *No Ordinary Journey: John Rae — Arctic Explorer 1813–1893*. Montreal and Kingston: McGill-Queen's University Press, 1993.

INDEX

Bruce, Tuinnaq Kanayuk, 9, 40, 42–52, 70, 72, 77, 92, 133, 134, 141, 147–48, 151, 155, 157–64, 172, 174–78, 185, 188, 189, 190, 191, 194, 197, 201, 202, 203, 204, 205, 208, 210, 211, 212, 234, 241

Buliard, Father, 142, 143, 144, 148, 221–28

Cape Fullerton. *See* Qatiktalik

Chesterfield Inlet, 9, 17, 26, 38, 39, 40, 43, 45, 47, 52, 57, 58, 59, 60, 61, 62, 71, 73, 74, 75, 76, 85, 88, 89, 93, 107, 108, 109, 111, 114, 125, 126, 128, 140, 144, 147, 167, 172, 173, 179, 181, 185, 190, 199, 203, 204, 210, 219, 230, 239, 248, 249, 250, 252, 253, 255, 256, 257, 263

Churchill (Fort Prince of Wales), 17, 30, 32, 43, 187, 223, 257

Cleveland, George W., 168, 171

Comer, George, 134, 166, 167, 169, 170, 171

Coral Harbour, 17, 38, 40, 42, 43, 62, 109, 114, 115, 151, 185, 212

Depot Island, 17, 140, 161, 166, 167, 252, 262

Didier, Father, 73, 74, 126, 173

Dobbs, Arthur, 30, 31, 32

Douglas Harbour, 19, 85, 92

Duke of York Bay, 17, 92, 140, 212

Erebus, HMS, 163, 164

Ford, J.L., 6, 133, 197, 258, 261, 262

Ford Lake. *See* Tasiujaq

Fort Chesterfield, 185, 186, 198, 246, 249, 256, 257

Fort Severn, 192, 193, 196, 198, 202, 264, 266, 270

Franklin, Sir John, 142, 155–64

Garry Lake. *See* Hanningajuq

Gilder, W.H., 160–64

Gjoa Haven, 17, 72, 75, 92, 140, 151, 159, 225

Hall, Charles Francis, 33, 162

Hanningajuq (Pelly and Garry Lakes, Back River), 17, 140, 141, 143, 144, 148, 221–28, 273

Heslop, W.A., 96, 197, 198, 268

Hudson Bay, 11, 17, 23, 26, 28, 29, 30, 31, 32, 58, 108, 134, 142, 143, 144, 159, 160, 161, 164, 166, 168, 171, 185, 192, 238

Hudson's Bay Company (HBC) (post), 9, 15, 27, 29, 30, 31, 33, 39, 40, 41, 42, 43, 44, 45, 46, 47, 48, 49, 50, 51, 52, 55, 57, 58, 60, 61, 62, 64, 65, 67, 70, 71, 72, 73, 76, 77, 80, 81, 85, 86, 87, 90, 91, 92, 103, 104, 105, 106, 108, 112, 114, 116, 119, 125, 128, 129, 130, 132–35, 142, 143, 147, 148, 155, 168, 172, 173, 175, 185–98, 199, 200, 201,

ALSO FROM DUNDURN

LOST
BENEATH
THE ICE
Andrew Cohen

When Sir John Franklin disappeared in the Arctic in the 1840s, the British Admiralty launched the largest rescue mission in its history. Among the search vessels was HMS *Investigator*, which left England in 1850 under the command of Captain Robert McClure. While the ambitious McClure never found Franklin, he and his crew did discover the fabled Northwest Passage.

Like Franklin's ships, though, *Investigator* disappeared in the most remote, bleak and unknown place on Earth. For three winters, its 66 souls were trapped in the unforgiving ice of Mercy Bay. They suffered cold, darkness, starvation, scurvy, boredom, depression, and madness. When they were rescued in 1853, *Investigator* was abandoned.

For more than a century and a half, the ship's fate remained a mystery. Had it been crushed by the ice or swept out to sea? In 2010, Parks Canada sent a team of archaeologists to Mercy Bay to find out. It was a formidable challenge, demanding expertise and patience. There, off the shores of Aulavik National Park, they found *Investigator*.

Lost Beneath the Ice is written with elegance and authority, and illustrated with archival imagery and startling underwater photographs of *Investigator* and its artifacts. It is a sensational story of discovery and intrigue in Canada's Arctic.

DUNDURN

VISIT US AT

Dundurn.com
@dundurnpress
Facebook.com/dundurnpress
Pinterest.com/dundurnpress